Neutrality of the Netherlands
During the World War

The
Neutrality of the Netherlands During the World War

BY

AMRY VANDENBOSCH

*Associate Professor of Political Science
in the
University of Kentucky*

Wm. B. Eerdmans Publishing Company
208 Pearl Street
GRAND RAPIDS, MICHIGAN

To

M. B. W. V.

Preface

༄

*T*HE *problems of "waging neutrality" under modern conditions of warfare are hardly less difficult and of less moment than those of waging war. And if war is under fire, neutrality is also. Moreover, if war is to be outlawed, neutrality will have to go with it. Thus both war and neutrality may be at the cross roads.*

This study represents a history and analysis of only the juridical phases of the neutrality of a country peculiarly situated near the theatre of the war. The political and social problems of such neutrality are in no way discussed, while the economic problems involved are only very incidentally touched upon. To get a complete picture of the problem a series of such studies from different points of view and for many countries will be required.

The writer wishes to acknowledge a very special debt of gratitude to Professor Quincy Wright of the University of Chicago under whom this study was made. In spite of his valuable directions and criticisms the study contains many shortcomings and errors for which the writer alone is accountable.

The writer is also indebted to the editor of the Kentucky Law Journal for publishing the substance of the chapter on "Neutral Convoy" which appeared in the May, 1927, number.

AMRY VANDENBOSCH.

TABLE OF CONTENTS

PART I

INTRODUCTION

PART II

ENFORCEMENT OF NEUTRAL DUTIES

PART III

CONTROVERSIES OVER NEUTRAL RIGHTS

PART IV

Conclusion

PART I

INTRODUCTION

CHAPTER I

IMPORTANCE OF THE STUDY

A STUDY of neutrality regulations during the World War clearly reveals a marked development in this branch of international law. The same new conditions which had so profoundly influenced all international relations were also naturally instrumental in causing new problems in the field of neutrality. The neutral governments in the last great war were confronted with new regulatory problems as a result of the tremendous developments in the science of electrical communication and the revolution in aerial navigation.

Industrialization and the vast extension of international trade had rendered the nations peculiarly dependent upon each other and made the maintenance of a strict neutrality more difficult than ever before. The improvements in overland transportation by means of canals and railroads had greatly increased the transit traffic of coastal states. This gave rise to vexatious problems with respect to the use of such territory for the transit of war material. The displacement of the sailing vessel and small steamer by the ocean liner of enormous tonnage brought forward new problems with respect to the question of search. New devices of naval warfare forced neutral governments to make fresh decisions as to the status of submarines and armed merchantmen and the treatment to be accorded them. The conditions of modern warfare which tend to reduce the distinction between the civil and military population also contributed to enlarge the number of new problems in the relations between neutral and belligerent powers.

Of all the states that remained neutral in the World War, the experiences of none offer a better opportunity for the study of the development of the law of neutrality than do the experiences of Holland.[1] Rarely a problem

---

[1] The terms "Holland" and "the Netherlands" are used interchangeably in this study.

3

of neutrality arose but what it affected Holland in some way; rarely a conflict over neutral and belligerent rights and duties but what Holland was sooner or later involved. This is in large part to be ascribed to her peculiar geographical position in the heart of western Europe. The country's frontiers marched with those of the greatest military power on the continent, while across a narrow channel her coasts faced those of the world's greatest naval power. Moreover, her coasts commanded access to some of the chief water-ways of western Europe, over which an enormous transit traffic was carried on with the great German industrial hinterland.

The threat to Dutch neutrality because of her strategical-geographical situation is apparent. The military advantages the occupation of Holland would give to Germany were considerable. "With Holland in the power of Germany," wrote an Englishman, "apart from any act of war, we could not defend India, nor our colonies, nor our trade routes, nor our coasts."[2] No less considerable would have been the military advantages to the Allied Powers had the Netherlands cast its lot with the Allied cause against Germany. The stream of food and military supplies passing into Germany through Holland from the outside world would at once have been cut off. The Allies also would have obtained the tremendous military advantage of a flank attack upon the German military forces in Belgium and northern France. The dangers to Holland of joining either group of belligerents are equally apparent. Had she taken the side of the Central Powers a swift and telling blow would at once have been struck at her overseas possessions and her overseas trade, and by joining the Allied Powers she would have invited an invasion from Germany and shared the lot of Belgium. To steer a straight course of strict neutrality was Holland's sole choice.

Aside from the geographical, there were other important factors which affected Holland's position as a neutral

---

[2] "A Letter to the Common People", by Robert Blatchford, *The Weekly Despatch*, September 11, 1910. Quoted by Van Hamel, *Holland Tusschen de Mogendheden*, p. 404.

power in a general European war. The economic life of the country in the years after 1890 tended more and more towards a closer relationship with the economic life of Germany.[3] The meager natural resources of Holland rendered her dependent on both parties of belligerents for essential supplies. By virtue of her overseas possessions this small country may be considered a world power. Her large merchant marine and her extended trade with the colonial possessions gave her many points of international contact. All the above were factors in making neutrality a highly important but also an extremely difficult role for Holland to play.

The neutrality of the Netherlands has a peculiar interest from yet another point of view. The Dutch, both as a nation and as individuals, have contributed much to the development of international law. From Grotius, the Father of the Law of Nations, until the present, Holland has never been without noteworthy representatives in this field of study. Indeed, it is doubtful whether any other country, in proportion to its population, has contributed as many outstanding authorities in international law. As a nation, Holland has taken a leading part in the development of specific rules and doctrines such as "free ships, free goods," contraband of war, and the right of neutral convoy. With the substitution, after 1870, of an international for a purely national foreign policy, the Netherlands became a leader in movements for international coöperation. Holland became an international center; many international conferences were held on her soil. Her capital became the seat of the Peace Palace, the Hague Court of Arbitration, and after the War, the Permanent Court of International Justice. The neutrality regulations of such a country can not but have an added interest and significance.

---

[3] Blok, *Geschiedenis van het Nederlandsche Volk*, VIII, p. 301.

Chapter II

BRIEF SURVEY OF THE DUTCH NEUTRALITY REGULATIONS

THERE are in the main two systems of neutrality regulations, though neither system is ever followed exclusively. By certain countries, of which the United States and England are the outstanding examples, the practice is followed of incorporating most of the regulations in a general neutrality law. The neutrality proclamations of these countries merely repeat the provisions of the neutrality law or confine themselves to a general statement of intention to preserve strict neutrality. The great majority of states, and practically all of the continental states, establish the neutrality regulations in proclamations issued upon the occasion. The proclamations issued under the latter system may be divided into two classes—those which make a mere statement of the state's intention to observe a strict neutrality, with a possible reference to the provisions of the Hague convention concerning the rights and duties of neutrals;[1] and those which describe minutely the government's intentions, and are of the form of a code of neutrality. The Dutch Neutrality Proclamation belongs to this latter class.[2]

As a result of the successive declarations of war the Dutch Government issued a proclamation of neutrality not once but nearly a dozen times during the course of the war. The first proclamation was issued on July 30, 1914, concerning the war between Austria-Hungary and

---

[1] Good examples of this class of neutrality proclamations are the Proclamations of Argentine and Chile, Naval War College, *International Law Topics*, 1916, pp. 9 and 16, respectively.

[2] Official proclamation in Dutch is found in *Dutch Orange Book*, I, 2–3. An official French translation is found in the *Recueil*, pp. 1–4. The Proclamation of Brazil is also an example of this class, Naval War College, *op. cit.*, pp. 10–14.

Serbia,[3] and the others followed with each new declaration of war. With the exception of a slight variation in the first, the contents of all are the same.[4]

Though a general or international standard neutrality proclamation is still lacking, there were at the beginning of the war, thanks to the Second Hague Peace Conference, two international conventions[5] which served as the main source of the various proclamations issued by the different neutrals. The question of whether the two Hague Conventions on neutrality form a part of positive international law may be waived here, since the conventions did roughly serve as a general standard of neutral rights and duties, and the peculiarities of a given proclamation can be most easily ascertained by a comparison of its provisions with those of the two Hague Conventions.

A comparison of the provisions of the Dutch Proclamation of Neutrality with those of the two Hague Conventions reveals that there are points in the first not covered by the second, and points in the second not touched upon in the first. An unusual feature of the Dutch provisions is the exclusion of warships or ships assimilated thereto belonging to any of the belligerents from the ports and coastal waters of the State.[6] The Hague Conventions contain no such provisions, nor do the neutrality regulations of any other power. However, this provision may be considered an extension of Articles 10 and 12 of the 13th Hague Convention.[7] The expression

---

[3] *Staatscourant*, No. 176.

[4] Art. 5, Cl. 2 of the later proclamations, granting belligerent warships a 24-hour stay in the ports or roadsteads of the colonies or overseas possessions exclusively with the object of completing their provisions of foodstuffs or fuel, is not found in the first declaration. Article 8, containing the so-called "24-hour rule", is also absent in the first proclamation, for the obvious reason that Serbia possessed no navy.

[5] The so-called 5th Hague Convention respecting the Rights and Duties of Neutral Powers and Persons in case of War on Land, and the 13th Hague Convention concerning the Rights and Duties of Neutral Powers in Naval War.

[6] Articles 4 and 17. See Appendix I.

[7] Article 10 provides that "the neutrality of a Power is not affected by the mere passage through its territorial waters of warships or prizes belonging to belligerents", while Article 12, "in the absence of special provisions to the contrary in the legislation of a neutral power", lays down the so-called "24-hour rule".

7

"ships assimilated thereto" also marks a peculiarity of the Dutch regulations, and the inclusion of armed merchantmen under the term caused one of the most extended diplomatic controversies of the War. This same article contains yet another variation from the ordinary rules of neutrality, in that it laid down one rule for the mother country and another rule for the colonies. As an exception to Article 4 only belligerent warships or ships assimilated thereto which were forced to enter the ports or roadsteads of the State on account of damages or the state of the sea were allowed a temporary stay, while the same vessels were allowed to enter the ports or roadsteads of the colonies or overseas possessions also for the purposes of completing their provision of foodstuff or fuel.[8]

Article 8 of the Proclamation, which deals with the simultaneous presence of warships and assimilated vessels of different belligerents in Dutch ports and harbors, is stricter than the corresponding Article 16 of the 13th Hague Convention. Article 8 provides that such vessels finding themselves at the same time, "in the same part of the world and within the territory of the State, a delay of at least 24 hours must elapse between the departure of each respective belligerent ship," while Article 16 of the 13th Hague Convention imposes the same rule only when such vessels are present simultaneously in a neutral port or roadstead.

The Dutch Proclamation contains two other articles which contain provisions which go far beyond similar provisions of the Hague Conventions. By Article 15 of the Proclamation "it is forbidden in State territory, failing previous authorization by the competent local authorities, to repair warships or ships assimilated thereto belonging to a belligerent, or to supply them with victuals or food," while by Article 16 "it is forbidden in State territory to take part in the dismantling or repairing of prizes, except in so far as is necessary to make them seaworthy; also to purchase prizes or confiscated goods, and

---

[8] Article 5, Sections 1 and 2. See Appendix I.

to receive them in exchange, in gift, or in deposit." In correspondence with this the second part of Article 17 of the 13th Hague Convention merely states that "the local authorities of the Neutral Power shall decide what repairs are necessary, and these must be carried out with the least delay possible."

The sanctions for the violations of these regulations are found in certain provisions of the Penal Codes of the mother country and the colonies, and of the law respecting the status of Netherlands nationality and domicile. Article 18 of the Proclamation calls attention to these, and similarly, "the attention of commanding officers, owners, and charterers of ships is called to the dangers and inconveniences to which they would expose themselves by disregarding the effective blockade of belligerents, by carrying contraband of war or military despatches for belligerents (except in the course of regular postal service), or by rendering them other transport services.

"Any person guilty of the acts afore said would expose himself to all the consequences of those acts and would not be able, as regards them, to obtain any protection or intervention on the part of the Netherlands Government."

The omissions in the Dutch Proclamation, as compared with the provisions of the Hague Conventions, were for the most part covered by royal decrees and special proclamations. Thus the Proclamation contains no provision corresponding to the provisions of Article 3 of the 5th Hague Convention regulating the installation and use of wireless stations on Dutch territory, but this deficiency was made good by a proclamation issued by the Minister of War in the *Staatscourant* of Aug. 5, 1914, No.181. So also the provisions in regard to the internment of belligerents and care of wounded in neutral territory, dealt with in Chapter II of the 5th Hague Convention, find no counterpart in the Proclamation except for the general rule of Article 3, but find regulation in a Royal decree of August 8, 1914.[9]

---

[9] *Staatscourant*, No. 185. See Appendix VIII.

For several articles of the 13th Hague Convention there are no corresponding articles in the Proclamation. Thus Articles 3, 4, 15, 22, and 23 do not appear in it,[10] for the reason that the regulations laid down in these articles are covered by the total prohibition of belligerent war vessels and prizes from entering Dutch ports and coastal waters. Omissions of neutral duties as laid down in other conventions are also found. Thus Articles 13 and 15 of the 10th Hague Convention, providing that "if sick, wounded, or shipwrecked persons are taken on board a neutral warship, every possible precaution must be taken that they do not again take part in the operations of war," and that such persons landed at a neutral port must "be guarded by the neutral State so as to prevent them again taking part in the operations of war," are also wanting in the Proclamation.

In addition to the special proclamation and royal decrees already mentioned there were several other royal decrees for the enforcement of neutral duties. Aerial navigation over Dutch territory was prohibited to all but fliers belonging to the Dutch army and naval forces by Royal decree of August 3, 1914.[11] This regulation was dealt with in neither the Hague Conventions nor the Dutch Proclamation. A Royal decree of July 30, 1914,[12] forbade all foreign warships from entering or anchoring in Dutch territorial waters. The regulations concerning the Scheldt are found partly in a royal decree[13] and partly in diplomatic correspondence between the Dutch and Belgian Governments.[14] An announcement of the Minister of War provides for an inspection service of all

---

[10] These articles, respectively, deal with the neutral's duties with respect to prizes captured in its waters, the prohibition of the establishment of a belligerent prize court in neutral territories or waters, the limitation of the maximum number of warships of the same belligerent simultaneously in the same neutral harbor to three, the neutral's duties with respect to prizes brought into its ports, and the sequestration of prizes in neutral ports.

[11] See Appendix VI.
[12] See Appendix III.
[13] See Appendix V.
[14] See Appendix II.

vessels entering Dutch territorial waters.[15] Regulations for the internment of persons belonging to belligerent forces coming upon Dutch territory are found in a proclamation of the Minister of War.[16] Provisions for the regulation of the interned on Dutch territory are found in a Royal decree of the 27th of March, 1914,[17] and a law of December 13, 1914.[18]

The unusual features and new departures of the Dutch neutrality regulations as outlined in part above, form the object of this study. The method pursued will be largely analytical, historical, and comparative. The neutrality regulations of the Dutch Government and the diplomatic correspondence with the belligerent governments with respect to them will in each case first be stated and analyzed. This will be followed by a brief history of the rule of international law with respect to the question, including a summary of the regulations of other neutrals during the World War with respect to the same question. And lastly, the compatibility of the regulations or positions maintained by the Dutch Government with the rule of international law will be considered.

---

[15] See Appendix IV.
[16] See Appendix VIII.
[17] See Appendix IX.
[18] See Appendix X.

PART II

ENFORCEMENT OF NEUTRAL DUTIES

Chapter III

TRANSIT OF MILITARY MATERIALS

History of the Case[1]

A. Transit of Sand and Gravel

THE TRANSIT across Dutch territory of materials susceptible of military use gave rise to a prolonged and bitter dispute between Germany and the Netherlands on the one hand, and between Great Britain and the Netherlands on the other. Holland and Belgium are covered with a large network of water-ways, canals, and estuaries, connecting the Rhine with the Scheldt and other rivers and affording an excellent system of cheap water transportation between Holland, Belgium, and Germany. This system of water routes came under international regulation with the Rhine Convention which was drawn up in 1831 in pursuance of the provisions of the Treaty of Vienna, and which was revised in 1868.

In the *Telegraaf* of October 29, 1915, there appeared an article stating that 20,000 tons of basalt and gravel were shipped to Ghent every week by way of Lobith, the Rhine, the Waal, and the Scheldt. According to this article the crews of the barges were totally exempted from military service by the German Government as being already employed in the service of the army. From Ghent the materials were transhipped into barges of shallower draught and carried up to the front.[2]

The French Minister at The Hague at once called the attention of the Dutch Government to this article and to the great increase in the traffic of sand and gravel from

---

[1] The diplomatic correspondence and related documents are found in the *Dutch White Book*, "Doorvoer door Nederland uit Duitschland naar België, en in omgekeerde richting", 1917 and 1918, and the *British White Book*, "Correspondence respecting the Transit Traffic across Holland of Materials Susceptible of Employment as Military Supplies", in *Brit. Parl. Papers*, Misc. No. 17 (1917), Cd. 8693, and Misc. No. 2 (1918), Cd. 8915. The White Books will hereafter be referred to as "D. W. B." or "B. W. B.", as the case may be.

[2] *B. W. B.*, Note 1.

Germany over the Rhine and Dutch water-ways to Belgium. The suspicion naturally arose that these materials, or at least a part of them, were not being used for peaceful purposes, especially since this material was suitable for making the cement blocks which were so extensively used in the German trenches and fortifications.

The Dutch Government brought the attention of the German Government to the matter and informed them that they would object to shipments of sand and gravel of any unusual amount, or which could be suspected of being used for military purposes, passing through the Netherlands' waters. From the beginning of the war the Dutch Government had prohibited the transportation of "provisions militaires" from Belgium by way of the Dutch canals into Germany. As regards these shipments from Belgium the Dutch Government required the guarantee of the German Government that articles coming from Belgium were not requisitioned goods, and also the certificate of the Netherlands' consul at Antwerp to that effect.

On February 12, 1916, the Dutch minister at Berlin presented to the German Government an Aide-Memoire in which it was pointed out that under Article 2 of the 5th Hague Convention belligerents are forbidden to move convoys of supplies across the territory of a neutral state, and that under Article 5 the neutral power is not to allow such passage. The Dutch Government had therefore the duty to prohibit the transit of such supplies across its territory from Germany to Belgium, or vice versa. It was also of the opinion that to take the character of convoys of supplies in the sense of Article 2 it was not necessary that the convoy be accompanied by persons forming a part of the armed forces of the belligerent; that Article 7, which states that a neutral power is not called upon to prevent the export or transport on behalf of one or other of the belligerents, applies only to commercial operations, and that the transport of material for the use of the armed forces or of material necessary for military works, and sent by one belligerent to its allies or army in

16

the field, did not fall under the term "commerce," and that therefore Article 7 did not apply to such transport.[3]

The Aide-Memoire of February 12 further called attention to the greatly increased transport of gravel and sand in the last five months of 1915. The number of tons of this material transported over Dutch water-ways during these five months was nearly four times as great as that transported during the whole year of 1913. The Dutch Government stated that it did not in any way wish to prohibit the legitimate transport of these materials in such amounts as would be used for peaceful purposes, but that it could not allow the transport of these materials in such amounts as could be suspected of being used for military purposes. The Dutch Government warned the German Government that before allowing barges to cross the frontier it would require a certificate by a competent German authority that the cargo was destined for peaceful usage.

On April 3 the German Government replied that inasmuch as there was a sufficient supply of sand and gravel in Belgium which could be used for military purposes, it would not discuss the question of law involved in the matter and declared that it was ready to give the desired certificates.[4] The British and French Ministers at The Hague continued to protest against the large amounts of sand and gravel still crossing Holland. They also informed the Dutch Government that reports had come to them that guns and ammunition had been concealed in the cargoes of sand and gravel, and further, that Germany had requisitioned many Belgian barges for the use of the transportation service over Holland.[5] It was later ascertained that these requisitioned barges were used only in Belgium. On May 26 a note was sent to the German Government pointing out that instead of diminishing, the amount of sand and gravel transited over Holland had greatly increased, and since the German

[3] *D. W. B.*, Note 1.
[4] *D. W. B.*, Note 3.
[5] *B. W. B.*, Notes 2 to 22 inclusive.

Government had failed to submit to the Dutch Government an estimate of the approximate quantities of material needed for non-military usage, the Dutch Government would shortly be obliged to fix the monthly quantity of material which it should permit to be transported over Holland.[6] When after another month the German Government had not made a satisfactory response to the demand for an estimate of its need of this material, the Dutch Government limited the total number of tons which would be allowed transit over Dutch waters to 75,000 tons a month.[7]

The German Government protested that the quantity of materials allowed to be transited across Dutch territory was much too low. An officer was sent to The Hague to explain the need for the transited materials for the repair of roads, quays, bridges, houses which had been destroyed during the invasion, and for the construction of bomb proof shelters against air raids. This work had been neglected for the first two years of the war and the need for these materials was therefore unusually great. Also, according to the German officer, much of the sand and gravel went for similar purposes to northern France, and, owing to strikes, the Belgian production of these materials was almost nothing. The German officer estimated the monthly quantity of sand and gravel needed for pacific purposes at from 400,000 to 500,000 tons.[8] As a result of these presentations the Dutch Government agreed provisionally to allow the transit of 420,000 tons monthly, under the condition that each cargo be provided with a certificate from the competent German officials that the materials were to be used for non-warlike purposes. In order to satisfy itself of the real need of, and the pacific use of these materials, the Dutch Government sent two engineering officers to Belgium to make a personal investigation on the ground.[9]

---

6) *D. W. B.*, Note 4.
7) *D. W. B.*, Note 5.
8) *Ibid.*, Notes 5, 6, 7, and 8.
9) *Ibid.*, Note 9.

Transit of Military Materials

The two Dutch engineering officers, who made their report on September 12, 1916, found the statements of the German officer to be substantially correct. The Dutch officers were convinced that a part of the materials transited before the system of certification had been put into effect, had been used for military purposes, but that none of the materials transited since had been so used. They concluded that the enormous reconstruction and improvement work carried on by Germany was sufficient to account for all the sand and gravel being transported over Holland, and that a very considerable amount would still have to be shipped in if that work was to be carried on to completion.[10] The Dutch Government thereupon sent a note to Berlin, October 9, 1916, declaring that it had no objections to the free transit of the materials, provided each shipment was accompanied by a declaration of the use for which the materials were intended.[11]

However, the British and the French were not satisfied with the report of the Dutch officers and continued to protest the free transit of material across Holland. The report of the Dutch officers was criticised as untrustworthy. The British also contended that even on the assumption that the materials were wholly devoted to the repair and construction of roads, railways, dykes, and bridges, the Dutch Government ought not to allow their transit across its territory, since the repairs and improvements were made to facilitate the traffic of troops and munitions, and were thus made for the sake of the German army, and not for the benefit of the Belgium population. The British Government submitted a report made by the French Inspector General of Bridges and Roads, showing that the quantities of sand and gravel already imported into Belgium were much greater than was necessary for the different works carried out throughout the occupied territory for pacific purposes. Consequently, the Allies protested that "no pacific purpose could justify the introduction into the occupied territories of France and Belgium, by way of Holland, of any

[10] *D. W. B.*, Note 11.
[11] *Ibid.*, Note 12.

19

quantity whatever of broken stones or gravel imported from Germany."[12]

The Dutch Government itself finally became disturbed over the enormous quantities of sand and gravel transited across Holland, and early in July, 1917, sent a note to Berlin stating that according to its calculations, the quantities of sand and gravel imported into Belgium during the first five months of 1917 exceeded the maximum limit of what was considered necessary for civil purposes for the year, and that therefore all further transit of these materials must cease after the 31st of July. Special permits for further consignments of these materials would be granted only after two Dutch officers had satisfied themselves by an examination on the spot, of the nature of the work for which the materials were required and the materials necessary for the purpose.[13]

The German Government issued a vigorous protest against these proposed measures, and submitted a carefully prepared statement by the German Governor General of Belgium in which the needs for the materials were presented. Three German delegates were sent to The Hague to discuss the matter. About the same time the Dutch Government sent the same two engineering officers to Belgium to make a new investigation. On the basis of this report the Dutch Government in September sent a note to Berlin stating that more than enough sand and gravel had already crossed Holland to meet all civil needs for the year. However, the Dutch Government would permit the advance quotas of January, February, and March of 1917, to be transited in October and November, in view of the possibility that on account of ice the transit might not be possible during the winter months. This quantity once attained, all transit of these materials would be prohibited until March 15, 1918, at which date the regular transports of the needs for 1918 might again be resumed.[14]

The German Government was not at all satisfied with

12) *D. W. B.*, Notes 30 and 31. *B. W. B.*, Notes 38–79 inclusive.
13) *D. W. B.*, Notes 14, 17, and 18.
14) *D. W. B.*, Notes 15, 16, and 19.

this arrangement and in October sent a note to The Hague contending for the legal right of free transit of these materials even for military purposes. The British continued their protests against the transit of sand and gravel in any quantity, and they also protested the export of Dutch sand into Belgium, declaring that this was just as objectionable as the transit of German sand across Dutch territory. The British Government informed the Dutch Government that the examination of thirty-nine samples of cement collected in German trenches in Flanders, thirty-two showed that they contained Rhine gravel. Thereupon the Dutch Government with increased vigor pressed its demand for permission to send a permanent commission of experts into Belgium to make sure that the gravel and sand would not be used for military purposes. It would consent to the resumption of the transit only on condition that it be allowed to control the usage of the materials. The German Government replied that in view of the actual military situation it would be impossible to allow the commission to move about freely in the occupied territory and demanded free transit under threat of ominous consequences. For a time the situation was very serious. Prime Minister Loudon made a statement before the States-General revealing the seriousness of the situation, the Lower House met in secret session, and the Dutch Minister to Berlin arrived at The Hague. On May 24 the Foreign Minister announced to the Chamber that a provisional agreement had been reached. Germany persisted in the refusal to admit the Dutch commission to Belgium, but agreed to a reduction in the annual amount of sand and gravel for which passage was demanded to 1,600,000 tons per year, which was about 600,000 tons less than the Dutch Government had deemed admissable before. Germany also undertook not to use the materials for military purposes.[15]

---

[15] *D. W. B.*, Notes 19, 90– 96 inclusive. *B. W. B.*, Notes 116–122, 125–127, 131, 132, 134, 135, 137, 141, 147. Barnouw, A. J., *Holland Under Queen Wilhelmina*, p. 133.

B. Coals, Minerals, and Metals

The Allies protested not only the transit of sand and gravel from Germany to Belgium, but also the transit of coal, metals, and minerals from Belgium to Germany. On June 21, 1916, the British Government demanded of the Dutch Government that it apply to the transit of coal, metals, and minerals the system of certification of peaceful usage which it applied to sand and gravel shipments. The Dutch Government replied on August 22 that it was unable to accede to the British demands, contending that this was an entirely different case from that of the transit of sand and gravel. From the beginning of the war the Dutch Government had required certificates from the Dutch consul in Belgium to accompany the cargoes, declaring that the goods were neither war booty, requisitioned goods, nor military supplies. But all other goods coming from Belgium were allowed free transit unless it was clearly shown that they were transported for military purposes. As regards the transit of sand and gravel from Germany to Belgium, the greatly increased quantities shipped and the fact that they were being sent in the direction of the theater of warlike operations, created the presumption that these consignments were of the nature of military supplies, although not recognizable as such, but this presumption did not exist in the case of coal, metals, and minerals transported from Belgium. The protests of the British Government continued, but the Dutch Government refused to modify its position. However, when the German authorities in Belgium actually commanded the requisition of various metals, the Dutch Government prohibited the passage of cargoes of all metals without distinction, for the reason that owing to the diversity of decrees regulating the requisitioning of metals in Belgium, it was practically impossible for the Dutch consuls to ascertain whether a cargo of these goods was or was not requisitioned.[16]

But soon after the question presented itself in another form when two cargoes of lead were sent from Belgium

---

[16] *D. W. B.*, Notes 43–55. *B. W. B.*, Notes 64–69.

to Germany. The Dutch Government replied to the British protest of the transit of these two cargoes that the metals had been extracted in Belgium from ores sent to Belgium from Germany for that purpose, and that the prohibition of the transit of metals applied only to metals originating in the occupied territories of Belgium and northern France, that the cargoes in question could in no wise be considered as either war booty or requisitioned goods, and that the Dutch Government therefore could not oppose the transit of these cargoes. However, the Dutch Government promised that in the future cargoes of ore going to Belgium from Germany would be tested and the content of pure metal calculated, and upon return, transit of pure metal would be allowed only for such quantities as could be extracted from the quantity of ore shipped into Belgium.[17]

II. RETORSIONARY MEASURES

The British Government backed up its protests with threats of retorsion, and in the end actually applied retorsionary measures against the Netherlands. In December, 1916, the British Government threatened to refuse facilities for certain imports into Holland if the Dutch Government continued to allow the transit of coal, metals, and minerals from Belgium to Germany across Holland.[18] In June, 1917, the British warned the Dutch Government that unless the shipment of metals over Holland was stopped they would be forced to cancel certain facilities whereby ships carrying metals to the Netherlands Government might be examined at Halifax. The metals were destined for the Dutch military arsenal which was practically shut down for lack of the needed materials. The British also refused to approve certain shipments to Holland of government goods by a Dutch ship from New York. It was only after the Dutch Government prohibited the further transit of these metals

---

[17] *B. W. B.*, Notes 67, 69, 79, 81, 89, 91, and 92. *D. W. B.*, Notes 58–61.

[18] *B. W. B.*, Note 51. *D. W. B.*, Note 50.

across Holland that the cargoes of metals consigned to the Netherlands Government on the steamships *Noordam* and *Zijldijk* were permitted to go forward.[19]

The British Government again threatened retorsion in a note of September 18, 1917. Holland was warned that unless all transports across the Netherlands of sand and gravel from Germany to Belgium and of metals from Belgium to Germany ceased completely and at once, the British Government would stop the transmission of cables between the Netherlands and overseas.[20] On October 3, 1917, the British Government instructed the cable censors to refuse the transmission over British lines of all commercial telegrams destined for, and emanating from Holland and Dutch possessions.[21] When on October 20 the Dutch Minister at London called at the Foreign Office to protest the cable embargo and to suggest some sort of compromise, Lord Robert Cecil hinted at even more far-reaching retorsionary measures. It was pointed out that the economic position after the war would be very serious, that neutral countries would only be able to procure necessary raw materials by the good will of Great Britain and her allies, and that if the Dutch Government did not comply with their demands, or tried to evade them, Holland's position after the war might easily become serious. However, when in the crisis with Germany in May, 1918, the Dutch Government withdrew its demand for a commission of control in Belgium to supervise the usage of sand and gravel and agreed to a maximum of 1,600,000 tons to be transited over Dutch water-ways, the Allies declared that they fully understood the seriousness of Holland's position, and although maintaining their original point of view, they would place no new obstacles in the way of the Dutch Government in the matter of the arrangements made with Germany.[22]

Great Britain also threatened Holland with the pro-

---

19) *D. W. B.*, Note 54. *B. W. B.*, Notes 69–70.
20) *D. W. B.*, Note 108. *B. W. B.*, Note 62.
21) *B. W. B.*, Note 113.
22) *B. W. B.*, Note 125.

hibition of the export of cement from the United Kingdom to Holland at the conclusion of the war. On October 8, 1917, the export of cement to Holland was prohibited except under license, and on the 13th of October the War Trade Department was requested by the Foreign Office to issue no further licenses for the export of cement to Holland.[23] The impression was current in England that there was a direct connection between the composition of the German "pill-boxes" on the Western front and the shipments of cement from England to Holland, and there was a wide-spread and vigorous agitation demanding that the export of cement to Holland be prohibited at once.[24] The prohibition of the export of cement to Holland except under license was probably not due to this agitation, which reached its height after the order of prohibition,[25] but it shortly became so strong that the Government felt compelled to take some sort of action. On November 28, 1917, Lord Robert Cecil, Minister of Blockade, appointed a committee "to enquire whether it is desirable that the export of cement to Holland should be resumed when the general embargo on exports to Holland is raised, and if so, upon what conditions."[26]

After investigation the Committee concluded that the British cement exported to Holland was not being re-exported to Belgium, nor was the export of this cement to Holland serving to release equivalent quantities of German cement for military purposes.[27] The Committee saw no reason why shipments of British cement should have been discouraged, but saw many reasons in favor of permitting it. Imported cement is a necessity for Holland. The life of the country depends upon maintenance and repair of the system of dykes and for this an extensive use of cement is necessary, and Great Britain could

---

23) Report of the Committee of Enquiry into the export of cement from the United Kingdom to Holland, *British Parliamentary Papers*, (1918), Misc. No. 9. Cd. 9023.
24) *Ibid.*, p. 1.
25) *Ibid.*, p. 2, paragraph 6.
26) *Ibid.*, p. 1.
27) *Ibid.*, paragraphs 7–16.

not afford any better than Germany to see Holland flooded for lack of cement. The Committee was of the opinion that wherever Great Britain had an "opportunity of competing with Germany in neutral markets, it is of great importance that every advantage should be taken of it, not only for the benefit of the trade concerned, for the improvement of the exchange, and for the general good of the country, but also to secure the political good will of the neutral country concerned, to weaken its dependence on Germany, and, above all, to combat as far as possible the dangerous system of specific exchanges."[28] The Committee recommended the immediate resumption of the export of cement to Holland as soon as the political situation permitted, and it saw no reason for applying to the export any more drastic conditions than those in force at the time when the export was suspended.[29]

III. THE GERMAN-DUTCH CONTROVERSY

As far as the controversy between the German and the Dutch Governments is concerned an examination of the correspondence indicates that in practice the difficulties raised by the transit of materials across Dutch territory between Germany and Belgium were amicably settled by provisional agreements, but that on the question of law there remained to the end a complete divergence in their points of view. This divergence arose largely from differences in interpretation and application of the 5th Hague Convention on the one hand and the Rhine Convention of 1868 on the other.

The German Government maintained throughout the controversy that under Articles 1 and 2 of the revised Rhine Convention of 1868,[30] Holland could not stop the transit of goods across its territory, regardless of the usage to which the transited goods were put, but that on the contrary, Holland was under obligation to give the

---

28) *Ibid.*, p. 8, paragraph 35.
29) *Ibid.*, p. 8, paragraph 36.
30) For the relevant articles of the Rhine Convention see Appendix XI.

navigation on the Rhine and other water-ways included in the Convention the freedom to which it was entitled under this agreement. The German Government held that the Convention permitted in an altogether general manner the transit of goods over the Dutch water-ways, and that no restrictions could be placed upon this freedom of transit.[31] The answer of the Dutch Government to this argument was that the Rhine Convention of 1868 did not by any of its articles guarantee the absolute freedom of the navigation of the Rhine and auxiliary waterways. The free navigation regulated by Articles 1 and 2 of this Act is restricted in the preamble to navigation which takes place "sous le rapport du commerce." Thus the Dutch Government held that it did not act contrary to the stipulations of the Rhine conventions in forbidding, in view of the obligations imposed upon her by the 5th Hague Convention, the free transit of convoys of munitions or supplies of war across her territory. The transit of such convoys by a belligerent power to its armies in the field could not be considered as taking place "sous le rapport du commerce."[32] The German Government also contended that the 5th Hague Convention could not be called in to restrict the freedom of navigation permitted by the Rhine Convention. Many belligerent states, and especially Great Britain, had either not ratified or had reserved upon many articles of the Convention, and it was therefore not applicable to the present war.[33] The Dutch Government held that the 5th Hague Convention was applicable, since the principles of the Convention were an established part of customary international law before the Convention was adopted. The Convention was merely declaratory of international law and therefore binding.[34]

The controversy then shifted to the interpretation of Articles 2, 5, and 7 of the 5th Hague Convention and their

---

31) *D. W. B.*, Note 10.
32) *Ibid.*, Note 12.
33) *Ibid.*, Note 10.
34) *Ibid.*, Note 12.

applicability in the present case.[35]   The German Government contended that Article 7 was alone applicable in this case, and that Article 2 was not applicable because Germany was not sending convoys of munitions or provisions across Dutch territory.   The difference between Articles 2 and 7 is merely whether the transit is made by persons forming a part of a belligerent army, or by private persons.   The term "convoy" clearly means a transport under official guard, while the term "transit pour le compte d'un belligerent" designates a transport made by private persons who may be in the employ of the state, but not forming a part of its armed forces.   Article 2 implies the exercise of the right of sovereignty on neutral territory, while Article 7 permits all kinds of traffic so long as the belligerent uses the ways and means of transportation of a neutral power under the same condition as other private persons.   All German shipments came exclusively under the second type and therefore could not be restricted.[36]

Nor, according to the German view, did the fact that the German Government stood at both ends of the transit as owner of the goods and that the goods were transited from one part of belligerent territory to another part of the same belligerent's territory, make any difference. This kind of traffic is distinctly permitted by Article 7.

The Dutch Government based the justification for its regulations of the transit traffic on Articles 2 and 5 of

---

[35] Art. 2. Belligerents are forbidden to move troops or convoys of either munitions of war or supplies across the territory of a neutral Power.

Art. 5. A neutral Power must not allow any of the acts referred to in Articles 2 and 4 to occur on its territory.

It is not called upon to punish acts in violation of its neutrality unless said acts have been committed on its own territory.

Art. 7. A neutral Power is not called upon to prevent the export or transport, on behalf of one or other of the belligerents, of arms, munitions of war, or in general, of anything which can be of use to an army or fleet.

Art. 9. Every measure of restriction or prohibition taken by a neutral Power in regard to the matters referred to in Articles 7 and 8 must be impartially applied by it to both belligerents.

[36] *D. W. B.*, Note 19.

the 5th Hague Convention. The Dutch Government held that under Article 2 it had the duty to prevent the transit across its territory of any cargo coming within the definition of military supplies sent from Germany to the occupied part of Belgium, or vice versa.[37] It admitted that the term "convoy" strictly construed meant cargoes under military guard, but contended that the term must also be construed to include goods owned by a belligerent government and sent to its armies in the field to be used for warlike purposes. The Dutch Government also held that it was its duty to forbid the passage across its territory from Belgium to Germany of all war booty and requisitioned goods for the reason that it would be contrary to the observance of a strict neutrality to allow one of the belligerents to continue on neutral territory to give effect to an act of war committed to the detriment of its adversary.

IV. THE BRITISH-DUTCH CONTROVERSY

The British and Dutch Governments were unable to reach either a provisional agreement in practice or to arrive at an agreement on the legal questions involved. For the most part the British Government discussed the legal questions involved from the broad point of view of the duties of a neutral power under general international law, while the Dutch Government brought the discussion to center more specifically around the neutral power's obligation under formal international conventions.

The British Government at first took the position that the transit of goods across Holland from Germany to Belgium was permissable in so far as the goods were used for peaceful purposes, but that it was the duty of the Dutch Government to ensure that no violations of Articles 2 and 5 of the 5th Hague Convention occurred. The Dutch Government could do this by satisfying itself that none of the goods transited over its territory was used for warlike purposes.[38] The Dutch Government to the contrary

---

37) *D. W. B.*, Note 12.   *B. W. B.*, Note 23.
38) *B. W. B.*, Note 39.

held that it should make sure that the goods transited were intended for peaceful usage only in case there was a presumption that they would be used for warlike purposes, and that to require more than this was equivalent to eliminating the distinction between the transit contemplated by Article 7 and that designated in Article 2 by the technical term "convoys of supplies." The fact that the goods were susceptible of use for warlike purposes did not by itself suffice to invest them with the character of "convoys of supplies" in the sense of Article 2.[39]

The British Government then moved over to the proposition that Holland should prohibit altogether the transit of goods susceptible of use for warlike purposes across her territory between Germany and Belgium on the ground that a belligerent power has no right to make use of neutral territory for purposes connected with war, and that a neutral power has not the right to allow a belligerent power to do so. By despatching the proceeds of an industry of an occupied territory, which it is exploiting for its own benefit, over neutral territory, the belligerent correspondingly relieves the railway system of its own territory, thereby obtaining a belligerent advantage from the use of neutral territory. The neutral government cannot escape liability for such improper use of its territory by demanding certification of peaceful usage.[40] The Dutch Government held the view that in consideration of Article 7 of the 5th Hague Convention the transit of goods and even of war materials for a belligerent across neutral territory is not sufficient to establish the use of its territory for warlike operations. The sole condition under which such transit takes the character of an illegal act is laid down in Article 2 of the Convention. With respect to the advantages of this traffic to belligerent transportation facilities, the Dutch Government declared that there exists in international law no rule which requires a neutral to take measures to deprive a belligerent of an advantage that arises from cir-

---

[39] *Ibid.*, Enclosure No. 2, Note 39.
[40] *B. W. B.*, Enclosure No. 2, Note 43.

cumstances independent of the law of neutrality. To deprive a belligerent of such an advantage would be to act arbitrarily to the prejudice of one belligerent to the advantage of the other.[41]

The two Governments differed in their interpretation of Articles 2 and 7 of the 5th Hague Convention. The British maintained that Article 2 is applicable in every case where the belligerent state itself is interested both in the despatch and the receipt of the troops, munitions, and supplies, and that Article 7 deals with the transport of goods acquired by a belligerent state as the result of commercial transactions with private persons in a foreign country. The British maintained that Article 7 does not apply to a case where the belligerent government is the owner of the goods and where it is sending it for its own purposes to its army in the field or to occupied territory. The Dutch took the position that the term "convoy" was a technical term by which was designated a consignment protected by a military escort and although this could not be taken to mean that only consignments protected by a military guide were included under the term, since an escort would not be needed in neutral territory and could not be allowed there, nevertheless the use of the technical term naturally excluded the application of the Article to consignments other than convoys of munitions of war or of supplies owned by a belligerent government and sent to its armies in the field or to occupied territory. Where supplies were sent into occupied territory for a peaceful usage they could not be classified as convoys of supplies.[42]

In support of its interpretation of these Articles of the 5th Hague Convention the Dutch Government quoted the following comment on the conventional disposition of the problem dealt with in these Articles, in the report drawn up at the Conference by Col. Borel, in the name of the Second Commission:

"The rule laid down by this article (Article 7)

---

[41] *Ibid.*, Note 144.
[42] *B. W. B.*, Note 144.

is justified in itself, independently of the reasons of a practical nature which militate in its favor. In principle, neutral States and their populations should not suffer from the consequences of a war with which they have no concern. Consequently the burdens which it imposes on them and the restrictions which it causes to their liberty of action should be reduced to a minimum. There is no reason to prohibit or impede the commerce of the inhabitant of the neutral State, even as regards the articles mentioned in the text quoted above. Every obligation which it may be attempted to lay upon the neutral State in this connection would cause in practice the greatest possible difficulties, and would place inadmissable obstacles in the way of commerce in general." *Acts and Documents,* I, p. 141.[43]

In further support of the contention that where supplies were sent into occupied territory for peaceful usage they could not be classified as convoys, the Dutch Government pointed to Article 43 of the 4th Hague Convention Respecting the Laws and Customs of War on Land. This Article made it the duty of the German military authorities in Belgium to keep the Belgian roads and railways in a state in which the Belgian people could use them since this is necessary for a safe, orderly, and normal life.[44] The Dutch Government, then, in allowing the sand and gravel to be transited across its territory for these purposes was only permitting Germany to fulfill its duty under international law.[45]

The British Government replied that they found it difficult to understand how the construction and upkeep of roads and railways was at all directly connected with the obligation of ensuring public order and safety, and

---

[43] *B. W. B.*, Enclosure No. 2, Note 121. *D. W. B.*, Note 41.

[44] Article 43 reads as follows: "The authority of the legitimate power having in fact passed into the hands of the occupant, the latter shall take all the measures in his power to restore, and ensure, as far as possible, public order and safety, while respecting, unless absolutely prevented, the laws in force in the country."

[45] *B. W. B.*, Enclosure in Note 144.

it pointed out that maintenance and reconstruction of railways and roads in reality had a military purpose. The Dutch reply to this was that only if the Belgian roads and railways were military works could the cargoes of sand and gravel passed in transit over Holland be considered as convoys of supplies in the terms of Article 2 of the 5th Hague Convention. However useful the Belgian railways might be to the German military authorities, they none the less retained the intrinsically non-military character they possessed before the war. Consequently the Dutch Government could not regard the upkeep and repair, nor even the transformation of these roads and railways, as military works.[46]

Another British contention was that the Netherlands Government, by its own interpretation of its duty as a neutral, was under obligation to prohibit the transit over its territory of all supplies from Belgium to Germany. The Dutch Government had laid down the regulation that no requisitioned goods would be allowed to be transported over its territory, and the British argued that all goods coming from Belgium were requisitioned goods since their exportation to all countries but Germany was prohibited. To this the Dutch replied that the act of requisitioning was an act apart, and the existence of an export prohibition in no way proved that goods which fell within the terms of such prohibition had been requisitioned. To this the British countered that the prohibition of exports in this case was the same as requisitioning since it had the same effect. The powers exercised by Germany in the occupied territory enabled it to dispose of the products of the country at will without having recourse to requisitioning. The Dutch maintained that the control of exports by the German authorities in Belgium did not constitute an act of war any more than similar control in other belligerent countries or in neutral countries.[47]

The British Government also attempted to convince

---

[46] *B. W. B.*, Note 146, Enclosure.
[47] *B. W. B.*, Enclosure No. 1 in Note 70.

the Netherlands Government of its duty to prohibit the transit of sand and gravel on the grounds that the Belgian stone quarries were worked by prisoners of war, and under Article 6 of the Land War Regulations such output can be utilized only for civilian purposes. Thus the Dutch Government had to assume that the output of the Belgian quarries was used for civilian purposes, and since this output was sufficient to supply all civilian needs, the imported stone and gravel could be used only for military purposes. The Dutch Government ought therefore to prohibit the transit. The answer of the Dutch Government to this argument was that they were under no obligation to enforce the observance of the rules of war by a belligerent, nor was it the duty of a neutral power to enquire into the use made by a belligerent of materials over which it had no control.[48]

As a final argument the British Government attempted to create the impression that the Netherlands had in some indirect way guaranteed the neutrality of Belgium. The Netherlands was a party to a treaty in which the perpetual neutrality of Belgium was expressly provided for.[49] The Dutch Government in tolerating this traffic across Dutch territory was in effect giving direct assistance to Germany in maintaining her military occupation of Belgium, which occupation was an act of war committed in flagrant defiance of Germany's solemn treaty obligation to respect and defend the perpetual neutrality of Belgium.[50] The Dutch Government strenuously opposed this interpretation of the treaty and the British Government modified its position by stating that it only meant to assert that Holland had a special interest in the maintenance of Belgium's neutrality since it was itself a party to a treaty in which her neutrality was expressly stipulated for. The Netherlands, though not one of the

---

[48] *D. W. B.*, Note 86. *B. W. B.*, Enclosure 2, Note 128.

[49] Dutch Belgian Treaty of April 19, 1839, in which the Netherlands recognizes the independence of Belgium. The treaty contains the following clause: *"La Belgique . . . . formera un etat independent et perpetuellement neutre"*.

[50] *D. W. B.*, Note 86. *B. W. B.*, Note 150.

guarantors of Belgium's neutrality, had at least recognized
the permanent neutrality of Belgium, and this recognition had the effect of intensifying her ordinary obligations of neutrality.[51]

V. SUFFICIENCY OF THE DUTCH REGULATORY MEASURES

A somewhat similar situation in the World War in
regard to the transit over other neutral territory is found
in the transit across Norway of materials from England
to Russia. Under the auspices of a Russian Committee in
London consignments of various supplies were sent over
to the so-called Skiboth sleigh route in northern Norway.
The Dutch Government did not lose the opportunity of
calling the attention of the British Government to this
incident, and pointing to the similar circumstances in the
two cases, reminded the British Government that Article
2 of the 5th Hague Convention places the first obligation
on the belligerents themselves to refrain from such
transit. The British Government granted that among the
goods forwarded over Norway there were some to which
the description of military supplies might have been applied, and the legality of the despatch of such consignments might have presented itself for consideration if
the Norwegian Government had made it an issue.[52]

Also during the World War the Canadian Government asked the United States Government for permission
to send equipment across Alaska to the sea. The American Government refused the request.[53]

During the Boer War Portugal allowed free passage
through Beira to Rhodesia. However, this permission
was based on the Anglo-Portuguese treaty of June 11,
1891. Under Article XII of this treaty, Portugal "engages
to permit and facilitate transit for all persons and goods

---

[51] *D. W. B.*, Notes 88 and 98. Also de Visscher, C., *Belgium's
Case.*
[52] *D. W. B.*, Notes 98 and 99.
[53] "Bryan–Stone Letters", *American Journal of International Law*
(hereafter referred to as *A. J. I. L.*), IX, Sp. Supp., 265.

of every description over the waterways of the Zambesi, the Shira, the Pungive, the Busi, the Limpopo, the Sabi, and their tributaries, and also over the landways which supply means of communication where these rivers are not navigable."[54] Had this been a grant of passage for a specific warlike purpose and not a general grant of passage made in peace time to afford a more convenient transit to a sphere of influence, it would clearly have been an unneutral act. It is a moot question whether even under the existing conditions it was not an unneutral act.[55]

As far as the issues were clearly joined they centered around the interpretation of Articles 2, 5, and 7 of the 5th Hague Convention, and the preamble and Article 2 of the Rhine Convention of 1868. It was the position of the German Government that since Great Britain had reserved on Article 20, the Hague Convention was not binding, and that anyway the transit in controversy did not fall under the term "convoy" of Article 2 of the 5th Hague Convention, since to come under that term the consignments would have to be accompanied by a military guard. According to the German contention all the consignments in question were permitted under the provisions of Article 7. Furthermore, under Article 2 of the Rhine Convention of 1868 the Dutch Government was under contractual obligation to facilitate the transit of all material without distinction.

The position of the British Government was that the German shipments across Holland were prohibited by Article 2 of the 5th Hague Convention. According to the British interpretation any consignment of goods in which a belligerent government stood at both ends of the transportation as owner of the goods was included under the term "convoy." The German consignments in question were not included under the provisions of Article 7, since that Article deals with the transport of goods acquired by a belligerent state as the result of commercial transac-

---

54) Moore, J. B., *Digest*, VII, 939, 940.
55) See Hall, pp. 594, 595.

tions with private persons in a foreign country. As far as Article 2 of the Rhine Convention of 1868 was concerned, its stipulations relate only to commerce in its ordinary sense, the passage of goods which are the subject of commercial transactions, and can have no bearing on the measure which a state may be bound to take in defence of its neutrality.

The Dutch Government maintained that from the point of view of international law it was under no obligation to hinder transit which in no way bears the character of consignments forbidden by Article 2 of the 5th Hague Convention, and that on the other hand, the Rhine Convention obliged it to allow such traffic. Whether or not a consignment of goods fell under the term "convoy" in the sense of Article 2 depended on the use to which the goods in the consignments were put upon arriving at their destination. As against Germany the Dutch Government took the position that the preamble of the Rhine Convention limited the freedom of transit stipulated for in Article 2 to goods included under ordinary commercial operations.[56]

The controversy failed to give any specific meaning to the ambiguous terms of Articles 2, 5, and 7 of the 5th Hague Convention. The distinction made by the Dutch Government between military and non-military use is unsatisfactory since it is difficult to apply and is open to much question. Clearly it is not necessary before a shipment by a belligerent can be called a convoy that it be accompanied by a military guard, since a neutral can not permit an armed soldier to come upon its territory, and must intern all belligerent soldiers crossing its frontier. If Articles 2 and 7 are not in opposition to each other they must apply to different kinds of shipments. According to the comments of Col. Borel, the reporter for the Commission which drafted this convention, Article 2

56) Article 8 of the Convention and Statute on Freedom of Transit signed at Barcelona, April 20, 1921, states: "This statute does not prescribe the rights and duties of belligerents and neutrals in time of war. This statute shall, however, continue in force in time of war so far as such rights and duties permit." *A. J. I. L.*, XVIII, 118 ff.

is addressed to the belligerents themselves, while Article 7 refers only to commercial enterprises of individuals.[57] This in its broadest terms would mean that Article 2 applies to any shipment which is organized by the belligerent state itself, and would still leave open the difficult question of whether supplies intended for peaceful usage also fall under its terms.[58]

[57] Carnegie Endowment for International Peace, *Hague Conference Reports*, III, 138.

[58] See article by de Visscher in *Revue General de Droit International Public*, XXVI, 142 (1919), for a general discussion of the transit controversy. Also Chamberlain, J. F., *Col. University Studies*.

Chapter IV

TRANSIT OF THE SCHELDT[1]

I. Diplomatic Correspondence in Respect to the Navigation of the Scheldt

OF ALL the controversies between the Netherlands and the belligerents during the war few were of greater importance than the controversy over the navigation of the Scheldt. The regulations imposed by the Dutch Government on this navigation undoubtedly had considerable influence on the course of the war, for the control of the mouth of the Scheldt by either belligerent would have been of great military significance. The Dutch-Belgian quarrel over the control of the Scheldt was of long standing, and the bitterness engendered during the war led Belgium to make strong annexationist demands at the Peace Conference. The strained relations between the two countries over this question continued until several years after the war when a treaty providing for a partial settlement of the dispute was finally signed.[2]

The Scheldt, though not a long stream, is an important international river. Rising in France near Catelet, the Scheldt flows through Belgium past Tournai, Oudenarde, Ghent, and Termonde, through Antwerp to the North Sea. Not far below Antwerp the island of Beeland divides the river into two channels, the East and the West Scheldt, and from this point on both banks of the Scheldt belong to Holland. Of the two channels, the West Scheldt, which enters the sea near Flushing, is the most navigable and is used for ocean commerce to Antwerp. From the date of its independence Holland has claimed and exercised jurisdiction over the mouth of this important river.

---

1) Correspondence found in the *Recueil*, the *Dutch Orange Books* (referred to as *D. O. B.*), I and IV, and the *British State Papers*, 1917–1918, III, 474–515, Pt. II, *British Parliamentary Papers*, Misc. No. 12 (1918).

2) April, 1925. See *Current History*, May, 1925, p. 323.

Neutrality of the Netherlands During World War

A. BRITISH–DUTCH CORRESPONDENCE

With the outbreak of the war a number of German and Austrian vessels fell into the hands of the Belgian Government. On September 2, 1914, the British Minister informed the Dutch Government that his Government proposed to transport these vessels with a non-military English crew to England by way of the West Scheldt. He drew the attention of the Dutch Government to the terms of the Treaty of London of 1839, which guaranteed the free navigation of the Scheldt, and expressed confidence that the Dutch Government would have no objections to the passage of these unarmed merchantmen. The Dutch Government replied that it could not permit the passage of these vessels over its territory. These vessels had fallen into the power of the Belgian Government by an act of war and the observance of a strict neutrality did not permit the utilization of Dutch territory for the perpetuation of this belligerent act. Furthermore, this kind of transport did not fall under the terms of the Treaty, which guaranteed free navigation of the Scheldt only "sous le rapport du commerce." Also, the Scheldt under the rules of international law formed a part of Dutch territory and not of the territorial waters. The Dutch Government declared that should the vessels enter its territory they would be interned to the end of the war when they would be turned over to those having the clearest right to them.[3]

Evidently the British Government thought that this decision was based upon the belief that these vessels should be treated as belligerent warships which have remained in a neutral port for a longer period than is sanctioned by the laws of neutrality, for in notes of the 8th and the 11th of September, the British Government vigorously combatted this position. It asserted that the vessels in question possessed none of the characteristics of public ships. Their commanding officers bore no commission, they flew no war flag, they were unarmed, and

---

[3] *Recueil*, pp. 170, 171. *D. O. B.*, I, 32, 33, and IV, 26. *British Parl. Papers*, Docs. 1–4.

they were to be engaged in non-military employment,—
that of transporting Belgian refugees to Great Britain.
According to the 6th Hague Convention these vessels
could not be confiscated, they could be merely requisitioned by the Belgian Government on payment of an indemnity or must be restored at the end of the war.[4] The
vessels were consequently not "prize of war" but only
enemy merchant vessels which had passed into the
ownership of the Belgian Government, either temporarily
or permanently, depending upon whether they were to
be restored, or to be requisitioned. But in either case,
under the Convention the Dutch Government could not
regard these as other than merchant ships, unless their
character had definitely been changed by some act of the
Belgian Government. Lastly, the British Government
called upon the terms of the Treaty of London, which
guaranteed the free navigation of the Scheldt. As long
as Belgium was at peace with Holland, Belgian merchant
vessels were as free to go down the Scheldt as were the
German vessels to go up the Rhine. The one could not
be restricted without restrictions upon the other also.[5]

The Dutch Government reiterated in a note of September 15 that the reason the vessels in question had been
denied the passage of the Scheldt was that they had fallen
into the control of the Belgian Government by an act of
war, and that the observance of a strict neutrality did not
permit its territory to be used to facilitate the hostile act
by which these vessels had passed into the ownership of
the Belgian Government. The passage over the Scheldt
of the vessels in question under these abnormal conditions did not fall within the terms of the Scheldt Treaty
which granted free navigation exclusively "sous le rapport du commerce." The decision of the Dutch Govern-

---

[4] Article 2: "A Merchant Ship unable, owing to the circumstances of *force majeure*, to leave the enemy port and within the
period contemplated in the above article, or which was not allowed to
leave, cannot be confiscated. The belligerent may only detain it, without payment of compensation, but subject to the obligation of restoring
it after the war, or requisition it on payment of compensation."

[5] *D. O. B.*, IV, 29, Notes 2 and 3. *British Parl. Papers*, Notes
6 and 7.

ment was in no wise based upon an analogy of these vessels with belligerent warships which have remained in a neutral port for a longer period than is sanctioned by the laws of neutrality, and hence the fact that these vessels had none of the characteristics of public vessels was irrelevant. The Dutch Government would apply the same principle in similar cases, as for instance, in case Germany should attempt to transport over the Rhine vessels seized from another belligerent. And should the vessels in question be recaptured by Germany, the attitude of the Dutch Government would be the same, and passage over the Scheldt likewise refused.[6]

On October 10, the day after the fall of Antwerp, the British Government sent a note informing the Dutch Government that it could not admit the validity of the arguments of the Dutch Government, but that it did not wish to pursue the matter any further in view of the assurance that the passage of these vessels down the Scheldt would also be prohibited in the event of their being recaptured by Germany.[7]

In the meanwhile, in a note of October 1, 1914, the British Government asked the Dutch Government to grant permission to the hospital ship "China" to take on sick and wounded at Antwerp and to return with these to England. Assurance was given that the vessel would transport neither personnel nor war material. The British Government referred to Article 14 of the 5th Hague Convention which states that a neutral may authorize such passage over its territory.[8] A week later the British Government asked the same permission for the naval hospital ship "Liberty." The Belgian Government joined in the demand for the authorization of the passage. The

---

[6] *D. O. B.*, IV, 29–30, Note 4. *British Parl. Papers*, Note 8.
[7] *D. O. B.*, IV, 30, Note 5. *British Parl. Papers*, Note 9.
[8] Article 14: "A neutral Power may authorize the passage over its territory of the sick and wounded belonging to the belligerent armies, on condition that the trains bringing them shall carry neither personnel nor war material. In such a case, the neutral Power is bound to take whatever measures of safety and control are necessary for the purpose."

Dutch Government replied that it gladly accorded the authorization subject to the conditions laid down in Article 14 of the 5th Hague Convention. Because of the sudden fall of Antwerp the project failed of execution. The "China" did not get beyond Flushing where it arrived on October 9, and on the next day it turned to strike out again for the high seas. The "Liberty" never reached the Dutch waters.

In November the question was again opened by a note from the British Government directing the attention of the Dutch Government to an alleged German plan to transport three of the German steamers detained at Antwerp by the Belgian Government at the beginning of the war, over Dutch water-ways, canals, and the Rhine to Germany. The Dutch Government was reminded of the assurance it had given that these vessels would not be allowed to pass through Dutch waters as long as the state of war should exist.[9]

The Dutch Government replied that the vessels in question would be prohibited from passing over the Dutch interior water-ways to Germany, but it also declared that as regards certain small German lighters which were used on the interior water-ways and which had been detained by Belgium at the beginning of the war, no such prohibition would be imposed, so long as they were not engaged in transporting war booty, military supplies, or requisitioned goods. There could be no reason for denying to these latter vessels their usual route over Dutch territory. Since the rules of maritime law did not apply to them, these vessels could not be made private property by the Belgian Government. Only when it became apparent that they had been requisitioned by the German military authorities could the transport over Dutch territory be denied them.[10]

This distinction between vessels used for internal navigation and ocean going vessels the British Govern-

---

[9] *D. O. B.*, IV, 30, 31, Notes 6 and 7; *British Parl. Papers*, Notes 10 and 11.
[10] *D. O. B.*, IV, 31, Note 8; *British Parl. Papers*, Note 12.

ment could not accept, and it protested this distinction and the difference in treatment based upon it. No distinction existed in practice between vessels which were subject to seizure by a belligerent and those which were not, and consequently there was no justification for a difference in treatment by a neutral.[11] Furthermore, the British Government undertook to point out that according to information it had received, certain lighters originally owned by Belgian subjects or nationals of other allied powers, which had been captured as war booty by the German forces at the fall of Antwerp, were being sold and would soon be used to transport antimony from Belgium across Dutch territory into Germany. The British Government demanded assurance that these vessels would be seized should an attempt be made to carry out this purpose.[12]

In February, 1915, the Dutch Government replied. It pointed out the difference between the rules which govern war at sea and those which govern war on land. In maritime war private property is to a certain extent subject to capture, while in war on land it is to a certain extent inviolable. River and canal boats are governed by the laws of war on land. The juridical status of the Austrian and German ocean-going vessels seized at Antwerp at the commencement of the war was uncertain. The vessels were governed by the rules of maritime warfare and were thus to a certain degree subject to capture; they had been seized by the Belgian officials and a number of them brought before prize courts, although definite information about this was lacking. Quite different was the status of the inland vessels belonging to German subjects. These were subject to the laws of war on land under which private property is inviolable. They retained their character of inviolable private property, notwithstanding the seizure by the Belgian authorities, and with the German occupation of Belgium they returned to their

---

[11] *D. O. B.*, IV, 31, Note 9; *British Parl. Papers*, Note 14.
[12] *D. O. B.*, IV, 32, Note 10; *British Parl. Papers*, Note 13.

original owners.[13] To the second note the Dutch Government replied by a note of the same month in which the British Government was reassured that no belligerent would be allowed to transport over Holland goods falling within any of the three categories: war booty, military provisions, or requisitioned goods.[14]

In a succeeding note of the 26th of February the British Government admitted that the distinction might be justified in the case of inland barges, coal flats or rafts, and similar vessels, but contended that in the case of the lighters in question the distinction was not justified, since they were vessels of considerable tonnage, capable of navigation in the narrow seas, and had doubtless been used for that purpose from time to time. Reference was made to the decision of the Japanese Prize Court in the case of the harbor launch *Juliette* in the Russo-Japanese war which, it was asserted, fully supported the view of the British Government. The British Government also complained that the Dutch Government did not indicate before the fall of Antwerp that this distinction would be made. It was in reliance upon the statement that these vessels would not be permitted to pass down the Scheldt that these vessels had not been wrecked.[15]

In a note of the 17th of March the Dutch Government replied to this contention that a vessel did not lose its character as an inland vessel by the fact that its tonnage is considerable or because it can without too great danger navigate the seas under unusual circumstances. The isolated case of the *Juliette* did not constitute sufficient grounds for the departure from a line of conduct which the Dutch Government considered just. Furthermore, it might well be asked whether the Japanese Prize Court would still render a similar decision after the 11th Hague Convention, which exempted from capture small boats employed in local trade. Also the *Juliette* was built for use in a seaport while the lighters in question were in-

---

13) *D. O. B.*, IV, 32, Note 11; *British Parl. Papers*, Note 15.
14) *D. O. B.*, IV, 32, Note 12; *British Parl. Papers*, Note 16.
15) *D. O. B.*, IV, 33, Note 13; *Britis Pharl. Papers*, Note 17.

tended only for use on canals and rivers. The British Government had no grounds for complaint that the Dutch Government had not, before the fall of Antwerp, declared that it would make this distinction between inland and ocean-going vessels, since both Governments in the exchange of correspondence before the fall of Antwerp, had reference only to the Austrian and German vessels still in the hands of the Belgians. Further proof that both Governments thought only of ocean-going vessels was found in the fact that the British Government had invoked the 10th Article of the Hague Convention concerning the Rights and Duties of Neutral Powers in Naval War, which Convention is applicable only to maritime vessels. The fact that the Anglo-Belgian forces in the month of October had damaged only inland vessels was of the nature of a confirmation of the correctness of this view.[16]

B. BELGIAN–DUTCH CORRESPONDENCE

1. *Navigation of the Scheldt*

After the German occupation of Antwerp several German ocean vessels came upon Dutch territory and were interned. In January, 1915, the Belgian Government demanded the return of one of these vessels, the *Delia*. The Belgian Government was under the impression that the Dutch Government regarded these vessels as prizes, even after the German recapture of these vessels, and since the Dutch government had not adopted the regulations contained in the 10th and 23rd Articles of the 13th Hague Convention[17] it was bound to send the vessels back to Antwerp under the terms of the 10th Article of the Dutch Neutrality Proclamation.[18] Moreover, if Holland allowed this sojourn of the *Delia* in its waters Germany would very probably send the remaining thirty-seven

---

[16] *D. O. B.*, IV, 33–34, Note 14; *British Parl. Papers*, Note 18.

[17] Article 10 states that the "neutrality of a power is not affected by the mere passage through its territorial waters of warships or prizes belonging to belligerents", and Article 23 relates to the sequestration of prizes in neutral ports pending the decision of a prize court.

[18] Prohibiting admission of prizes into Dutch territory.

vessels into Dutch waters in order thus to prevent their recapture by Belgium in case the Allies should retake Antwerp.[19]

The Dutch Government held that in accordance with the provisions of the 6th Hague Convention these vessels could not be regarded as prizes, and that consequently should these vessels come upon Dutch territory they could not be returned to their original German owners. Neither Articles 10 and 23 of the 13th Hague Convention nor Article 10 of the Proclamation were applicable since the Scheldt did not form a part of the Dutch territorial waters but a part of Dutch territory itself. The juridical status of these vessels was uncertain, and for this reason the regulation for internment was imposed.[20]

When three other German vessels had left Antwerp and had been interned at Rotterdam, the Belgian Government asked what disposition would be made of these vessels at the conclusion of the war. It trusted that the vessels would be sent back to Antwerp in order that the Belgian Prize Courts might decide on the legality of the seizure. Any other solution would disregard the rights of Belgium.[21] The Dutch Government replied in a note of July 16, 1915, that it could not in the course of the war open a discussion with either of the belligerent parties as to what disposition would be made of the interned vessels at the conclusion of the war, but that the Belgian Government could rest assured that when that time came the Dutch Government would render an impartial decision.[22]

---

[19] *D. O. B.*, IV, 34, Note 15.

[20] *Ibid.*, IV, 34, 35, Note 16.

[21] *D. O. B.*, IV, 35, Note 17.

[22] *Ibid.*, IV, 35, 36, Note 18. In September, 1917, some Belgian subjects navigated the motor boat *Scheldt* from the occupied portion of Belgium to Dutch territory. Investigation disclosed that the vessel had belonged to the Belgian Government and after the German occupation had been seized by the German authorities and put into service by them. The Dutch Government decided not to return the vessel to the Belgian Government, for so doing would be granting to the Belgian Government the use of Dutch territory to recover by an act of war goods lost by an act of war. Nor was it thought proper to send the vessel back to Antwerp, for this would have the same effect, only in favor of the other belligerent party. It was thus decided to intern the vessel. *D. O. B.*, IV, 50.

2. *War-buoying on the Scheldt*

When the situation in Europe became grave the Belgian Government was informed that the Netherlands Government might soon be obliged to institute war buoying on the Scheldt in order to maintain the neutrality of Dutch territory. The arrangements for the buoying were such that navigation to Antwerp would still be possible by day, but only with Dutch pilots furnished with the necessary instructions. Should war buoying be instituted the presence of the Belgian light-ships could be dispensed with since there would be no reason to enter the tidal waters of Flushing by night. The Dutch Government would therefore be much obliged if these two vessels would be withdrawn in that event. It was convinced that by these measures it could serve equally the Dutch interests in the defense of Netherlands territory and the Belgian interests in the navigation of the Scheldt to Antwerp.[23]

On August 5, the Dutch Government informed the Belgian Minister at The Hague that war buoying was about to be instituted.[24] In subsequent notes the Belgian Government suggested a few changes in the interests of convenience. These details were amicably adjusted,[25] and in a note of August 7, the Belgian Government thanked the Dutch Government for the measures taken to secure navigation on the Scheldt, and stated that it was "in agreement with the Netherlands Government on the subject of the extent of the navigation."[26]

C. GERMAN–DUTCH CORRESPONDENCE

1. *Navigation of the Scheldt*

On October 3, 1916, the German Government requested permission for the German vessels which lay at Antwerp at the commencement of the war, to pass over the Scheldt.

---

[23] *Belgian Grey Book*, Annex to No. 29; reported in *A. J. I. L.*, IX, Sp. Supp., 50–100.
[24] *Ibid.*, Document 50. See Appendix II.
[25] *Ibid.*, Documents 54 and 55.
[26] *Ibid.*, Document 56.

The policy in regard to these vessels would necessarily be different now that they were again in German possession. The juridical status of these vessels was now the same as before the war, since they were again in the possession of their original owners. The passage over Dutch waters could consequently not be considered as a violation of neutrality.[27]

The Dutch Government replied in November that the fact that the German Government had restored these vessels to their original owners did not change the juridical status of these vessels so far as the duties of a neutral power was concerned. These vessels had fallen into the hands of the German Government by an act of war, and these vessels could not, therefore, be allowed to enter Dutch territory any more than before the fall of Antwerp.[28]

2. *Disposition of Vessels Coming from Antwerp into Holland Territory After the Armistice*

A number of vessels from Antwerp entered the Dutch waters after the Armistice. Among these vessels were several German warships, which were immediately interned upon their arrival, and several river and canal boats which belonged to Belgian or unknown owners, and which had been denied passage to Germany by Dutch officials. The French Government on the 22nd of November, asked that these vessels be conducted back to Belgium. The French Government contended that under Article 28 of the Armistice Terms the German Government had no right to sequester these vessels in neutral harbors after the Armistice, and that the river and canal boats had been brought into Dutch territory contrary to the terms of this Article.[29]

Since the terms of the Armistice were still unknown to the Dutch Government no immediate reply was sent to the French note. The Dutch Government was also very

---

[27] *D. O. B.*, IV, 36, Note 19.
[28] *Ibid.*, IV, 36, Note 20.
[29] *Ibid.*, V, 5–6.

49

uncertain as to how far the terms of the Armistice were legally binding upon a neutral power. However, the Dutch Government decided to offer no objections to the request to conduct the vessels back to Antwerp, since it would establish a situation between the belligerents as nearly as possible like that in which they found themselves at the conclusion of the Armistice. After an exchange of notes with the Belgian Government with respect to the manner of its execution the vessels were sent to Antwerp.[30]

The Dutch Government had notified Berlin of its intention to cause the return of these vessels to Antwerp.[31] The German Government in reply recognized its obligation upon its evacuation of the coasts and ports of Belgium to abandon in the place where found, and intact, all vessels of war and commerce. But it wished to point out that this evacuation had already started before the conclusion of the Armistice, and that many of these vessels anchored in Belgian ports had quit these ports before November 11, and at the time of the conclusion of the Armistice were on their way to Holland or Germany. All of these vessels did not arrive in Dutch waters before November 11, but nevertheless they did not come under the terms of the Armistice as having been surrendered to the Allies.[32]

The Dutch Government replied that it did not care to carry on an extended discussion to ascertain whether Article 28 of the Armistice Agreement was also applicable to the vessels which had quit their anchorage in Belgian harbors before November 11. However, it doubted whether Germany had the right to sequester in neutral territory any of these vessels which arrived in Dutch waters after the conclusion of the Armistice. A study of the text of the Armistice Terms confirmed this view, and the Dutch Government had therefore decided to take measures which would tend to reëstablish in regard to

---

[30] *D. O. B.*, V, 6–7.
[31] *Ibid.*, V, 7.
[32] *Ibid.*, V, 7.

these vessels the state of affairs in which they found themselves at the conclusion of the Armistice.[33]

The German Government protested this action, contending that the difference in opinion in the present case was a matter for Germany and the Allied Powers to settle, and that the Dutch Government was wrong in taking the initiative in the matter. Furthermore, the Dutch action did not reëstablish the situation as it was at the time of the Armistice, but gravely prejudiced the interests of the German Government, for which the Dutch Government would be held responsible in case damages resulted.[34]

II. HISTORY OF THE SCHELDT[35]

The control and navigation of the Scheldt has been a bone of contention since the middle of the 17th century when the independence of the United Provinces from Spain received recognition in the Treaty of Westphalia. At the signing of the first peace treaty between Spain and Holland, in 1609, no stipulation was made that the navigation of the Scheldt should be free, and the Dutch fleet which commanded the channel simply closed the Scheldt to navigation. Antwerp was the great rival of Amsterdam and the Dutch did not lose the opportunity to punish the rival city which had remained loyal to the king of Spain. At the next European peace conference the States-General succeeded in securing from the powers the ratification of their right to close all the channels of the Scheldt to ships of all nations. This clause of the Treaty of Munster, 1648, was ratified in every subsequent European treaty up to 1795.

---

[33] *D. O. B.*, V, 7.
[34] *Ibid.*, V, 8.
[35] The best account is found in Kaeckenbaeck, *International Rivers*, published as Vol. VII, *Transactions*, Grotius Society. There are several books by Belgians on the Scheldt: Nys, *L'Escaut en temps de guerre*, 1911; Linquet, *Dissertation sur L'Ouverture et la Navigation de L'Escaut;* Baron Quillaume, *L'Escaut depuis 1830.* See also the paper by Omond, "The Scheldt and the Wielingen", *Transactions,* Grotius Society, VI, 80 ff. A good summary for the legal history of the Scheldt is found in *Holland, Belgium and the Powers*, by Prof. A. A. H. Struycken.

This action, though in complete accord with the international law of the day, for it was then the recognized right of a state owning both banks of the mouth of a navigable river to close it at will, was disastrous for Antwerp. When Napoleon visited it in 1803 he found it little more than a ruin. Joseph II made an attempt to open the Scheldt, but failed. In 1784 he sent an ultimatum to the Dutch States-General demanding the opening of the Scheldt with complete freedom of navigation and the additional privilege of the right of trade and navigation for his subjects with the Dutch East and West Indies. The States-General promptly rejected the demands. Joseph remained obdurate and the Dutch asked France and England to mediate. As a result of the mediation of France the Treaty of Fontainebleau was signed. This Treaty confirmed the Treaty of Munster and the Emperor was compelled to give up his demands. The Emperor was merely awarded an indemnity of nine and a half million florins for the insult inflicted on his flag when the Dutch fired upon the squadron sent down the Scheldt from Antwerp.

A change came with the French Revolution. In 1792 the French troops occupied Antwerp. The French Convention in proclaiming the principle of the freedom of rivers declared, "That the stream of a river is the common, inalienable property of all countries which it bounds or traverses; that no nation can without injustice claim the right exclusively to occupy the channel of a river and to prevent the neighboring riparian States from enjoying the same advantages." This principle was immediately applied to the Scheldt. By decree of 1792, the Scheldt and the Meuse were opened to navigation. In 1794, Holland fell under the influence of France and by Treaty of The Hague signed in May, 1795, between France and Holland, the navigation of the Rhine, the Meuse, and the Scheldt was declared free to the two nations. Under this Treaty, Holland ceded the territory on the left bank of the Scheldt to France.

The 5th Article of the Treaty of Paris, 1814, provided

for the freedom of the navigation of the Rhine and in a secret clause provided for the freedom of the Scheldt for purposes of commerce, but with the stipulation that Antwerp should cease to be a naval arsenal. This was inserted at the demand of England, who had learned to fear the possibilities of Antwerp as a threat to England, or as Napoleon called it, "a pistol levelled at the heart of England."[36]

The Treaty of Vienna proclaimed the principle of the freedom of the navigation of international rivers, but qualified the words "with respect to commerce." The secret clause in respect to the Scheldt was confirmed, and it was furthermore provided in regard to this river that, "Everything relating to the navigation on this river specified in Article 1, shall be definitely regulated in the manner most favorable to commerce and navigation, and the most analagous to the regulations established on the Rhine."

The Treaty of Vienna, however, provided for the Union of Holland and Belgium under the Prince of Orange, and, since under this arrangement the Scheldt would be wholly under Dutch control, no special articles were concluded to provide for the regulation of this river as was done for the Rhine, the Meuse, the Main, the Neckar, and the Moselle.

In 1830, the Belgians revolted and the Dutch, as a punitive measure, at once revived the provisions of the Treaty of Munster of 1648 and closed the river. The matter was brought before the conference of the powers at London, which in January, 1831, ordered the immediate withdrawal of the blockade. The Dutch King gave way only under protest. This situation lasted throughout the period of the protracted negotiations over the final settlement of the separation. Holland was permitted to retain both banks of the Scheldt, but Belgium insisted that the piloting, buoying, police, and repairs of the river from Antwerp to the sea be placed under the joint supervision of

[36] Maeterlinck, M. A., *Transactions*, Grotius Society, IV, 258.

the two states. Holland refused to subscribe to these clauses on the ground that they were "derogating to the rights of sovereignty of any independent state." The Dutch declared themselves willing to adhere to the same kind of a convention as that which was signed at Mayence in 1831 in regard to the Rhine.

The Conference, in taking the side of Belgium, pointed to the fact that there already were agreements providing for the joint supervision of the navigation of other rivers and that these agreements were evidence of a modification of the original right of a nation to close the navigation of its international rivers. Further, a free navigation could not be ensured if this supervision were to be left in the hands of one of the riparian states. The Conference also pointed out that Belgium had a more vital interest in the navigation of the Scheldt than in the navigation of the Rhine, and for this reason it would be dangerous to set up a system of "assimilation" such as was set up for the Rhine. The transit traffic on the Rhine was so vital to several of Holland's largest cities as to ensure a liberal policy in the execution of the agreement.

Articles were drawn up providing for the common supervision of piloting, buoying, and for the repair of the river. The dues of pilotage would be fixed in common and were to be the same for the vessels of all nations. The Netherlands Government was permitted to levy certain dues for the right of the navigation of the Scheldt and its mouth, but vessels doing a coastwise or fishing business would not be subject to any duty. Not only was the Scheldt opened to navigation but also the intermediate channels between the Scheldt and the Rhine, though subject to moderate tolls. The tolls which the Dutch Government was permitted to collect were capitalized and paid off in a lump sum in 1863. Belgium was aided by contributions from twenty-one nations and free towns in paying off this sum.

Important supplementary conventions were later added in regard to the buoying of the Scheldt. The Convention of 1866 provides that the Netherlands shall see that the constructions, lighting apparatus and whatever depends on them, shall be kept in good repair. It shall neither take them away, displace them, nor divert them from the use for which they are intended without the consent of Belgium. The Convention of 1881 further provides that, "The Dutch Government shall see that the beacons, high and low water marks and buoys are preserved in good working order. It shall neither take them away nor divert them from their intended use without the consent of Belgium."

Holland later objected to these provisions in so far as they extended to war time. The Dutch Government demanded full liberty of action "in war time, or in the eventuality of war." To this demand Belgium yielded in 1892, confirmed by statutes of 1905 and 1907, and thus henceforth Holland became entitled to take away the lights, beacons, and high and low water marks in time of war, and even in contemplation of war, without Belgium's consent.

The atmosphere again became tense when in 1910 the Dutch Ministry introduced a bill in the chamber providing for a general fortification of the coast. A storm of criticism and protest broke forth from the press of London, Paris, and Brussels. The fortification of Flushing was regarded as of special significance. Belgian opinion saw in the undertaking "a veiled design to revive the old pretension to close the Scheldt." It was generally believed by critics in those countries that the guarantor powers of Belgium's neutrality had the right of passage up the Scheldt to come to the aid of Belgium against an invading German army. Holland's fortifications, it was held, would be injurious to everybody but the Germans; and it was even hinted that Germany was the instigator of the proposal, and that one of the main purposes was to block the Scheldt against a British fleet which might be sent in to the support of Antwerp. Rumors even had it that there was a secret treaty between Germany and Holland by which the former promised military support for the defence of the forts.[37]   This suspicion and criticism caused the Dutch Government to greatly modify its proposals and to delay its program for two years.[38]

With the opening of hostilities the Dutch Government took prompt and energetic action for the protection of its neutrality. War buoying on the Scheldt was instituted in the first few days of the war. From the exchange of notes between Holland and Belgium it appears that the latter recognized the sovereignty of the Netherlands over the mouth of the Scheldt. Great Britain also seems to have recognized the Dutch control, for early in October, before the fall of Antwerp, the British Government requested passage up the Scheldt to Antwerp for two British hospital ships.

But there were officials in the British Government who felt that the Dutch control of the Scheldt ought not to be respected in case the request for free passage up the Scheldt for the relief of Antwerp was denied. As early as August, 1911, on the occasion of the crisis of Agadir, Winston Churchill wrote a letter to Sir Edward Grey in which he urged the necessity of aiding Belgium in the defence of Antwerp in case of hostilities.[39]   In the early days of the war Churchill again urged this action. In a memorandum to the Prime Minister, Sir Edward Grey, and Lord Kitchener, on September 7, 1914, Churchill emphasized the importance of saving Antwerp, and that to

---

[37] See article by "Y" in *Fortn. Review*, Vol. 89, 314 ff, for a typical example, and den Beer Portugael, *La Neutralite sur L'Escaut*, for the Dutch view.

[38] Barnouw, *Holland Under Queen Wilhelmina*, pp. 63–68. The Dutch proposals for increased fortifications may have been influenced in a measure by a threat or warning from Berlin that Dutch territory would be occupied in case of war between Germany and Great Britain. See Barnouw.

[39] "We should be prepared at the proper moment to put extreme pressure on the Dutch to keep the Scheldt open for all purposes. If the Dutch close the Scheldt, we should retaliate by a blockade of the Rhine.

"It is very important to us to be able to blockade the Rhine, and it gets more important as the war goes on. On the other hand, if the Germans do not use the 'Maastricht Appendix' in the first day of the war, they will not want it all all." Winston Churchill, *The World Crisis*, pp. 62, 63.

save Antwerp "true uninterrupted communication with the sea was necessary." He proposed that the British Government request "the Dutch Government to give a free passage up the Scheldt to Antwerp for whatever troops and supplies were needed." He did not believe it possible to supply an army at Antwerp from Ostend and Ghent. He was ready to go far in the application of pressure upon Holland, for in his memorandum he dwelt at some length on the disadvantages to the Allies of a neutrality which kept the Rhine open for Germany but closed the Scheldt to the Allies. Churchill's proposal was turned down for two reasons. Sir Edward Grey did not feel that he could put this grave issue to the Dutch Government, and Lord Kitchener did not wish to use the British Territorial Divisions to reinforce the Belgian army.[40] However, that some such action was at one time contemplated in the very early days of the war may be inferred from the Belgian Grey Book, Document No. 49, in which the British Government announced on August 5, 1914, that the British Great Fleet would insure the free passage of the Scheldt for provisioning Antwerp.[41]

---

[40] *Ibid.*, pp. 360–362. Churchill concludes: "I still think that strong presentations to the Dutch Government might have induced them to grant relief to Antwerp and the Belgian nation in their agony. . . . . a neutral Holland was of far more use to Germany than a hostile, a conquered, or even an allied Holland. Once Holland was attacked by or allied to Germany we could close the Rhine, and if we were in alliance with Holland, the Texel and other Dutch islands of enormous strategic importance would become available for the forward action of the British Navy. We should, in fact, have that overseas route without which a British Naval offensive was impossible. I do not therefore, believe that if Holland had agreed to open the Scheldt for the succor of Antwerp, Germany would have declared war on her. There would have been a long argument about interpretations of neutrality in which the Germans, after their behavior, would have started at a great disadvantage. I still think that if Holland would have said to Germany the English are threatening us with a blockade of the Rhine if we do not open the Scheldt', Germany would have accepted the lesser of two evils."

[41] *A. J. I. L.*, IX, Supp., 80.

III. COMPATIBILITY OF THE DUTCH MEASURES WITH THE RULES OF INTERNATIONAL LAW

Assuming that the mouth of the Scheldt is in Dutch territory,—that is, under the sovereignty of the Netherlands,—and that Belgium is a belligerent, the Dutch regulation of the navigation of the Scheldt, was according to the rules of international law and was impartially administered.[42] The Dutch Government applied to the navigation of the Scheldt the same principles and regulations that it applied to the transport over Dutch territory between Belgium and Germany.

Unofficial attacks on the Dutch neutrality measures in regard to the closing of the Scheldt to anything but commerce were made from two angles. The first of these is based upon the rather ingenious theory that Belgium was not a belligerent since Belgium's perpetual neutrality had been guaranteed. Under Article 10 of the 5th Hague Convention even the use of force by a neutral power to resist any attempt to violate its neutrality can not be regarded as a hostile act. According to Article 5 of the same Convention, Belgium was under obligation to resist the violation of her territory, and according to Article 10 this resistance did not make her a belligerent. Holland had thus no right to treat Belgium as a belligerent to whom Articles 2 and 5 of the 5th Hague Convention applied. In fact, according to this view, these Articles of the 5th Hague Convention instead of justifying the Dutch measures, unequivocally condemned them. And any one of the guarantor powers coming to the aid of Belgium while defending its neutrality, could not be considered a belligerent.[43]

---

[42] For a contemporary view see Phillipson, Coleman, *International tional Law and the Great War*, pp. 301–307.

[43] Maeterlinck, M. A., "The Freedom of the Scheldt", *Transactions*, Grotius Society, IV, 253. This view is found in many Belgian and British writers. See, for instance, Churchill, *op. cit.*; de Visscher, *The Case of Belgium;* "En Vendette", in a number of articles in *Fortnightly Review*. This argument was set forth in Belgium as early as 1911. *Transactions*, Grotius Society, IV, 272.

The answer to this argument is that none of the powers engaged in the war confined themselves merely to resisting Germany's attempt to violate Belgian neutrality. Also at the very commencement of hostilities Germany declared war on Belgium and England declared war on Germany. However unjustifiable and reprehensible may have been the German attack on Belgium it can not be contended that a state of war did not exist. It is not necessary for both parties to declare war before a state of war exists.[44] Whether war exists or not has nothing to do with the nature of the controversy. International law recognizes war as a fact, or as an event,—and the really important question from the legal point of view is the time at which war begins and ends. "War begins when any state of the world manifests its intention to make war by some overt act, which may take the form of an act of war, a declaration of war, or an ultimatum with a time limit."[45]

From a legal standpoint it can not be doubted that a state of war existed and that Holland had to shape her actions accordingly. It should also be remembered that in signing the Treaties of London, Holland merely recognized Belgian neutrality but did not guarantee it. The Dutch Government was therefore under no obligation to aid the powers in the defense of Belgian neutrality. Had Holland permitted the use of the Scheldt for warlike purposes, hostilities might have taken place within her territory. Holland certainly was free to take measures to prevent that.[46]

The second attack upon the Scheldt regulations is

---

[44] "War is the state or condition . . . . It can be set up only by the will to do so, but that will may be unilateral, because that state of peace requires the concurrent wills of two Governments to live together in it, and is replaced by the state of war as soon as one of these wills is withdrawn." Westlake, *International Law*, II, 2.

[45] Wright, Q., "Changes in the Conception of War", *A. J. I. L.*, XVIII, 758.

[46] For the Dutch view on this question see the paper of Bisschop, W. R., *Transactions*, Grotius Society, IV, 271 ff. See also the interesting comments following Maeterlinck's and Bisschop's papers by leading British writers and students of international law.

made by a group of writers who hold that the Treaties of 1839 never intended to give Holland the right to prevent Belgium from using the Scheldt for the purpose of defense any more than for commerce.[47] According to these writers it could never have been the intention of the powers which drafted the Treaties to give Holland sovereign rights over the mouth of the Scheldt, since such an arrangement would clearly be contrary to reason and common sense, as well as justice and equity. It could never have been intended to trust the sovereignty of the Scheldt, the key to a great port, to a state which has a rival port of its own, and which for 200 years had closed the Scheldt to the disadvantage of its rival. Nor could the powers have intended to give such absolute control of the Scheldt to Holland that it could bar the guarantor powers from sending aid to Belgium in case an attack was made upon her neutrality. These writers see also in the facts in the case and in the memoranda of the negotiations substantiation for their claim that the Dutch Government did not again acquire an absolute sovereignty over the Scheldt in 1839. Just what the legal situation has been since 1839 these writers are not certain. Some thought it ought to be regarded as a co-ownership of a co-sovereignty, and others again, like Westlake, thought of it as a servitude in favor of Belgium.[48] But whatever the exact legal situation, these writers are of the opinion that the Netherlands Government was under no obligation to prevent the powers from using the Scheldt to go to the aid of Belgium, and that the guarantor powers would not have exceeded their rights in sending a fleet to Antwerp.

Has the free navigation on international rivers become a right under the customary rules of international law?

---

[47] See Maeterlinck, *op. cit.;* Nys, *Le Droit International,* 129–170; Boulger, *Fortnightly Review,* LXXXVII–LXXXIX, 317 ff; Omond, *Transactions,* Grotius Society, VI, contend that the waters of the Wielingen are Belgian territorial waters.

[48] *Revue de Droit International et de Legislation Comparee,* XIII. This is also the view of Lemonon, *Journal de Droit International,* (Clunet), 1911, p. 850.

On this question there is a difference of opinion. Hall,[49] Oppenheim,[50] Roxburgh,[51] and Lawrence[52] conclude that from the practice in regard to the free navigation of international rivers a right of free navigation can not be deduced.

Westlake[53] and Hershey[54] take the opposite view. The Treaty of Versailles goes a long way in the direction of the internationalization of rivers. Upon the commissions of control even non-riparian states are given representation.[55] Article 23 states that "Subject to and in accordance with the provisions of international conventions existing or hereafter to be agreed upon, the members of the League; . . . . (e) will make provision to secure and maintain freedom of communications and of transit and equitable treatment for the commerce of all members of the League . . . ." This Article would seem to accept the present practice as having crystalized into a principle, and that at least between members of the League it would be an obligation to extend free navigation. The Barcelona Convention is an attempt to put this principle into practice.[56]

But can it be said that either the customary rules of international law or the Treaties of 1839 give Belgium, more than full rights over the river for all purposes of commercial navigation or beneficial enjoyment in time of peace? Since 1829 Holland has not attempted to take away or hamper the exercise of the economic rights given to Belgium under those treaties. Belgium's grievances are political and strategic and not economic. The main question is whether Holland is obligated to grant the use of the Scheldt for warlike purposes.[57]

---

49) *International Law*, pp. 141–142.
50) *International Law*, I, 228–229.
51) *International Conventions and Third States*.
52) *Principles of International Law*, pp. 188–189.
53) *International Law*, I, 157.
54) *Essentials on International Law*, p. 206.
55) Articles 327–362.
56) Convention and Statute on Freedom of Transit, Barcelona, April 20, 1921. *League of Nations Treaty Series*, No. 171.
57) For a statement of Belgian grievances see de Visscher, C., *The Stabilization of Europe*, pp. 68 ff.

The right to the free use of international rivers, if it is an established right under customary international law, has reference only to peace time and for peace needs. And as the Dutch Government frequently had occasion to point out, the terms of the treaties grant freedom of transport over the Scheldt only with respect to commerce. The consensus of opinion among writers and students of international law seems to be that Holland was justified in closing the Scheldt to warships. Among British writers who hold this view are Professor Goudy,[58] Lord Reay,[59] Dr. H. Peason Pyke,[60] and Dr. Bellot.[61] Phillipson sums up the correctness of the Dutch position in the following words:

> "According to the principles we have already set forth, it would be a violation of neutrality to transport armed forces over the portion of the Scheldt below Antwerp. . . . In the large amount of correspondence that went on relative to the separation of the two countries the discussion was confined to securing to Belgium only commercial advantages. Nothing in these arrangements was said about co-sovereignty, nothing was said about warships; nothing was said with an intention to deprive Holland of the right to take necessary measures of self-defence even though the closing of her territorial waters be thereby demanded. The essential point emphasized was that there should be no barrier to commercial navigation; and it was stated expressly that Antwerp should be only a commercial port. Moreover, as Holland was not one of the guarantors of the neutrality of Belgium, she is not obliged to allow foreign warships to pass through her territorial waters for the purpose of protecting Belgium or any other reason. The conclusion, then, to be drawn from all these considerations is that though exclusive sovereignty over the Scheldt cannot be claimed by Holland in respect of commercial navigation . . . . . yet her sole

---

58) *Transactions*, Grotius Society, IV, 282–284.
59) *Ibid.*, IV, 284–286.
60) *Ibid.*, IV, 287–288.
61) *Ibid*, IV, 288.

sovereignty with regard to men of war has not been impaired. Accordingly, the prohibition enforced by the Dutch Government in reference to the warships of the present belligerents were legally justifiable."[62]

---

[62] *International Law and the Great War*, pp. 304–307.

CHAPTER V

TRANSIT OF BELLIGERENT TROOPS AND SUPPLIES AFTER THE ARMISTICE

I. DIPLOMATIC CORRESPONDENCE

A. ALLIED–DUTCH CORRESPONDENCE WITH RESPECT TO THE PASSAGE OF GERMAN SOLDIERS ACROSS DUTCH LIMBURG

PROJECTING far downward between Belgium and Germany is a narrow strip of Dutch territory which comprises the province of Limburg. It has an area of 850 square miles and a population of about 300,000 people. The River Meuse enters this province at the extreme southwest tip where for a short distance both banks of the river are a part of Dutch territory. For the remaining distance up to where the Meuse enters the main body of the Netherlands territory, the river forms the boundary between Dutch Limburg and Belgium. On the west bank of the river near the tip of this salient is situated the city of Maestricht, the capital of the province.

Immediately after the armistice German troops arrived at the frontier of Dutch Limburg and demanded admission to Dutch territory. Before the armistice all belligerent soldiers coming upon Dutch territory were interned, but the Dutch Government decided that there was no longer any object in interning them after the signing of the armistice. The German soldiers coming upon Dutch territory were completely disarmed and their weapons sequestrated. In order to prevent the dispersion of the soldiers over a wide area and to prevent them from sojourning upon Dutch territory for a longer time than was necessary, entrance and passage was restricted to a narrow strip of territory.[1]

When the Allied and Associate Governments were informed of this action by the Dutch Government, individual protests were made by the Belgian, British, United States, French, and Italian Governments. The United

---

[1] *D. O. B.*, V, 9.

States Government in its note stated that the act of permitting the return of German troops across Dutch territory was a violation of neutrality, but that under the circumstances it was not disposed to object. However, it was to be understood that this attitude of the United States was not to be considered as a precedent for the future or an admission of the rightfulness of the Netherlands Government in this matter.[2] The Governments of Great Britain and Italy merely made a formal diplomatic protest.[3] But the Belgian Government reserved the right to provide against the consequences of the decision of the Dutch Government and to employ, should the occasion arrive, all the rights to which this decision might give rise.[4]

The French Government went into some detail as to the grounds of its protest. The armistice had put an end neither to the state of war nor to neutrality. The passage of the German troops across Dutch territory was contrary to the rules of neutrality and should have been prohibited, for in case of failure to evacuate Belgium in the time stipulated these troops would under the terms of the armistice have been subject to capture. The failure to observe these principles permitted Germany to dispose of important forces at a time when peace had not yet been concluded. The French Government, like the Belgian Government, reserved the right to provide against the consequences of the action of the Dutch Government and to assert in case of eventualities, all the rights to which this action was open.[5]

The Netherlands Government replied to all these protests with identic notes. In its opinion the situation in fact and in law had been greatly modified by the armistice. The conditions accepted by Germany were of such a nature as to preclude the resumption of hostilities. The maintenance of internment of belligerent soldiers in-

---

[2] *D. O. B., V,* 9.
[3] *Ibid.,* V, 10 and 14, respectively.
[4] *Ibid.,* V, 8.
[5] *D. O. B.,* V, 10.

terned in the Netherlands conformably to the 5th Hague Convention and the prisoners of war interned in the Netherlands by virtue of the arrangement concluded between Great Britain and Germany, had become without object. The Dutch Government the more readily arrived at this decision because of the fact that the British Government had informed it that all prisoners of war transferred to Holland under the Hague Agreement of 1917 and those interned under international law were all entitled to repatriation.[6]   Moreover, it could not intern these German soldiers at a time when the general liberation of the interned was admitted.   The Dutch Government might have availed itself of the right to deny the request of the German soldiers. This refusal would have been difficult to reconcile with the line of conduct followed in similar circumstances during the war with respect to all belligerents without distinction, but the general situation of the country would have justified it, in view of the excitement of a part of the population at this time, the transport and hospitalization of numerous civil refugees arrived from the north of France, and the passage from Germany of thousands of liberated prisoners of war. If, in spite of this situation, the Dutch Government decided not to object to the entrance of German soldiers it was largely, if not solely, because this decision would be contrary to the best interests of the population of the north of Belgium, from the point of view of food supply and public order. Dutch authorities along the frontier had received reports of impending armed conflicts among the various German soldiers which would have been of fatal consequence to the inhabitants of the country.[7]

The French Government in continuing the correspondence made a distinction between the different interned soldiers in Holland on November 12. One class of interned soldiers, termed "indirect interns," had been entrusted to Holland by virtue of a special arrangement and the Dutch Government was in no way accountable for

---

6) *Ibid.*, V, 9–10, Note to Dutch Government, Nov. 12, 1918.
7) *D. O. B.*, V, 8–9.

these except to the belligerents concerned. Entirely different was the situation of those interned soldiers which Holland had interned for violation of its territory. Over these the Dutch Government had the duty of exercising a close surveillance, and for these,—"direct interns,"— Holland was equally responsible to all the belligerents, and the liberation of these could not be effected except by the consent of all the belligerents, of which France was one. Moreover, Article 10 of the Armistice Terms absolutely limited the liberation of the interned soldiers in Holland to the execution of those engagements concluded anterior to November 11. The British authorization of November 11 to liberate all interned soldiers in Holland applied only to those already interned and did not apply to those soldiers which Holland would be under the necessity to intern later by virtue of its neutrality, to which the armistice had not put an end.[8]

By the time the Dutch Government replied to this note the Allied and Associated Governments had requested and received the permission of the Dutch Government to send troops and supplies across Dutch territory to and from the occupied areas in Germany and to use the port of Rotterdam as a base of supplies for the army of occupation, and the Dutch Government in its note pointed out that the same reasons which were advanced by the Allied Governments to obtain this permission also justified the action of the Dutch Government in regard to the passage of the German troops across Limburg. The Dutch Government accepted the distinction between "direct" and "indirect" internments but failed to see how this distinction opposed the point of view it had adopted. The British Government had held that both the direct and indirect interned soldiers were equally entitled to repatriation.[9] The Dutch Government regarded as illogical the proposi-

---

[8] *Ibid.*, V, 11, Note of December 20, 1918.

[9] *D. O. B.*, V, 9–10, British note of Nov. 12: "Thus all prisoners of war transferred to these countries [Holland and Switzerland] under the Hague Agreement of 1917 and those interned in this country under international law by the Netherlands Government are entitled to repatriation."

tion that it had the right to liberate the prisoners of war already interned, but was under the obligation to continue to intern those who came later.[10]

In support of its contention that though it did not put an end to the state of war the armistice did greatly modify the situation, the Dutch Government included in the above note an annex on the juridical character of the armistice. It was true that the convention was expressly designated as an armistice by its first article, and the expression was repeatedly used in succeeding articles, but the terms of the convention were of such a character as to correspond very little to an armistice convention and were even contradictory to such a convention. The object of an armistice convention, properly speaking, is the suspension of hostilities with the military disposition remaining reciprocal throughout the period of the armistice. But the object of the convention in question, to the contrary, had as its first object to place Germany, during the suspension of hostilities, in a position such that it would not be able to continue the war. This intention of the Allied and Associated Governments was already evident in the note of President Wilson of October 23, in which he stated that the only armistice which he was authorized to propose would be the one that would render Germany incapable of resuming hostilities. This same purpose was also evident from the large number of the stipulations of the convention by which Germany abandoned in law and in fact its means of carrying on war while the Allied and Associated Powers conserved and fortified theirs. Taken together, all these stipulations could mean only one thing —that the so-called armistice convention had as its object the general capitulation of Germany as a belligerent power. The surrender of enormous supplies of war material, of railroad rolling stock, the surrender of the German fleet, the evacuation of Allied territory, the free entry and exit in the Baltic, the occupation of German territory, the liberation of prisoners of war without reciprocity, and the stipulation that the neutral powers were

---

10) *Ibid.*, V, 11–12, Note of April 19.

to be advised that the liberty of navigation conceded to Allied and Associated warships, would not raise questions of neutrality—all these conditions marked the convention as something besides a mere armistice convention.

As far as a neutral was concerned there was no longer any war in the true sense of the term, nor was there yet a state of peace. International law recognizes many similar situations, as for instance the so-called "pacific blockade" and the opposition by armed force of a neutral state against the violations of its neutrality by a belligerent.[11] Moreover, it has often happened that neutrals have considered armistice conventions, because of their special tendency, practically in many respects, as treaties of peace. Always respecting the principles of impartiality and maintaining its proper sovereign rights, and abstaining as such from any part in the war, the neutral must shape its conduct so as to adapt itself as quickly as possible to the very special situation, intermediary between peace and war, created by the convention. Naturally, in a matter of this kind, precise rules are lacking and differences of opinion easily result. The Dutch note ended by showing that the Dutch actions after the armistice were such as to facilitate the objects of the convention.[12]

B. ALLIED–DUTCH CORRESPONDENCE IN RESPECT TO THE TRANSPORT ACROSS DUTCH TERRITORY OF MEN AND SUPPLIES

The United States Government on January 27, 1919, requested permission for the use of the port of Rotterdam and the river Rhine as a means of supplying the armies of occupation.[13] The Dutch Government consented to this request with the understanding that the transport was to take place under the flag of commerce.[14] On February 1 the American Government requested permission to send American troops and supplies down the

---

11) 5th Hague Convention, Art. 10 and 13th Hague Convention, Art. 26.
12) *D. O. B.*, V, 12–14.
13) *Ibid.*, V, 14.
14) *Ibid.*, V, 14.

Rhine and to tranship them at the port of Rotterdam.[15] The Dutch Government also granted this request, but under the following conditions: that it was to be regarded as a special case and not as a precedent; that the transport would take place only under the flag of commerce; that only officers would carry arms; and that the Dutch officials would be furnished with all convenient information in regard to the transport.[16]   A little later the United States Government was granted permission for a similar use of the Scheldt, subject to the same conditions.[17]

The Belgian and British Governments regarded this use of the Rhine and the Scheldt not so much a privilege as a right.   In a note of December 1, 1918, the Belgian Government stated that it had, notwithstanding the fact that the armistice had not put an end to the state of war, transported supplies and materials from the Belgian military base at Calais to Antwerp by way of the Scheldt, and that it reserved the right to transport by the same way military supplies and material in general.   This decision could meet with no objection on the part of the Dutch Government since the same right had been accorded to German troops and military supplies in the passage across Limburg.[18]   The Dutch Government replied that the statement that the right of transporting war material had been accorded to German soldiers was inexact, and that Belgium's claim for a similar right, based upon analogy, was not well founded.   However, it had no objection to the navigation of the Scheldt for the purposes mentioned in the note.[19]

The Belgian Government persisted that its statement was exact—that its truth was established by photographs which had been published even in Holland showing an important military train had crossed Limburg with baggage, rolling kitchens, motor trucks, animals, forage, and

---

15) *Ibid.,* V, 15.
16) *D. O. B.,* V, 15.
17) *Ibid.,* V, 15.
18) *Ibid.,* V, 16.
19) *Ibid.,* V, Note of Dec. 12.

other provisions, if not arms and munitions.[20]   On December 27 the Belgian Government informed the Dutch Government that it faced the necessity of sending supplies to its troops stationed in Germany by way of the routes traversing Limburg and by the Anvers-Gladbach railway and that since the Dutch Government had permitted the passage of German troops across this territory, it could have no objections to the proposed transit by Belgium.[21]   The Dutch Government acceded also to this last request but again made plain that it did so without reference to the claim made by Belgium in regard to the passage of German soldiers across Limburg.   Until the Belgian Government made more specific reference to actual photographs, so that the Dutch Government could determine their authenticity, it could not accept them as evidence as to what had taken place.   As proof that the German soldiers passing through Limburg had been completely disarmed the Dutch Government gave a list of the number of rifles, revolvers, machine guns, anti-aircraft guns, artillery, automobiles, and other military supplies which had been sequestered at this occurrence. Moreover, many of the 70,300 soldiers admitted into Limburg had previous to admission abandoned their arms and equipment in Belgium.[22]

France and Great Britain were accorded the same privilege of transporting and sending supplies across Dutch territory to the armies of occupation and to demobilize troops across Dutch territory subject to the same conditions.[23]   But when the British Government asked permission also to send men on leave to England and back to the area of occupation, and in particular, to move troops with their arms across Dutch territory, the Dutch Government advanced objections.   It believed that the concessions demanded surpassed those which it could accord without prejudice to primordial interests of the state.

---

20) *D. O. B., V,* Note of Dec. 21.
21) *Ibid.,* V, Note of Dec. 27.
22) *Ibid.,* V, 17, Notes of January 16 and 22.
23) *Ibid.,* V, 18–21.

The Dutch Government refused to grant the concession of transporting soldiers across Dutch territory except under the conditions stipulated, but stated that the conditions would be complied with if the arms were placed in the hold of the vessels transporting the soldiers or were placed on board auxiliary vessels accompanying the troop transport vessels. But the Dutch Government felt that it could not consent to the passage of British soldiers returning to Germany.[24]

The British Government continued to press the demand, arguing that the passage of these troops across Dutch territory was directly essential to the establishment of the general peace. It was of the highest importance in the interests of an early peace that the occupation of the German territory on the left bank of the Rhine should be effectually carried out. The extreme congestion of railways in Belgium and northern France placed serious hindrances in the way of executing the armistice agreements, and

> "It is in order that the efforts of the Associated Powers to bring about the speedy conclusion of a desirable peace for the benefit of the whole community of nations may not be brought to naught that the Netherlands Government is earnestly requested to coöperate towards this end by facilitating in every way the movement of troops and supplies across Dutch territory strictly for the purpose agreed upon with the German Government under the terms of the armistice."[25]

On March 1st the Dutch Government sent a note to the British Government stating that in view of the grounds upon which the permission was demanded, namely, that this measure would help to bring about more promptly the return of normal relations and that to this end the Dutch Government ought to coöperate as much as possible while still remaining within its rights and duties, and taking cognizance of the statement that the measure

---

[24] *D. O. B.*, V, 19, Note of February 20.
[25] *Ibid.*, V, 20, Note of February 20.

in question had in view only the execution of the purposes agreed upon with the German Government under the armistice terms, and considering the affirmation of the British Government that the passage of these troops was not open to objection on the grounds of neutrality, the Dutch Government saw fit to defer to the British demands. However, the permission was granted subject to the condition that the troops reascending the Rhine would not exceed in number those descending. The authorization would have to be limited to the duration of the armistice, and the Dutch Government reserved the right to withdraw the authorization at any time.[26]

II. THE RULE OF INTERNATIONAL LAW WITH RESPECT TO THE TRANSPORT OF TROOPS AND SUPPLIES ACROSS NEUTRAL TERRITORY

The passage of belligerent troops or the transport of war material across neutral territory was a common occurrence in the 18th century, and there were instances of it even in the Napoleonic wars. Bernadotte, upon the order of Napoleon, marched French troops through the Prussian territory of Anspach without asking the consent of Prussia. Austrian troops passed through Swiss territory in 1815, and upon the renewal of the war in 1815 allied troops passed through Swiss territory with the consent of the Swiss Government.[27] In 1870 Switzerland denied passage across her territory to groups of Alsatians which had enlisted for service in the French army but were traveling without arms or munitions. Germany in the same war asked Belgium for the permission to transport wounded soldiers across Belgian territory by railway. France vigorously protested on the ground that the concession would facilitate German military operations by the relief this transport across Belgium would give to the German railways. After consultation with Great Britain Belgium refused the request.[28] During the World

---

26) *D. O. B.*, V, 20.
27) Oppenheim, II, 345–347.
28) Hall, pp. 594–596.

War the United States refused to grant permission to Canadian wounded demobilized soldiers, soldiers returning home on furlough, or those being invalided home for convalescence, passage across Maine.[29] Portugal granted free passage through Beira to Rhodesia in the war between Great Britain and Transvaal, but this permission was based on the Anglo-Portuguese treaty of June 11, 1891.[30]

Modern writers on international law unanimously agree that a neutral can not allow a belligerent to convoy troops or war materials across its territory, and that it can not permit this even though it should grant the same privilege to both belligerents.[31] Even the existence of a state-servitude or of a treaty made previous to the war can not justify permission of this passage, since it is now generally accepted that a qualified neutrality is no longer admissable.[32] This concensus of opinion was finally embodied in the 5th Hague Convention, Article 5, which states that "A neutral Power must not allow belligerents to move troops or convoys of either munitions of war or supplies across its territory."

III. COMPATIBILITY OF THE DUTCH MEASURES WITH THE RULES OF INTERNATIONAL LAW

That a neutral may not permit the convoy of belligerent troops or war materials across its territory in time of war is generally accepted and this the Dutch Government never denied. Can such convoy be permitted during an armistice? The Dutch Government seemed to assume that under the conditions it imposed in the case of the German soldiers the passage was perfectly proper. It had received orders from Great Britain to release the interned soldiers. What was the logic or use of interning German soldiers coming upon Dutch territory when all

---

29) *A. J. I. L.*, IX, Sp. Supp., 229–230.
30) Moore, *Digest*, VII, 939–940.
31) Halleck, pp. 517–518; Woolsey, pp. 278–279; Hall, pp. 623–624; Westlake, II, 233; Lawrence, p. 635; Oppenheim, II, 391.
32) Oppenheim, II, 392.

the other soldiers already interned in Holland were being released? After disarming these soldiers entering Dutch territory, the Dutch authorities merely let them go their way homeward like the previously interned soldiers. But in the case of the transport of the British troops the Dutch Government conceded about as much as it is physically possible to concede. British soldiers were allowed to go up the Rhine to the army of occupation and British soldiers coming down the Rhine were permitted to carry their arms.

If the armistice convention was what it purported to be by its own terms—an armistice—the passage of armed British soldiers across Dutch territory, and in particular the passage to Germany was a clear violation of neutrality. But armistices are sometimes treated as practically an end of war, as for instance after the conclusion of the armistice between the United States and Spain in 1898 many neutral powers permitted American public ships freely to enter their ports for the purpose of docking and taking in supplies.[33] And as the Dutch Government insisted in its note to France, the terms of the armistice from a juridical as well as from a practical point of view partook more of the nature of a capitulation than of an armistice.

The permission of the Dutch Government to allow the transportation of British troops under arms across its territory involved a technical violation of neutrality, but the matter ought to be judged upon the broader ground of international policy. The four years of war had brought Europe to the point of exhaustion and it was highly important for all of Europe, neutral as well as belligerent, to restore normal conditions as soon as possible. The Dutch Government therefore decided to work along as much as possible in the liquidation of the war. The actual situation, juridical and practical, with which the Dutch Government was confronted, is well summed up in the British note of February 3, 1919.

---

[33] Moore, *Digest*, VII, 335.

"Though technically we are still at war with Germany and Holland remains neutral no real infraction of any neutral obligation on the part of Holland is in fact involved. The obligation of a neutral to prevent passage of armed forces of a belligerent across his territory is but the application of the principle that a neutral must not allow his territory to be used by one belligerent in order to further military operations directed against the other. In the present case the returning troops are coming home to be demobilized; their passage therefore, so far from promoting military operations against Germany, is in accordance with the terms of the armistice to which Germany is a party. Germany therefore cannot and does not object to their arrival in German territory and it cannot affect Germany in any way whether or not such troops, on their way to occupied provinces where their position is stipulated for, pass through neutral territory. Germany is in no way disadvantaged by Holland permitting the passage.

"On the other hand, Holland is herself interested in easing general transportation facilities which must be successfully overcome as a whole in order that the provisioning of Western Europe with food and necessary supplies is to be assured. A general breakdown of essential lines of communications is as little to the Dutch as to the Allied interests."[34]

---

[34] *D. O. B.*, V, 19.

Chapter VI

AERIAL REGULATIONS

I. Regulations and Measures of Control

THE NEUTRALITY PROCLAMATION contained no regulations with respect to the control of aircraft. By royal decree of August 3, 1914, all airships not belonging to the Netherlands' land or sea forces, were prohibited from crossing the Dutch frontier.[1] The reason for the general prohibition was stated in the decree to be the necessity of preventing foreign armies from acquiring information about the military preparations of the Dutch Government. The decree was thus apparently issued in the first instance as a protective measure, though it was afterwards regarded as a neutrality measure as well.[2]

At the time the prohibition was issued the Dutch Government sent a warning to the belligerent governments that it would oppose by force any violation of the prohibition, and that it would not be responsible for whatever consequences might follow. In several instances violators of the prohibition were forced to land by fire from Dutch anti-aircraft guns. All aircraft and their crews landing in Dutch territory were interned. Every known violation was immediately followed by a protest from the Dutch Government. Where damages were suffered as a result of the violation, indemnities were demanded and obtained.[3]

All belligerent aircraft and their crews landing on Dutch territory, even when they had come above Dutch territory by mistake or by force majeure were interned. When in July, 1915, a German aviator on a practice flight had come above Dutch territory through faulty orienta-

---

[1] See Appendix VI. Carsten, *op. cit.*, pp. 164–165. The indefinite term "land frontier" (lands grenzen) is used in the decree and was construed to include territorial waters.

[2] *D. O. B.*, I, 26; *Recueil*, pp. 134–135.

[3] *Ibid.*, I, 26.

tion and had been compelled to land, the German Government protested the subsequent internment on the ground that no military operation was here involved. The German Government sought to establish an analogy between this case and that of the belligerent soldier who crosses the neutral frontier by mistake and without any military end. Release of the flier and his plane was demanded. The Dutch Government refused to make any exception in its rules of belligerent aircraft internment, rejecting the analogy of the airship with the soldier on the ground that the two cases differed essentially. The circumstances under which the soldier crosses the neutral frontier allow the authorities guarding the frontier to determine if his presence upon Dutch territory is or is not due to a mistake and without relation to military operations, while the circumstances which caused the aviator to land on Dutch territory or to fly over it escaped the control of the Dutch authorities, and moreover, there are reasons for a special and strict treatment of aircraft. They enjoy great liberty of action, unusual facilities for making observations, and practically complete freedom from control.[4]

A serious consequence of the Dutch regulations was that aircraft not belonging to the land or sea forces of the Netherlands were exposed to immediate fire upon crossing the Dutch frontier, without any warning from the Dutch military authorities that they were above Dutch territory, and without being given opportunity to depart. This regulation led to a grave disaster in the case of the German dirigible L-19 which, as a result of the damage sustained by it from fire of the Dutch coast guard, fell into the North Sea, with the loss of its entire crew.[5] The German Government contended that in firing upon the L-19 without warning the Dutch military authorities had conducted themselves in a manner contrary to the principles of international law and the laws of humanity. It ought to be presumed that every German airship found above Dutch territory was there because of circumstances

---

[4] *D. O. B.*, III, 25. *Recueil*, pp. 139–140.
[5] February 1, 1916.

beyond its control, since the German Government had repeatedly assured the Dutch Government that it had given its aviators strict orders not to fly above Dutch territory.

The Dutch Government replied that it had frequently protested the violation of Dutch territory by German aircraft, but that notwithstanding, violations were constantly increasing. The only effective way for German aviators to avoid coming over Dutch territory would be always to remain sufficiently distant from the Dutch maritime and territorial frontiers so as to avoid the possibility of being carried over Dutch territory even by mistake, damages, or atmospheric conditions. A neutral power is not obliged to determine by what cause the belligerent aircraft find themselves above its territory. In the interest of the defense of the state, not less than in the interest of the maintenance of a strict neutrality, a neutral power is within its right in opposing by force all crossing of its frontiers by belligerent aircraft unless they indicate by a signal, a white flag or other distinctive sign, their intention to land. The L-19 had been repeatedly warned that it was above Dutch territory and it had given no signal of distress. The Dutch authorities had every reason to oppose the violation of Dutch sovereignty by force, for the L-19 had been for hours above the northern frontier without indicating any intention of landing.[6]

The German Government refused to accept both the Netherland Government's statement of the facts and the correctness of its regulations under international law. The German Government insisted that the circumstances clearly indicated that the L-19 was in distress. An international distress signal was lacking, and moreover airships can not immediately land under all circumstances. As regards the regulations themselves, the German Government could not in any way admit that flying over neutral territory violated either the sovereignty or the neutrality of the state concerned. There was not a single generally recognized principle in international law in re-

---

6) *D. O. B.*, III, 25–26. *Recueil*, pp. 140–144.

gard to the regulations a neutral must impose on belligerent aircraft. The German Government had not protested the Dutch prohibition at the time of its announcement, not because it accepted the principles underlying the prohibition, but because it wanted to avoid anything that might disturb neighborly relations. The war constituted a hindrance to bringing this matter to clarity upon an international basis, and for this reason the German Government wished to hold its definitive opinion in abeyance.[7]

The Dutch Government then proposed that a distress signal be agreed upon for the use of German aviators when they wished to alight upon Dutch territory. The German Government agreed with the view of the Dutch Government that the flier ought to indicate his distress by a convenient signal, indicating that he would land upon Dutch territory. The German Government would not, during the existing war, protest the internment of aircraft and their crews landing upon Dutch territory. Distress signals were agreed upon in December, 1916,[8] and these same signals were later accepted by France and Belgium. Great Britain because of technical objections accepted them only for their marine planes.[9]

There were many violations of the Dutch aerial prohibition by belligerent aircraft.[10] When protests were lodged with the government to which the offending aircraft belonged expressions of regret were invariably obtained. In every case it was alleged that no violation of Dutch sovereignty had been intended and that the unfortunate occurrence was to be ascribed to bad weather or atmospheric conditions, damages, or faulty orientation. The Dutch Government refused to accept these explanations in all cases, contending that the frequency of the violations could not be accounted for on these

---

[7] *D. O. B.*, III, 25–27.
[8] *D. O. B.*, III, 26–27.
[9] *Ibid.*, IV., 51.
[10] *Ibid.*, I, 26–28 and III, 23–25.

grounds, and that the circumstances in many cases clearly disproved the explanations given.[11] Where the Dutch Government did accept the explanation that no violation was intended, it frequently protested the conduct of the aviators after they had become aware of being above Dutch territory. The Dutch Government took the position that when a belligerent aircraft did cross the Dutch frontier by error it should return to the place where it crossed the frontier along the same route by which it had come, even though that might not be the quickest and shortest way to the Dutch border. The guiding principle should be the violation of as little territory as possible.[12]

The violation of the Dutch aerial prohibition did not stop with a mere crossing of the frontier by the belligerent aircraft. Several bombs were dropped on Dutch towns, causing much material damage and even loss of life. Much damage was thus caused one night in the little town of Zierikzee. Both the British and German Governments made denials of guilt, but the fragments of bombs found in the debris indicated British origin. The Admiralty in London then admitted the mistake and agreed to pay damages to the victims.[13] British aircraft also dropped bombs on the towns of Goes, Axel, and Sas van Gent. The British Government paid damages totaling nearly 30,000 florins to the victims of these attacks.[14]

The Dutch Government's resort to force to compel respect for its neutrality and sovereignty was evidently without much success. Violations were repeated and frequent. So long as the aircraft did not come within the range of the Dutch anti-aircraft guns or were forced to land on Dutch territory because of force majeure or mistakes, they escaped all control of the Dutch author-

---

[11] *Ibid.*, I, 26–27.

[12] *D. O. B.*, I, 27; *Recueil*, pp. 135–139.

[13] Barnouw, *op. cit.*, p. 116. *D. O. B.*, 1921–1922, p. 22. Garner, *op. cit.*, I, 477, wrongfully ascribes these attacks to German craft.

[14] *D. O. B.*, 1921–1922, p. 22.

ities.[15] Diplomatic protests brought no marked diminution in the number of violations.

II. History of Aerial Regulations

The use of aircraft for the purpose of combat and the dropping of bombs on towns and military works was a development of the World War. Balloons had been used for over a century for the purposes of observation, signaling, and the sending of despatches. During the Turco-Italian and Balkan wars airplanes began to be used for similar purposes, but it was not until the World War that both dirigibles and airplanes were used for purposes of attack.[16] As a result the World War opened with very few positive international rules of aerial regulation whether in peace or in war. Nor were there any precedents for guidance.

Other neutral powers laid down aerial regulations similar to those of the Netherlands. Switzerland and Denmark forbade belligerent aircraft to fly over their territories and ordered their military authorities to fire upon all aircraft violating the order. Norway, Spain, and Italy also formally prohibited the passage of belligerent aircraft, non-military as well as military, over its territory. A formal prohibition against passage over its territory of foreign aircraft without its permission was not issued by the Swedish Government until July, 1916.[17] President Wilson by proclamation of November 13, 1914,

---

[15] Garner, *op. cit.*, I, 475, states that in October, 1915, the Dutch authorities adopted the expedient of permitting the despatch of warning telegrams to England announcing the approach of German Zeppelins which were guilty of passing over Dutch territory, and the expedient is said to have been fairly successful in deterring German aviators subsequently flying over Holland in the course of their raids upon England. Garner probably has reference to the Dutch regulation whereby the transmission of news concerning the movements of belligerent forces, observed from the territory of Holland was forbidden, but in regard to the violation of Dutch territory the immediate publication of the news by telegraph was entirely free. *Recueil*, p. 168.

[16] Garner, *International Law and the World War*, I, 458–459.

[17] *Ibid.*, I, 476–478. Garner, *A. J. I. L.*, XVIII, 76–80. Fenwick, *International Law*, pp. 286–287, 571–572.

denied the use of the air spaces over the Panama Canal Zone to all belligerent aircraft, private as well as public.[18]

All the neutral powers, with the exception of Norway, refused to grant belligerent aircraft the privilege of temporary sojourn in their territory for any purpose whatsoever. All belligerent airships and their crews landing on their territory, no matter for what reason, were interned. This regulation is in direct contrast with the treatment generally accorded belligerent warships, which may sojourn in neutral ports twenty-four hours and even longer if repairs are necessary to render them seaworthy. Norway was apparently the only neutral government which did not intern airships and the crews of airships forced to land on its soil.[19]

III. COMPATIBILITY OF THE DUTCH AERIAL REGULATIONS WITH THE RULES OF INTERNATIONAL LAW

Very little customary and no conventional rules governing the rights and duties of a neutral over belligerent airships above its national domain were in existence at the outbreak of the World War. Much had been written on the control of aerial navigation and warfare, but it took the experience of the World War to put to test the various theories held by the different writers. There was a considerable school of writers who maintained that the air space, like the open sea, is, because of its very nature, free, and that subjacent states have no control over it. One of these writers, Fauchille, in his proposed code would even allow hostilities in the air space over neutral territories, subject to certain conditions.[20] The analogy of the air space with the open seas is an unsound one and was rejected in practice during the World War and in the conventions formulated since. Neutrality is not only involved, but also the safety of the inhabitants beneath. The question of national defense is also involved. The

---

18) *Am. White Book, European War*, II, 18; *A. J. I. L.*, IX, Sp. Supp. 205.
19) Fenwick, *op. cit.*, p. 52. Garner, *A. J. I. L.*, XVIII, 79.
20) Garner, *Recent Developments of International Law*, p. 177.

neutral should be free to take measures to prevent members of the belligerent forces from making observations above its territory in regard to the state of its military preparations.[21]

Fortunately, there is now in existence a proposed international convention by which the compatibility of the Dutch aerial regulations with the rules of international law can be objectively tested. A resolution adopted by the Washington Conference, February, 1922, provided for the appointment of a commission of jurists to formulate rules governing the use of aircraft and radio in war. The commission, composed of representatives of Great Britain, France, Italy, Japan, the United States, and the Netherlands, completed its work in February, 1923.

The rules proposed by the commission give a rather complete outline of the rights and duties of a neutral with respect to the air space over its territory.[22] Article 12 gives the neutral the right to forbid the entrance within its jurisdiction of all aircraft, while Article 42 imposes the duty to exclude entry within its jurisdiction of belligerent military aircraft, to compel them to alight if they have entered such jurisdiction, and to intern any belligerent aircraft which is within its jurisdiction no matter for

---

[21] The two main schools of thought, with their subdivisions, were as follows:
A. Those who maintain that the air space is by its nature free
  1) Air freedom without restriction.
  2) Air freedom restricted by some special rights (not limited as regards height), of the subjacent state.
  3) Air freedom restricted by a territorial zone.
B. Those who maintain the theory of the sovereignty of the subjacent state in the air above its territory.
  1) Full sovereignty without any restrictions.
  2) Full sovereignty restricted by the right of innocent passage for aerial navigation.
  3) Full sovereignty up to a limited height only.
See "Report of Committee on Aviation", International Law Association, *Proceedings*, 28th Conference, Madrid, 1913, pp. 529–530. For an excellent review of the extensive literature on the subject see Garner, *Recent Developments of International Law*, Lecture V. See also Hyde, *International Law*, I, 324–334.
[22] For the text of the proposed rules see Moore, *International Law and Some Current Illusions*, pp. 182–288. For comments on the proposed rules see Garner, *A. J. I. L.*, XVIII, 56 ff.

what reason it may have alighted, together with its crew and passengers. Article 39 imposes upon the belligerent non-military aircraft, if permitted to enter within neutral jurisdiction, the obligation to abstain from such acts which it is the neutral's duty to prevent. Belligerent military aircraft under Article 40 are forbidden to enter the jurisdiction of a neutral state, but Article 41 provides that aircraft on board vessels of war, including aircraft carriers, shall be regarded as part of such vessels, and come therefore under the rules governing the treatment of belligerent warships in neutral ports.

Article 43 provides for the internment of the personnel of a disabled belligerent aircraft rescued outside neutral waters and brought into the jurisdiction of a neutral state by a neutral military aircraft. Other articles provide that the neutral must not supply a belligerent, directly or indirectly, aircraft, parts of aircraft, or material, supplies or munitions required for aircraft,[23] but a neutral is not under obligation to prevent the export or transit on behalf of a belligerent, of aircraft, parts of aircraft, or material, supplies or munitions for aircraft.[24] However, a neutral must prevent the use of its territory as a base of operations by a belligerent. It is bound to prevent the departure from its jurisdiction of hostile expeditions.[25] A neutral must also prevent within its jurisdiction aerial observations of the movements, operations or defences of one belligerent, with the intention of informing the other belligerent.[26] The use of force or other means at its disposal by a neutral in the exercise of its rights or duties under these rules can not be regarded as a hostile act.[27]

It will be noticed that the Dutch aerial regulations in no way conflict with the rules of the code proposed by the commission of jurists; in fact, the code embodies the

---

[23] Article 44.
[24] Article 45.
[25] Article 46.
[26] Article 47.
[27] Article 48.

general practice of neutrals in the World War. The acquiescence of the belligerents in this practice established a customary rule. It may be expected that most neutrals will, like Switzerland, Holland, and Denmark, avail themselves of the right to forbid the entrance of all belligerent aircraft, military and non-military alike, and thus avoid most of the possibilities of controversy in regard to the duties of a neutral provided for under Articles 44-47 of the proposed code.

Chapter VII

ADMISSION OF BELLIGERENT WARSHIPS

I. Provisions of the Neutrality Proclamation

ONE of the most unusual features of the Dutch neutrality regulations was the treatment under its provisions of belligerent warships, armed merchant vessels, and vessels acquired as a result of an act of war. On July 30, 1914, the Dutch Government by royal decree prohibited all warships, regardless of nationality, from entering Dutch territorial waters.[1] More detailed provisions with respect to this general prohibition were placed in the Proclamation of Neutrality which was issued six days later. Article 4 of the Proclamation provided that no warships or vessels assimilated thereto belonging to belligerents would be allowed to enter the jurisdiction of the state. In the next article three exceptions were made to this general prohibition. A temporary sojourn was allowed these vessels in case they were forced to enter ports or roadsteads of the state on account of damages or the state of the sea. So also the belligerent warships and assimilated vessels were permitted to anchor in a port or roadstead of the colonies or overseas possessions exclusively with the object of completing their provisions of foodstuffs or fuel, but under no circumstances could their stay exceed twenty-four hours. A different rule was laid down for the home territory and the overseas possessions. The third exemption from the general prohibition applied to vessels employed exclusively on a religious, scientific, or humanitarian mission.[2] Belligerent warships violating these regulations would be interned for the duration of the war.[3]

---

[1] *Staatsblad*, No. 332.

[2] The customary restrictions as laid down in the 13th Hague Convention were imposed in the event that warships entered the territorial waters under the exceptions of Article 5.

[3] Article 3.

Out of these regulations many controversies arose. Germany protested the regulations for the treatment of warships, particularly submarines, while Great Britain protested the action of the Netherlands Government in assimilating armed merchantmen to warships. In March and April, 1917, a few notes were exchanged between the United States and the Netherlands with respect to the application of the rule to neutral armed merchantmen.

II. Correspondence with Respect to the Non-Admission of Warships[4]

The first German protest of this regulation was occasioned by the internment in November, 1915, of the German submarine "UC-8," which had been stranded on the Noordergronden within the Dutch territorial waters.[5] The German Government contended first of all that the entrance of this submarine into the Dutch waters was due to a defective electric compass, and that therefore this case fell under the exceptions of Article 5. The second and main contention was that this entrance into Dutch waters was prohibited neither under international law nor under the rules of the Dutch Proclamation of Neutrality. The German Government invoked the 10th Article of the 13th Hague Convention which states that the "neutrality of a power is not affected by the mere passage through its territorial waters of warships or prizes belonging to belligerents." And the German Government was of the opinion that the Dutch proclamation nowhere contained a prohibition of passage through territorial waters since Article 2 could refer only to passage through interior Dutch waters. As a consequence, on the basis of paragraph 1, Article 5, the submarine should be given permission freely to leave the territorial waters of the Netherlands. Should the Dutch Govern-

---

[4] Found in the *Dutch White Book*, "Diplomatieke Bescheiden betreffende de toelating van oorlogsschepen en bewapende Handelsvaartuigen der oorlogvoerenden binnen het Nederlandsche Rechtsgebied"; *Recueil de diverses communications;* and *D. O. B., passim.*

[5] *D. O. B.*, II, 18 and *Recueil*, pp. 148–149.

ment interpret Article 2 to prohibit also the passage through territorial waters, the German Government would be forced to reject this interpretation since under international law belligerents have the right of passage through the territorial waters of neutrals and this right could not be taken away from them by a unilateral declaration such as the Neutrality Proclamation.[6]

To these contentions, Mr. Loudon replied that the internment of the "UC-8" was based on the provisions of Articles 4, 17, 3, and 2 of the Dutch Proclamation and that Article 3, upon which the German contention was based, did not diminish the prohibition found in Article 4, but on the contrary was an amplification in that it expressly excluded passage through Dutch interior waters. The prohibition found in Article 4 was in no way contrary to international law. Article 10 of the 13th Hague Convention merely states that the neutrality of a power is not affected by the mere passage through its territorial waters of warships. Nowhere is the neutral prohibited from denying the right to belligerent warships of passage through its territorial waters. The neutral is free to make such restrictions as it sees fit. Mr. Loudon admitted that the prohibition contained in Article 4 might be contrary to the rules of international law if applied to ordinary navigation, but the territorial waters of the Netherlands at no point of their entire expanse constitute a passage for ordinary navigation. Furthermore the "UC-8" did not fall under any of the exceptions in Article 5 of the Proclamation, under which the entrance of warships into the territorial waters would be permissable. A defective compass would not justify such entrance. The commander should have taken a more vigorous precaution against such an eventuality. The commander had, according to his own declaration, already doubted the correct functioning of the compass while in the open seas. Under these circumstances he should have taken the precaution to navigate by sounding in order to keep outside of the Dutch territorial waters. And finally Mr. Loudon

---

[6] *D. O. B.*, II, 19, 20. *Recueil*, pp. 150, 153, 154.

rejected the German interpretation of the word *toege-laten,* used in the Dutch text, to mean "sojourn" as contrary to its plain meaning.[7]

In the case of the German submarine "UB-30," which was stranded in Dutch waters in February, 1917, a peaceful settlement was reached only after a Commission of Inquiry had been instituted to determine the actual conditions under which the vessel had entered Dutch jurisdiction. The Dutch Government was convinced from the findings of its own investigation that the "UB-30" could have avoided entering Dutch waters if it had taken reasonable precautions. The entrance was due to the fact that the German commander had mistaken the identification of various beacon lights along the Dutch shore and because he had failed to consult the Dutch light-list. Since the circumstances of the entrance into Dutch waters did not fall under the last exception under Article 5 of the Proclamation the submarine and its crew were interned.

The German commander protested the internment on the ground that the "UB-30" had entered the Dutch territorial waters without knowledge or blame on the part of the commander. The report of the commander to his government stated that the entrance had been in part due to a defective compass and that the Dutch officials had refused to make an investigation of this matter after he had requested them to do so. A second investigation by the Dutch Government revealed no new details. The German commander was interviewed by several Dutch naval officials in the presence of the naval attaché of the German Legation. But it did not appear that the commander had requested the Dutch officials to personally convince themselves of the defect in the compass. Upon the outcome of this investigation the Dutch Government notified the German Government that the "UB-30" must remain interned.[8]

On the night of March 12, another German submarine, the "UB-6," was found stranded in Dutch territorial

7) *D. O. B.,* II, 19–23. *Recueil,* pp. 150–158.
8) *Dutch White Book,* p. 3.

waters and likewise was interned by the Dutch naval authorities. The circumstance under which the "UB-6" entered Dutch territorial waters was much the same as that of the "UB-30"[9] and the German Government protested its internment on the same ground as that of the internment of the first submarine.

Since further exchanges of notes brought the two Governments no nearer to an agreement as to the facts of the case and the consequent validity of the internment, it was decided to submit the matter to an International Commission of Inquiry.[10] The Commission was charged with the sole duty of settling the factual dispute, that is, of determining whether the entrance of the two submarines into Dutch territorial waters was or was not due to neglect of the commanders to take the necessary precautionary measures to prevent entrance into the Dutch territorial jurisdiction. The Commission, which convened at The Hague on July 12, 1917, was composed of the following: Captain Block of Denmark, Chairman; Captain H. J. Surie of the Netherlands; Captain Vansdow of Germany; Lieutenant Lisbeck of Sweden. The Dutch Government appointed as its representative before the Commission Vice-Admiral W. C. J. Smit, and the German Government appointed as its representative Dr. Scheurer of the Admiralty Staff.[11]

The Commission which reported its findings on the 20th of July, decided that the entrance of the "UB-6" was due to neglect on the part of the commander to take necessary precautions, but that the entrance of the "UB-30" was not due to neglect.[12] In conformity with

---

[9] *Ibid.*, p. 7.

[10] Van Eyzinga in the *Annuaire Grotius*, 1917, p. 139, calls the commission a Commission of Arbitration and not of Inquiry, upon the ground that both powers agreed to accept the findings of the Commission, but it is to be noted that the Commission was a mere fact-finding body.

[11] *D. O. B.*, IV, 64.

[12] *Ibid.*, IV, 64–67.

this decision the Dutch Government released the "UB-30."[13]

In addition to the submarines mentioned above, the Dutch Government interned the German patrol boat, *Nurnberg,* which was found anchored only a short distance from the Dutch coast in August, 1918. When discovered by Dutch torpedo boats the *Nurnberg* attempted to escape, but it was brought into a Dutch harbor, and after an investigation by Dutch naval authorities, was duly interned. The German Minister sent a note to the Dutch Minister of Foreign Affairs inquiring the cause of the delay in the liberation of the *Nurnberg,* erroneously referred to in the note as the *Nymwegen.* The note contained the assertion that the vessel's presence was due to a defective compass and a heavy fog. The Dutch Government in proof of denial of these assertions, enclosed the proces verbal of the investigation made into the case by its naval commission and a copy of the report of the commander of the Dutch torpedo boat which had brought the *Nurnberg* into port. These documents clearly proved that the entrance of the German patrol boat was due neither to the state of the weather nor on account of damages suffered at sea. The German Government did not reply to this note.[14]

B. ALLIED–DUTCH CORRESPONDENCE

The increasing use and effectiveness of the submarine as an agent of warfare brought from the Allied Governments a general demand addressed to the neutral governments for "efficacious measures tending to prevent belligerent submarines, regardless of their use, to avail themselves of neutral waters, roadsteads, and harbors." The reasons advanced to justify this demand were that no surveillance or supervision could be kept over submarines

---

13) *Ibid., IV,* 64. One German submarine which had entered the Dutch territorial waters in January, 1917, while lost in a heavy fog, was detained for a while by the Dutch authorities but later released as coming under the first exemption of Article 5. See *Dutch White Book,* p. 1.
14) *D. O. B.,* V, 23–25.

due to their facility to navigate and sojourn in the seas while submerged, and that it was practically impossible to identify them and determine whether they were neutral or belligerent, combatant or non-combatant. Furthermore, it was held that the usual facilities granted to warships in neutral ports would give the submarines such advantages as to make those ports "a veritable basis of naval operations."[15]

In its reply the Dutch Government pointed out that positive international law, notably the 13th Hague Convention, did not contain a single regulation relative to the application of special rules for combatant belligerent submarines, even though most navies in 1907 possessed boats of this type. Neutrals have, therefore, the same rights and duties with respect to belligerent submarines that they have with respect to other belligerent warships. The Dutch Government could not apply to belligerent submarines any other regulations than were laid down by the Dutch Proclamation of Neutrality for belligerent warships in general. The Dutch note further pointed out that in accordance with this Proclamation, except under certain circumstances, belligerent warships were prohibited from entering the Dutch territorial waters, and that all such warships entering the Dutch waters contrary to these rules were interned.[16]

In January, 1916, a British submarine, the "H-6," stranded in Dutch territorial waters, due to a mistake in the computation of her position, and was likewise interned. Part of the crew was picked up by a motor boat sent out by three British submarine chasers cruising outside of the Dutch territorial waters. The Dutch Government protested this action which was held to be entirely unnecessary to save the crew since the Dutch life guard boat was already on the spot. The Dutch note stated that it was only because the Dutch life guard boat had no mili-

---

[15] Identic memoranda received from the embassies of France, Great Britain, Italy, Portugal, and Russia, August 31, 1916.
[16] *D. O. B.*, III, 27–28. Note sent October 14, 1916.

tary authorities on board that these members of the crew were allowed to leave the Dutch jurisdiction.[17]

A controversy arose in the early part of 1917 over the entrance into Dutch territorial waters of the German torpedo boat, "U-69," suffering from heavy damages sustained in a fight with British warships. Several wounded were handed over within Dutch territorial waters to a fisherman of IJmuiden in order that they might the sooner obtain medical aid. While the Dutch Government was still making an investigation of the case in order to determine whether or not the "U-69" should be allowed to leave the Dutch jurisdiction after repair of her damages, a note was received from the British Minister in which the British Government stated that in its opinion the Dutch Government was under obligations to intern the enemy torpedo boat, since international law prohibited repairs in neutral harbors of belligerent warships when the damages were the result of a naval battle. The British Government also held that the rules of neutrality placed upon the Dutch the obligation to intern the wounded brought to shore by the Dutch fisherman, since the Dutch fishing boat had clearly been used by the "U-69" as a tender in order to rid herself of her wounded.[18]

In a later memorandum the British Government named several cases in which belligerent warships, which had entered neutral harbors after having sustained damages in a naval battle, were not allowed to depart after the damages had been repaired. The cases cited were those of the *Juncal* in the harbor of Baltimore in 1828, the Russian warships *Aurora*, *Oleg*, and *Zemchug* in the harbor of Tsing-Tau during the Russo-Japanese war. The memorandum made reference to the proposal made by Great Britain at the Second Hague Peace Conference to declare repairs of naval battle damages in neutral harbors to be inadmissable. The British delegation had accepted the wording of Article 17 of the 13th Hague Con-

---

[17] *Ibid.*, V, 24. *Recueil*, pp. 162–163.
[18] *Dutch White Book*, p. 1.

vention only upon the understanding that the meaning would be the same as that of their proposition, namely, that repair of damages which were clearly due to a battle would not be permitted in neutral harbors. In a note a few days later the British Minister stated that the geographical position of IJmuiden, where the "U-69" was anchored, was an added reason for interning this vessel because of the great danger allied merchantmen run from the eventual departure of the German torpedo boat.[19]

The Dutch Government decided to give the "U-69" a definite period within which to repair its damages in so far as such repairs were necessary to restore the vessel to seaworthiness without increasing its fighting strength. Within this period the "U-69" and its crew would be allowed to depart. In a note to the British Government on February 6th, the Dutch Government answered the objections raised by the British notes. It maintained that its decision was in strict conformity with Article 17 of the 13th Hague Convention,[20] and that in spite of the cases cited by the British in which certain neutrals had not allowed belligerent warships to make repairs due to a contest with the enemy, international law allows damages to be repaired in neutral ports without distinction as to cause. In support of this the Dutch note cited a number of authorities. The note further called attention to the fact that the British delegates sought to introduce this distinction in Article 17 at the Second Hague Conference, but that this proposition had been rejected by the delegates of the other countries and that Great Britain had signed Article 17 without reservations. The Dutch note further pointed out that Brazil, though a proponent of the British proposition at the Second Hague Conference, had, nevertheless, in the present war allowed a British cruiser

---

[19] *Dutch White Book*, pp.1–2.

[20] Article 17, 13th Hague Convention: "In neutral ports and roadsteads belligerent warships may only carry out such repairs as are absolutely necessary to render them seaworthy, and may not add to their fighting force. The local authorities of the neutral power shall decide what repairs are necessary."

at Rio de Janeiro to repair damages received in combat with the enemy. In regard to the wounded taken off the "U-69" and rushed to shore by a Dutch fishing vessel, the Dutch Government stated that these would not be interned unless the vessel after its repairs again took them on board. This decision was based upon Article 15 of the 10th Hague Convention.[21]

The ruling made by the Dutch Government in the case of the German torpedo boat was cited the next year by the British Government to secure a ruling in its favor in the case of several British motorboats which had entered Dutch jurisdiction under somewhat similar circumstances as the German "U-69." An August 11, 1918, a contest took place outside the Dutch waters near Terschelling between several British motorboats and a number of German seaplanes, whose number had increased to fourteen before the battle ended. When, partly due to lack of ammunition and partly from the shock of the firing, the motorboats could no longer return the fire of the enemy planes, they changed their direction with the purpose of withdrawing from the contest. Three of the motorboats were destroyed by the crew, two entered the Dutch waters with their crews, and one was found abandoned drifting within the Dutch waters. Of the members of the crews of the abandoned boats, several swam to the Dutch shores and others were picked up by Dutch torpedo boats and brought to land.[22] One German seaplane pursued the motorboats even after they had entered the Dutch jurisdiction and did not stop its pursuit until within a mile of the shore, when it was driven off by the fire of the coast guard.[23]

Very soon after the British Minister at The Hague presented a note to the Dutch Government expressing the expectation that just as the German boat "U-69" had been allowed to depart after having repaired its damages, so the motorboats and their crews would be allowed to leave

---

[21] *Dutch White Book*, pp. 2–3.
[22] *D. O. B.*, V, 25.
[23] *D. O. B.*, V, 25.

the Dutch jurisdiction after the boats had again been rendered seaworthy. In its reply the Dutch Government
pointed out that the entrance of the motorboats into
Dutch jurisdiction did not fall under any of the exceptions found in Article 5 of the Dutch Proclamation of
Neutrality. The "U-69" had entered the Dutch jurisdiction not while in direct flight from the enemy, but merely
as a result of damages sustained in a combat and while
unpursued. The British motorboats were in full flight
from the enemy and entered the Dutch waters to escape
pursuit by the protection of neutral waters. These boats
clearly had not entered Dutch waters to repair damages,
since their crews had even attempted to destroy them.
Since the British boats had not entered Dutch jurisdiction under any of the exceptions of Article 5 of the
Proclamation, the Dutch Government held that in conformity with the maintenance of a strict neutrality the
boats and their crews must be interned, which was accordingly done.[24]

A note was sent to the German Government vigorously
protesting the violation of neutral territory by the German seaplanes which had continued the pursuit of the
motorboats until driven back by the coast guard guns.
The German Government expressed its regret at the conduct of the seaplane which in the heat of the fight, in conflict with specific orders, had continued hostilities above
Dutch territorial waters.[25]

Probably the most flagrant violation of Dutch neutrality, and particularly of Article 4 of the Neutrality
Proclamation, occurred in July, 1916, when British warships attacked some German merchantmen within the
Dutch territorial waters off Bergen. According to the
findings of the Dutch Government four German merchant
vessels were captured within the Dutch waters and led
away by British warships, while two other German
merchant vessels were pursued by British warships within the Dutch waters where they were finally fired upon

24) *Ibid.*, V, 25–28.
25) *D. O. B.*, V, 25.

97

and forced to shore. More than twenty projectiles landed upon the Dutch coast, some far inland.[26]

The Dutch Government at once protested this violation of Dutch sovereignty and neutrality and expressed the confident hope that the British Government would give complete redress in conformity with international law, in particular with the third paragraph of the 13th Hague Convention, which provides that when a ship has been captured in the territorial waters of a neutral, the captor government, on the demand of the neutral whose neutrality has been violated, must liberate the prize with its officers and crew.[27] Balfour, the British Secretary of State for Foreign Affairs, informed the Dutch Minister at London that the four captured vessels would be brought before the British prize courts, and as regards the two stranded vessels the British Government would make complete amends if upon investigation it appeared that the British commanders had acted unlawfully.[28]

To this procedure the Dutch Government objected on the ground that under the rules of international law the neutral government whose sovereignty has been violated can not be made to appear before a prize court. The Dutch Government offered to send a naval officer to London, who with the proper British naval authorities, should make a joint investigation into the facts of the case.[29] The British Government replied that an investigation by the British naval authorities revealed that the four vessels had been captured outside of Dutch waters, but that if the Dutch Government continued to maintain that the captures took place within Dutch waters, it could make an appeal to the British Prize Court for the release of these vessels.[30] In a later memorandum the British Government cited many judicial decisions[31] and state-

---

26) *Ibid.*, IV, 51–52.
27) *Ibid.*, IV, Note No. 1, pp. 53–54.
28) *D. O. B.*, IV, 52.
29) *Ibid.*, IV, Note No. 2, p. 54.
30) *Ibid.*, IV, Note No. 3, p. 54.
31) Case of the "Anne", *Wheaton* 435; "La Christina" and "Saint Michel", De Boeck, *Propriete privee enemie sous pavillion enemie*, Section 225, p. 256.

ments from many publicists on international law to indicate that for more than a century it had been the practice of neutrals when they believed that their neutrality had been violated by a capture within their waters to demand the release of such vessels before the prize court. The British Government also stated as its opinion that this method was superior to the diplomatic method since the prize courts were in much better position to handle such cases.[32] In regard to the two vessels which had been fired upon after they had run aground, the British Government admitted an infraction of Netherlands territorial jurisdiction, for which it expressed sincere regrets and offered to pay due compensation for any damage caused by the infraction.[33] The Dutch Government finally consented to hand in a demand to the British Prize Court for the release of the four German vessels, but with the understanding that they retained all their previous rights in case the Prize Court should return an unfavorable decision.[34]

After these points had apparently been satisfactorily settled the controversy was renewed over the unwillingness of the British Government to pay for the repairs to the German vessels which had been damaged by the British fire within the Dutch territorial waters although willing to pay for any damages sustained by Dutch subjects. The British Government admitted the obligation of a belligerent to make compensation to a private ship owner for damages done while the vessel is under the protection of a neutral state, even though he is an enemy subject, but refused to give practical effect to the principle in this case because the Germans had not shown the same respect for British ships when within the protection of neutral territorial waters. Many cases were cited in which the British vessels had either been sunk or damaged by German submarines while within neutral waters and for which the German Government had re-

---

[32] *D. O. B.*, IV, Notes 3 and 4, pp. 54–57.
[33] *D. O. B.*, IV, Notes 5 and 7, pp. 57–58.
[34] Ibid., IV, 57–58. The vessels were ordered restored to Holland. Decision rendered July 30, 1919—Lloyd's *Cases*, IX, 170 ff.

fused to make reparation.[35]   To this the Dutch Government replied that no British vessel had ever been captured or damaged within the Dutch territorial waters, and whatever attitude the German Government might take toward attacks upon British vessels in the territorial waters of other neutral powers had no bearing whatever on this case.   It was the respect for Dutch sovereignty which put the British Government under obligation to make this reparation and to restore the conditions to what they would have been had this violation of neutral territory not taken place.[36]

III.   Rule of International Law with Respect to the Admission of Belligerent Warships to Neutral Waters

A.   History

Previous to the World War there have been cases of neutral states closing certain of their ports to belligerent warships, but the Netherlands is the first, and so far, the only state on record which has prohibited all warships from entering the territorial waters of the home territory.

President Jefferson, after the *Leopard* and *Chesapeake* in 1807, issued a proclamation excluding British warships from United States ports.[37]   Austria in 1834 closed the port of Cattara and in the same war the Danish Government closed the port of Christiansand to belligerent warships.[38]   Lubeck in 1850 ordered the warships of Denmark and Schleswig-Holstein not to come within cannon shot of her shores.[39]   The rules of neutrality adopted by Brazil during the American Civil War provided that no warships of any belligerent which had once violated its neutrality could be admitted to its ports for the remainder of the war.[40]   The Scandinavian states

---

[35] *D. O. B.*, IV, Note No. 9, p. 59.
[36] *D. O. B.*, IV, 59–60.
[37] Moore, *Digest*, VI, 1035.
[38] Garner, *op. cit.*, II, 430–431.
[39] Francois, *op. cit.*, p. 294.
[40] Hall, *International Law*, p. 619; Bernard, *Neutrality of Great Britain*, p. 414.

during the Russo-Japanese War denied entrance to certain of their ports to belligerent warships, excluding hospital ships, except in case of distress.[41] The Danish Royal Decree concerning the neutrality of Denmark, in case of war, promulgated in 1912, prohibited belligerent warships from entering the Danish interior waters whose entrances were closed either by mines or means of defense. The Danish Government also reserved the right to prohibit entrance to other ports, roadsteads, and interior waters. This decree was incorporated without change in the neutrality regulations of all the Scandinavian states during the World War.[42]

In the World War the Netherlands alone of the neutrals prohibited all belligerent war vessels from entering her territorial waters, but several other neutrals later in the war imposed certain prohibitions upon the entrance of belligerent submarines into their waters. The attacks of Russian submarines on enemy ships in Swedish waters led the Swedish Government to supplement the neutrality regulations by a Royal decree of November 29, 1915, prohibiting the entrance of belligerent submarines except in the narrow passage in the Sound leading into the Baltic. In case of forced entry on account of the state of the sea, or because of damages, the belligerent submarine must keep to the surface, fly the national flag, and show the international signal indicating the reason for its entrance into the territorial waters. July, 1916, the decree was amended so as not to apply to commercial submarines.[43]

Norway, by Royal decree of October 13, 1916, prohibited belligerent submarines from entering Norwegian territorial waters except to save human lives in case of damage or on account of the state of the sea. All other

---

[41] Lawrence, *War and Neutrality*, p. 133.

[42] Francois, *op. cit.*, p. 294. Also Garner, *op. cit.*, II, 430–431.

[43] For the different municipal regulations in regard to the exclusion of warships, see *A. J. I. L.*, X, Sp. Supp. No. 3 (1916), pp. 121 ff. For the treatment of submarines in neutral waters see Garner, *op. cit.*, II, 430–438. See also 44 *Clunet* 90 ff., *Du Regime a imposer aux sonsmarins dans les Eaux Territoriales et ports Neutres*. Naval War College, *International Law Topics*, 1916, 1917 *in passim*.

submarines were prohibited from navigating the Norwegian waters except in the day time and in clear weather, and in any case they must all keep to the surface and display the flag of their country. This regulation gave rise to a diplomatic controversy with Germany which ended by an amendment to the regulation by which belligerent war submarines were given freedom to enter the prohibited waters, in case of damages, or on account of the state of the sea, or in order to save human lives.[44]

Denmark put into effect, without change throughout the war, the decree of 1912 discussed above. Belligerent warships were prohibited from the Danish interior waters which had been closed by mines or other means of defense.

Spain issued no formal declaration of neutrality upon the outbreak of the World War in 1914. By Royal Decree of November 23, 1914, it was proclaimed that for the purpose of maintaining neutrality all state authorities would carry out their duties in conformity with the regulations established by the 13th Hague Convention of 1907. Due to the destruction of many Spanish merchant ships by German submarines, public opinion became very bitter and a Royal decree was published on June 30, 1917, by which it was announced that all belligerent submarines, no matter what kind, entering the Spanish jurisdiction, no matter for what reason, would be interned. By Dahir of July 18, 1917, similar regulations were proclaimed in Spanish Morocco.[45]

One other country, Uruguay, took action in regard to the admission of submarines, but here the conditions were different from those in any of the other countries cited. The president of Uruguay was empowered by law of October 7, 1917, to suspend all diplomatic and commercial relations with Germany, but without a declaration of war. In pursuance of this law a presidential de-

---

44) Francois, *op. cit.*, p. 342. Naval War College, *International Law Topics*, 1917, pp. 194–195.

45) Francois, *op. cit.*, pp. 343–349. Naval War College, *International Law Topics*, 1917.

cree was issued on November 9th ordering interned all
commercial or war submarines flying the German flag or
belonging to the German navy coming within the territorial waters of the Republic.[46]

B. RULE OF INTERNATIONAL LAW AT THE TIME OF THE WORLD WAR

History previous to the World War throws little
light on the question of whether a neutral power has the
right to prohibit the entrance of belligerent warships into
its territorial waters. Previous to the World War there
was not a single case of a power as a general neutrality
measure prohibiting all belligerent warships from entering its waters.

Publicists are divided on the right of neutrals to impose such a prohibition. In the first place, publicists are
not agreed as to the nature of the jurisdiction of a state
over its territorial waters. Some writers hold that the
jurisdiction of a state over its territorial waters is the
same as that over its land.[47] Others deny this complete
jurisdiction.[48] The question of the nature of territorial
jurisdiction has little importance in practice, since the
writers of the first group admit that the coastal states are
obliged to recognize within this territory certain servi-

---

46) Francois, *op. cit.*, p. 350.

47) Among those who hold this view are Bynkershoek, *De Dominio
Maris*, Cap. 2; Vattel, L. I., par. 288; G. F. De Martens, par. 34; Klu-
ber, par. 130; Hautefeuille, I, 57; Pradiere Fodere, II, 158; Hall, 6th
edition, p. 152; Schucking, *Das Kustemeer in Internationalen
Rechte*, p. 14; Einicke, *Rechte und Pflichten der Neutralen Machte in
Seekrieg*, p. 38; Kleen, I, 508; Fenwick, *International Law*, p. 251.

48) Grotius, *De Jure Belli et Pacis*, lib. II, C, III, par. 13; Heffter,
par. 74; Bluntschli, par. 322; Calvo, par. 244; Ortolan, *Dip. de la
Mer*, Bk. II, Chaps. 7 and 8; Twiss, I, par. 173; Rolin, *Le Droit Moderne de la Guerre*, p. 1079. Hall criticizes this view by saying that it
is open to the objections that: "1. It does not account for the fact
that a state has admittedly an exclusive right to the enjoyment of the
fisheries in its marginal waters; 2. As the rights of sovereignty or
jurisdiction belonging to a state are in all other cases except that of
piracy, which in every way stands wholly apart, indissolubly connected with the possession of international property, a solitary instance of their existence independently of such property requires to be
proved like all other exceptions to a general rule, by reference to a
distinct usage, which in this case can not be shown." Note, pp. 152–
153.

tudes under international law, and the writers of the second group hold that the coastal states can likewise lay claim to certain coastal servitudes in this territory.[49] Thus a discussion of this matter does not settle the matter in question.[50]

On the direct question as to whether a neutral has the right to close its waters to belligerent warships, writers are likewise divided. First there is a group of modern writers who hold that belligerents have the right of passage through neutral territorial waters.[51] A second group of writers recognize the right of neutrals to prohibit all passage or entrance of belligerent warships within neutral waters.[52] A third group of writers go so far as to contend that it is the duty of a neutral to forbid the passage of belligerent warships through its territorial waters.[53]

The Institute of International Law in a resolution in 1894 lays down the rule that "all ships without distinction have the right of innocent passage through the territorial sea ... saving to neutrals the right of regulating the passage of ships of war of all nationalities through the said sea."[54] One of the resolutions adopted by the Institute in

---

[49] Francois, *op, cit.*, p. 288.

[50] Fenwick, for instance, states that "within the limits of the marginal sea the jurisdiction of the state is, with but one exception (the right of innocent passage on the part of foreign ships) as exclusive as its jurisdiction over the land itself", p. 251. But the exception here stated is just the point involved.

[51] Among those who compose this group are Ortolan, II, 285; Ferguson, II, 445; Calvo, IV, par. 2653; Perels, p. 212; Walker, p. 168; Westlake, II, 235; Ullman, p. 522; Nys, III, 560; Rivier, II, 401; Wilson, 6th ed., p. 296; and Von Liszt, 11th ed., p. 343.

[52] Among these writers are Bluntschli, p. 20; Wheaton, Dana's, p. 520; Woolsey, pp. 278–279; Phillimore, III, 283; Hall, 6th ed., p. 619; Oppenheim, II, 393–394; De Louter, II, 423; Lawrence, p. 636 (position somewhat uncertain); Einicke, p. 158; and Rolin, *op. cit.*, Section 1081.

[53] Heffter, who in the first edition of his work still recognized the right of innocent passage even over land, holds this view, p. 323. Others belonging to this group are: Bulmerincq, in Marquardson's *Handbuch*, p. 358; Kleen, *Lois et Usuages de la Neutralite*, I, par. 119; Wehberg, *Das Seekriegsrecht*, p. 417; and Kebedgy, *Ann. I. D. I.*, XXIII, p. 17, p. 176.

[54] *Annuaire*, 1894, p. 114.

104

1898 provides that "Granting of asylum to belligerents in neutral ports, although depending upon the pleasure of the sovereign state and not required of it, shall be presumed, unless previous notification to the contrary has been given.

"With regard to warships, however, it shall be limited to cases of real distress, in consequence of: 1. defeat, sickness or insufficient crew; 2. perils of the sea; 3. lack of means of subsistence of locomotion (water, coal, provisions); 4. need of repairs."[55]

It would seem from these regulations that the Institute was of the opinion that entrance into the ports and interior waters of the neutral may be regulated and even prohibited, but that mere passage through its waters could be regulated but not prohibited by the neutral state. Kleen, in preparing the Avant-Projet for the 1906 meeting at Ghent, included an article making it the duty of a neutral state to deny belligerent passage through its territory whether continental or maritime, of all armed forces, prisoners of war, wounded or sick, or any material susceptible of military use. The article never reached discussion.[56]

The conflicting interests of the powers in regard to the treatment of belligerent warships in neutral ports was clearly brought out at the Second Hague Conference.[57] In regard to the length of stay of belligerent warships in neutral ports the maritime powers and their satellites wished to fix twenty-four hours as the universal rule, but this was strenuously opposed by the continental powers.[58] Much the same alignment took place in respect to the number of belligerent warships to be allowed in a neutral port at the same time—Great Britain and Japan proposed to limit the number to three, while Germany contended in the name of sovereignty that the neutrals should be

---

55) Scott, *Resolutions of the Institute of International Law*, Carnegie Endowment for International Peace, p. 154.

56) Francois, *op. cit.*, p. 291.

57) *The Proceedings of the Hague Peace Conferences*, Carnegie Endowment for International Peace, I, 276–324.

58) *Ibid.*, I, 302–304.

free to set the number themselves.[59]   In the matter of provisioning and fueling the continental powers contended that the belligerent vessels should be permitted to fill their bunkers, whereas Great Britain proposed that they should be permitted only to take in fuel enough to reach the nearest port of their own country.   Great Britain even proposed that a ship should not be allowed to venture twice into the same neutral country within three months, which was bitterly opposed by Germany and France.[60]

When Article 8 came up for discussion in the committee of examination, Sir Ernest Satow explained the necessity of making a distinction between access and simple passage. By access or admission was meant the entrance into territorial waters for the purpose of hovering there or continuing on its way to a neutral port, and by simple passage was meant merely the navigation through the waters at an even distance from the shore. The original British proposal recognized the right of a neutral to prohibit admission to its waters, but denied the right of a neutral to impair simple passage in any way. This proposal was rejected because it might be understood to mean that a neutral had no right to forbid warships from passing through its waters.[61]   In fact, Admiral Sperry of the American delegation declared that he could not accept even the mild language of the drafts as finally adopted by reason of the political considerations involved in the question of passage through territorial waters.[62]   From the opinions expressed in the committee of examination "it seems that a neutral state may forbid even innocent passage through limited parts of its territorial waters so far as that seems to it necessary to maintain its neutrality, but that this prohibition can not extend to straits uniting

---

[59] *Ibid.*, I, 305–306.
[60] *The Proceedings of the Hague Peace Conferences*, Carnegie Endowment for International Peace, I, 309–312.
[61] *Ibid.*, I, 297.
[62] *Ibid.*, I, 298.

two open seas."[63]   As finally adopted, the Articles relating to this subject admit by implication the right of a neutral state to impose whatsoever conditions, restrictions, or prohibitions it sees fit in regard to the admission of belligerent warships or their prizes into their ports or territorial waters, but in regard to simple passage it is merely stated that the neutrality of a power is not affected by such passage.[64]   It is not impossible to deduce from the negative phraseology of Article 10 the right of a neutral to regulate or prohibit such passage.

The nearest approach to a direct discussion of whether a neutral may exclude the warships of a belligerent from its ports and waters is found in the case of the *Exchange versus M'Faddon,* a case decided by the United States Supreme Court in 1812, and in which Chief Justice Marshall delivered the opinion of the Court.[65]   The *Exchange,* owned by M'Faddon and Greetham of Baltimore, had been seized in December, 1810, by the order of Napoleon and then armed and commissioned as a public vessel of the French Government. In July, 1811, the vessel put into the port of Philadelphia and soon after was libelled by the original owners.

The decision of the case rested upon the answer to the question of whether an American citizen can assert in an American court a title to an armed national vessel found within the waters of the United States, but incidentally Chief Justice Marshall was forced to discuss the right of a power to regulate or even prohibit the entrance of such

---

63) 13th Hague Convention, 1907, Art. 9: "A neutral Power must apply impartially to the two belligerents the conditions, restrictions, or prohibitions made by it in regard to the admission into its ports, roadsteads, or territorial waters, of belligerent warships or of their prizes. Nevertheless, a neutral Power may forbid a belligerent vessel which has failed to conform to the orders and regulations made by it, or which has violated neutrality, to enter its ports or roadsteads.

"Article 10. The neutrality of a Power is not affected by the mere passage through its territorial waters of warships or prizes belonging to belligerents."

64) *The Proceedings of the Hague Peace Conferences,* Carnegie Endowment for International Peace, I, "Report of the Eighth Plenary Meeting".

65) 7 *Cranch,* 116, 3 L. Ed., 287.

vessels into its waters. The Chief Justice started with the proposition that "the jurisdiction of the nation within its own territory is necessarily exclusive and absolute," and then proceeded to discuss the exceptions to this absolute jurisdiction which a nation sometimes makes by its own consent. In discussing these exceptions, Chief Justice Marshall was clearly of the opinion that the ports of a nation may be closed or opened entirely at the will of the sovereign. The language of the eminent jurist upon this point is as follows:

> ". . . If, for reasons of state, the ports of a nation generally, or any particular ports be closed against vessels of war generally, or the vessels of any particular nation, notice is usually given of such determination. If there be no prohibition, the ports of a friendly nation are considered as open to the public ships of all powers with whom it is at peace, and they are supposed to enter such ports and to remain in them while allowed to remain, under the protection of the government of the place.

> . . . .

> "If there be no treaty applicable to the case, and the sovereign, from motives deemed adequate by himself, permits his ports to remain open to the public ships of foreign friendly powers, the conclusion seems irresistible, that they enter by his consent."[66]

Summing up the rules of international law at the time of the World War with respect to the right of a neutral to prohibit the admission into its ports of belligerent warships it appears that both in practice and in the writing of publicists this right of the neutral was generally recognized. Judicial decisions and international conventions recognize this right by implication. Prior to the World War there is no case of a neutral prohibiting the general passage of belligerent warships through its waters. Only particular ports had been closed. Writers on international law were about equally divided as to the right of a neutral to prohibit such passage. But most significant is the fact

---

[66] 7 Cranch 116, 3 L. Ed., 287. Also in Scott, *Cases*, p. 305.

that there was a small but gradually increasing number of writers who believed that it was the duty of the neutral to prohibit the passage of belligerent warships through its territorial waters. One can trace here the same development of the neutral's duties in regard to its maritime waters as took place in regard to its duties on land.

IV. COMPATIBILITY OF THE DUTCH REGULATIONS WITH THE RULES OF INTERNATIONAL LAW

There is of course no contention that the Dutch regulations prohibiting the simple passage of belligerent warships through its waters was an obligation under the rules of international law, but there may be some slight question as to whether the Netherlands regulations are compatible with the rules of international law as they stood in 1914. In regard to this question it is first to be noted that the Dutch regulations prohibiting the admission were not absolute. Asylum was allowed on account of damages or the state of the sea. The right of all ships, no matter of what character, to the hospitality of ports for the purpose of saving human lives, may be considered such a fundamental right as to be an established part of international law,[67] and may even be considered a part of the concept of the freedom of the seas.[68] Whether the exceptions made by the Dutch Government are broad enough to satisfy this principle may well be doubted, since the exceptions listed under Article 5 of the Neutrality Proclamation do not include the right of admission for the purpose of revictualing and refueling. This may be considered a serious handicap to belligerent states which have few harbors of their own outside of their home territory. If the vessels of such a power could not make use of neutral harbors for the purpose of coaling and revictualing, the power of navigating for great distances would be greatly impaired. But on the other hand, is the neutral expected to supply the belligerent forces with

---

[67] Oppenheim, II, par. 342. La Pradelle, *Annuaire, I. D. I.,* XXIII, 113.
[68] Visser, *De Territoriale Zee,* p. 299.

vital supplies for the carrying on of hostilities? This may entail great hardships for a neutral, which like Holland had difficulty in getting sufficient supplies for its own population, and may tend to make the neutral serve as a base of operations for the belligerents.

Secondly, it is to be noted that none of the belligerents affected seriously disputed the Dutch prohibitions, nor were the similar prohibitions of other neutrals in regard to the admission of belligerent fighting submarines during the war seriously disputed. And these regulations with respect to the exclusion of submarines are certainly more open to dispute since they involve the prohibition laid down some considerable time after the commencement of hostilities and making a distinction between different kinds of warships to the plausible disadvantage of one of the belligerents.

Thirdly, the reasons which led the Netherlands Government to impose this prohibition ought to be considered. As stated in the Dutch note to the French Minister the main reasons for the prohibition were two. One was to safeguard the country against precipitate and masked agression, and the other to maintain a very strict neutrality. The prohibition gave the strongest guarantee to both groups of belligerents that its adversary would not be able to use any part of Dutch territory as a base of naval operations.[69] The neutral power is under obligations not to allow any part of its territory to be used as a base of operations for either belligerent and it is certainly free to use any methods not prohibited by the rules of international law to enforce this obligation.[70] The peculiar geographical position of Holland with reference to the seat of the World War gives added force to this argument.

And lastly, it is to be noted that this prohibition is in direct line with the neutral duties in regard to the passage

---

[69] *Dutch White Book*, "Diplomatieke Bescheiden betreffende de Toelating van Bewapende Handelsvaartuigen der Oorlogvoerenden en Onzijdigen Binnen het Nederlandsche Rechtsgebied", p. 7.
[70] Francois, *op. cit.*, pp. 296–297.

of belligerents over land. And the same reasons which argue for the neutral's obligations to prohibit such passage over its land apply with almost equal force to its maritime jurisdiction. The entrance to both can be used to escape an attack from the enemy or to plan a sudden attack upon the enemy while under the protection of neutral territory. This last would have been peculiarly true of the territorial waters of Holland because of their situation on a great ocean channel.

In commenting on the Dutch regulations prohibiting belligerent warships the right of simple passage through its territorial waters, Garner states, "There is a growing opinion in favor of the view that neutrals should be required to prohibit belligerent warships from entering their ports or making use of their waters except where considerations of humanity require such entry or use, and the results of the recent war will probably strengthen the opinion. Had this measure been adopted at the outbreak of the war by all neutrals, as it was subsequently by a few of the Powers, many irritating controversies would have been avoided and the requirements of a true neutrality would have been more fully met."[71]

The project of the Maritime Convention submitted in 1925 by the American Institute of International Law to the Governing Board of the Pan American Union contained the *voeux* that "belligerent warships shall not have access to the ports, roadsteads, and territorial waters of neutral American Republics except in case of duly proven *force majeure.*"[72]

---

[71] *International Law and the World War*, II, 436–437. See also Cole, "Neutrals and Belligerents in Territorial Waters", *Grotius Society*, II; M. Perrinjaquet, XXIV, *Revue General de Droit International Publique*, p. 230.

[72] *A. J. I. L.*, Sp. Supp., XX, 367.

CHAPTER VIII

ADMISSION OF BELLIGERENT ARMED MERCHANTMEN

I. THE DUTCH REGULATIONS

A. BRITISH–DUTCH CORRESPONDENCE INTERPRETING THE REGULATIONS

THE DUTCH neutrality regulations covering the treatment of belligerent armed merchant ships caused a long and bitter controversy with Great Britain. Soon after the issuance of the Neutrality Proclamation, Grey, on August 8, 1914, sent a note to the Netherlands Government insisting that British armed merchantmen could not be interned, nor be required to put to sea or land their guns. These ships were neither actual nor potential warships since the British Government did not allow conversion in foreign ports.[1] Grey, in this note, also pressed the claim that the neutral government must intern all German armed merchant vessels because the German rules permitted conversion on the high seas. If the neutral did not intern the German merchant vessels it must be prepared to assume responsibility for a binding assurance that no such conversion would take place.

It would appear from a communication of Mr. Chilton, the British representative at The Hague, to Sir Edward Grey, that the Dutch Government had not in the beginning fully determined upon the policy it would pursue in the treatment of belligerent armed merchantmen. The

---

[1] *A. J. I. L.*, Supp. XII, 196, "The British–Dutch correspondence is found in the *Dutch White Books*, "Diplomatieke Bescheiden betreffende de Toelating van Bewapende Handelsvaartuigen der Oorlogvoerenden en Onzijdigen Binnen het Nederlandsche Rechtsgebied. Augustus, 1914, tot November, 1917" (referred to as *Dutch White Book—Armed Merchantmen*) and "Diplomatieke Bescheiden betreffende de Toelating van Oorlogsschepen en Bewapende Handelsvaartuigen der Oorlogvoerenden Binnen het Nederlandsche Rechtsgebied". Also *Brit. Parl. Papers*, Misc. No. 14 (1917), cd. 8690.

Dutch Minister of Marine in a conversation with the British Naval Attache stated that he fully realized the difference between auxiliary cruisers and merchant vessels defensively armed, but that since the Netherlands Government had already issued instructions not to admit to Dutch territorial waters merchantmen that were capable of performing any warlike act, the Dutch Government was placed in a difficult position by the British demand. The Marine Minister feared that any modification of the instructions would be regarded by the people, who were in fear of a violation of their territory by the English, as a departure from the Dutch attitude of strict neutrality. This would have the effect of throwing the Dutch nation into the arms of Germany.[2]

But whatever the causes which led the Dutch Government to include armed merchant vessels under the provisions of Article 4, and however much it may have doubted the justification of this inclusion in the beginning, it never wavered from the position then taken. It was not until the next March, when the German submarine became a menace, that the question again became a matter of diplomatic discussion. The British Government again protested the treatment of armed merchantmen on the same basis as warships.[3] Mr. Loudon, the Minister for Foreign Affairs, replied that the Queen's Government was still of the opinion that the observance of a strict neutrality obliged them "to place in the category of vessels assimilated to belligerent warships those merchant vessels of the belligerent parties that are provided with an armament and that consequently would be capable of committing acts of war."[4]

The British Foreign Office pointed to the fact that every other neutral recognized the legality of arming merchantmen in self defense, and that they admitted ships so armed into their ports on the same footing as

---

[2] *A. J. I. L.*, Supp. XII, 197.
[3] *A. J. I. L.*, Supp. XII, 197–198.
[4] *A. J. I. L.*, Supp. XII, 198–199; *Dutch White Book—Armed Merchantment*, p. 2.

ordinary merchant vessels.[5]   A memorandum on the right of arming merchant ships, prepared by Dr. A. Pearce Higgins, Professor of International Law at Cambridge and Lecturer at the Royal Naval War College, was also presented to the Dutch Foreign Minister for his perusal. In reply to this note Mr. Loudon took the position that there was no connection between the rule of international law which permits belligerent merchant ships to arm in self defense against enemy warships and the question whether admission into neutral ports of belligerent armed vessels is or is not compatible with the observance of a strict neutrality. The first question, he held, lies within the province of the law of war; the latter is part of the law of neutrality. The Dutch Government did not question the right of a merchant vessel to arm in self defense, but pointed out that "a belligerent vessel which fights to escape capture or destruction by an enemy warship commits an act the legitimacy of which is indeed unquestionable, but which is none the less an act of war."[6]

The discussion again lapsed, this time for over a year and a half. But in March, 1917, the *Princess Melita,* a British steamship with a single gun mounted aft, entered the Dutch territorial waters at the Hoek of Holland. The vessel was promptly ordered out, but shortly after returned, with her gun dismounted, with a request for water. Still the Dutch would not allow the vessel to enter the territorial waters. It was only after the *Princess Melita* had dropped her gun overboard that she was allowed to proceed into port. This incident, made the more prominent by the increasing destructiveness of the submarine, re-opened the whole diplomatic controversy.[7]

The British contention is indicated in a series of notes beginning in March, 1917 and ending with the note of November 14, 1917. Since the Dutch had adopted the rule

---

[5] *A. J. I. L.*, Supp. XII, 199–201; *Dutch White Book—Armed Merchantmen*, pp. 2–3.

[6] *A. J. I. L.*, Supp. XII, 202–203; *Dutch White Book—Armed Merchantmen*, p. 3.

[7] *A. J. I. L.*, Supp. XII, 204.

of assimilating belligerent armed merchant ships to warships, the circumstances had been changed by the proclamation by Germany of its intention to sink at sight all merchant ships going to or coming from Great Britain. If the Dutch did not relax their rule they would be assisting the Germans in their lawlessness, since the only way that the unlawful practice could be combatted was by arming the merchantmen.[8] Neither the natural nor the reasonable construction of the language of Article 4 of the Proclamation of Neutrality would include British defensively armed merchant vessels. Nor did the observance of a strict neutrality require that the Netherlands Government treat these defensively armed ships as assimilated to warships, since the rule went beyond the requirements of international law. No writer of repute held that it was necessary for a neutral to exclude armed merchant ships from its ports. Nor did any other neutral think that it was required to do so, judging by their practice.[9]

The British admitted the right of the Dutch Government to make such an enactment as a rule of internal legislation provided the rule did not conflict with treaty rights and provided it was impartial as between the belligerents, but the Dutch rule played into the German hands. The few German vessels that ventured on foreign voyages were not armed. "A rule which closes Dutch ports to merchant ships armed in self defense must operate with complete want of equality as between the two belligerents, because it opens Dutch ports to all German merchant vessels without opening them to all British vessels. A British merchant vessel will not, in fact, be allowed that freedom of trade with Holland which the commercial treaty between the two countries guarantees to it unless it deprives itself of the safeguards which, by

---

[8] *Ibid.*, Supp. XII, 204–205; *Dutch White Book—Armed Merchantmen*, p. 45.

[9] *A. J. I. L.*, Supp. XII, 209–214; *Dutch White Book—Armed Merchantmen*, pp. 8–10.

the law of its own country, not less than by international law, it is entitled to adopt."[10]

The argument of the Netherlands that the country was in an exceptional geographical position in regard to the belligerents, and that therefore it was required to take added precautions, was rejected by the British on the ground that the geographical position of the Netherlands differed in no material way from that of the other belligerents, and that in any case, a defensively armed merchantman was utterly incapable of committing acts of aggression in foreign ports. Unarmed merchantmen, if they minded to do so, would be just as capable of committing such acts as armed ones. The rule really did nothing to safeguard the country from acts of aggression.[11]

The British Foreign Office did not confine itself exclusively to arguments based on precedent, present practice, and the views of publicists. It threatened the Dutch with a retorsionary measure. The Netherlands Overseas Trust had made an agreement with the British Government that its vessels should go into British ports for the exercise of visit and search. The Dutch Government and the Overseas Trust were asking to be released from the terms of the agreement because the Germans threatened to sink all merchantmen coming from British ports. Mr. Balfour stated that the Dutch were unreasonable in asking the British to forego both their belligerent and contract rights in order to increase the safety of the Dutch vessels while insisting on rules which increased the danger of the British vessels. Mr. Balfour hinted that the British Government might not be able to make concessions to the Dutch Government "unless they are prepared to show greater good-will toward us."[12]

To all these arguments of the British Government the

---

10) *A. J. I. L.*, Supp. XII, 209–214; *Dutch White Book—Armed Merchantmen*, pp. 8–10.
11) *A. J. I. L.*, Supp. XII, 209–214; *Dutch White Book—Armed Merchantment*, pp. 8–10.
12) *A. J. I. L.*, Supp. XII, 209–214; *Dutch White Book—Armed Merchantmen*, pp. 8–10.

Dutch Foreign Office made extended replies. Mr. Loudon pointed to the very geographical position in which the Netherlands found itself in relation to the belligerent nations, and that in order to ensure respect for the neutrality of the territory under its jurisdiction, it was necessary to exclude from its territory not only warships but also all armed vessels. This rule of the exclusion of all armed vessels from its territorial waters ensured respect for Dutch neutrality in that it safe-guarded the country against any concealed aggression; it prevented acts of violence between belligerents within Dutch territorial waters; and it offered to each belligerent the most effective guarantee that the adversary would not be able to use any part of Dutch territory as a base for naval operations.[13)]

Mr. Loudon further pointed out the impossibility of revoking a rule of neutrality which had been established at the beginning of the war, and which had been notified to the two belligerent parties.

"Nothing could be more contrary to the very principle of neutrality than to revoke during the course of a war, and at the demand of one of the belligerents, a rule of neutrality which, owing to the course of events, whatever they may be, proves to be disadvantageous to that belligerent only.

"This revocation would unquestionably assume the character of a favor, and would consequently be incompatible with the impartiality which is the distinctive feature of neutrality.

". . . Your Excellency's government will further recognize that it was the British delegates who, at the Second Peace Conference, laid particular stress on the fact that the English doctrine does not admit that a State has the right of modifying its rules of neutrality in the course of the war, except with a view to rendering them more strict. (*Actes*, Vol. I, p. 326; Vol. III, p. 621)"[14)]

Nor was the matter altered by the fact that the Dutch

---

13) *A. J. I. L.*, Supp. XII, 206–209.
14) *Dutch White Book—Armed Merchantmen*, pp. 5–6.

Proclamation did not specifically enumerate the categories of vessels which were regarded as assimilated to warships. A modification of the interpretation of a neutrality declaration would be no less serious from the point of view of neutrality than a modification of the declaration proper, or a rule enacted to meet cases not provided for in the declaration.[15]

In reply to the argument that the Dutch Government alone of all the neutrals assimilated belligerent armed merchantmen to warships, Mr. Loudon called attention to the fact that the Governments of Denmark and Sweden had made no pronouncement on the matter, and that Mr. Lansing's confidential letter to the belligerent governments, January 18, 1916,[16] indicated that the Government of the United States was convinced of the correctness of the view that armed merchant vessels should be treated by neutrals as vessels of war. The publications of the United States Department of State clearly indicated that the Government "entertained grave doubts as to whether any admittance of such ships was not incompatible with a strict observance of the duties of neutrality." Attention was drawn to the case of the *Merrion* which had been ordered to dismount her guns before putting to sea from a United States port in September, 1914. After this incident no British armed merchantmen called at ports of the United States for over a year. "This same paper (European War No. 2, pp. 45-46) contains a letter in which the United States Government, while fully admitting that a merchant ship has the right to arm for purposes of self defense, makes it known that they disapprove of a practice which compels a neutral to express an opinion as to the intended use of a vessel, and thus to incur responsibility in the event of this opinion subsequently proving wrong."[17]

In answer to the British threat of refusing concessions in the matter of compelling Dutch vessels to go into Eng-

---

15) *Ibid.*, pp. 5–6.
16) *A. J. I. L.*, Sp. Supp. X, 310–313.
17) Note of October 22, 1917, *A. J. I. L.*, Supp. XII, 229–230; *Dutch White Book—Armed Merchantmen*, p. 15.

lish harbors for the exercise of visit and search, the Dutch Government attempted to show that the British request for a modification of the Dutch neutrality rules would involve a breach of Dutch neutrality obligations, whereas the British Government was under no obligation under international law to effect the examination of Dutch vessels in a British port, instead of carrying it out on the high seas, or in a British overseas port.[18]

And as regards the treaty rights of Great Britain under the Treaty of Commerce existing between the two states the Dutch Government held that the treaty could not be construed to mean that the contracting governments were under obligations "to receive in all circumstances into their ports, the vessels flying the flag of the other contracting party." The British Government could not itself hold this opinion and justify various measures they had taken in the course of the war. The British Government had even closed certain ports of the United Kingdom to Dutch shipping.[19]

B. FRENCH–DUTCH CORRESPONDENCE

The protest of the French Government followed a slightly different line of argument. The Dutch Neutrality Proclamation could not have intended to assimilate armed merchantmen to warships, for the question of armed merchantmen as it now presented itself was an absolutely new question, and one which should not have arisen since the Treaty of Paris of 1856. The illegal and inhuman methods of submarine warfare had revived the insecurity at sea which had formerly prevailed. "Under these conditions Governments would be seriously failing in their duty of protection toward the sailors of their merchant marine and the passengers sailing under their flag if they refused, contrary to the traditions formerly followed in all countries, to allow merchant ships the means of defending themselves on the high seas. To pro-

---

18) Note of April 4, 1917, *A. J. I. L.*, Supp. XII. 206–209.
19) Note of June 18, 1917, *A. J. I. L.*, Supp. XII, 215–220; *Dutch White Book—Armed Merchantmen*, pp. 10–12.

hibit them from entering ports would be equivalent to either denying them this right, or refusing to allow them to have intercourse with countries exercising this right. This would be an unfriendly attitude. . . ." This eventuality could not have been considered at the time the Dutch Neutrality Proclamation was drawn up and therefore the Dutch Government was still entirely free to decide that question.[20]

The French Government in its note further contended that even if the conditions or restrictions with regard to admission imposed upon belligerent vessels by a neutral were a matter for domestic legislation, it was nevertheless on condition that these restrictions did not violate international law. Whether or not a foreign vessel has the character, the rights, and the obligations of a warship "is a question of an international nature governed by international law." In order to be regarded as a warship, "a vessel must be under the direct authority, immediate control, and responsibility of the state, its captain must be in the service of the state, and its crew must be under military discipline." Consequently, only merchant ships converted into warships according to the provisions of the 7th Hague Convention could be assimilated to warships, and assimilation of other merchant vessels was inadmissable under international law, for it would have the effect of giving defensively armed merchantmen the same rights as warships. Neutral powers adopting this point of view would by their acts, at least by implication, reëstablish privateering.[21]

The institution of armed merchantmen, the Dutch Government replied, had not arisen in the course of the present war, but had been inaugurated before the war by the British Government, in spite of the fact that it had been regarded as excluded at the Second Hague Peace

---

[20] *A. J. I. L.*, Supp. XII, 236–238; *Dutch White Book—Armed Merchantmen*, p. 6.

[21] *A. J. I. L.*, Supp. XII, 236–238; *Dutch White Book—Armed Merchantmen*, p. 6.

Conference.[22]   As a result of this action by the British Government, the question of the treatment of such vessels in time of war and in time of peace was submitted by the Dutch Government, May, 1913, to the commission drawing up the Netherlands proposals for the program for the Third Peace Conference.   The commission, presenting its report in March, 1914, expressed the opinion that armed merchantships of a belligerent power should not be admitted to the dominion of the Netherlands except on the same footing as belligerent warships.[23]

The Dutch Government fully shared the French Government's point of view that it was not lawful for a state to confer the character of a warship upon a vessel which had not that character under the rules of international law.   But it was not conferring that character upon armed merchantmen.   It was confining itself to assimilating them to warships, in so far as their admission to its waters was concerned.   It conferred upon them no other right than that of being admitted to the Netherlands jurisdiction in the cases in which warships were also admitted thereto.   "If privateering were reëstablished, it would certainly not be by the act of the Powers that refuse to receive in their dominion vessels which, though they do not fulfill the conditions required of vessels of war, are nevertheless provided with an armament that enables them to commit acts of war."[24]

The 7th Hague Convention, according to the Dutch Government, governs the legal status of auxiliary cruisers duly incorporated into the navies of belligerents and does not deal with the legal status of vessels which can not claim to be warships, but which are none the less suitable for war operations.   This Convention in no way affects the rights and duties of neutral powers with regard to belligerent vessels, which, though they can not be con-

---

[22] The Dutch note referred to the observations of Captain Ottley, delegate of Great Britain, and Captain Behr, delegate of Russia, *Acts*, III, 1010.
[23] *A. J. I. L.*, Supp. XII, 238–242; *Dutch White Book—Armed Merchantmen*, pp. 7–8.
[24] *Ibid.*

sidered warships, are adapted for military purposes. Such vessels are subject to the 13th Hague Convention and to the general principles of neutrality.[25]

C. German–Dutch Correspondence

In a note to the Dutch Government on August 2, 1915, the German Government stated that according to information it had received the English steamer *Brussels* was armed during its stay at Rotterdam early in the year, and many British merchantmen were similarly armed. Armed resistance was contrary to international law and would give warships the right to sink the boat in question, together with its crew and passengers. The German Government regarded as doubtful whether such boats might demand admission to the ports of a neutral state. They should not, in any case, enjoy more favorable treatment than that accorded by such a state to warships intended for legitimate warfare.[26]

The reply of the Dutch Government to this note is important for the further explanation it gives with regard to the Dutch Government's attitude on the question of armed merchantmen. After stating that belligerent armed merchantmen had been assimilated to belligerent warships, by the Dutch Government, and that neither had been admitted to a port of the kingdom during the war, with the exception of cases of damages or of stress of weather at sea, the Dutch Government stated that it did not share the opinion of the German Government that armed resistance was contrary to the laws of nations. On the contrary, it held that international law permitted belligerent merchantmen to defend themselves against enemy warships but that resistance to visit and search by an enemy warship constituted an act of war.[27]

---

[25] *A. J. I. L.*, Supp. XII, 238–242; *Dutch White Book—Armed Merchantmen*, pp. 7–8.

[26] *A. J. I. L.*, Supp. XII, 234; *Dutch White Book—Armed Merchantmen*, pp. 3–4.

[27] *Dutch White Book—Armed Merchantmen*, p. 4; *A. J. I. L.*, Supp. XII, 235.

Admission of Belligerent Armed Merchantmen

D. AMERICAN–DUTCH CORRESPONDENCE

On March 13, 1917, the United States Government through its minister at The Hague asked the Dutch Government whether American vessels armed for self-protection would be permitted to stop at Dutch ports without hindrance.[28] A few days later the United States Government asked further if it was the intention of the Dutch Government to draw a distinction between vessels which were armed privately by the respective owners and American merchantmen which carried an armed guard on board for protection by the Government of the United States.[29] The Dutch Government replied on March 22, 1917, that by order of the royal decree of July 30, 1914, the presence of warships or assimilated vessels of foreign powers in Dutch territorial and interior waters was prohibited. Armed merchantmen came within the category of assimilated vessels, without distinction as to whether armed privately or by the government.[30] The United States Government was still uncertain as to the meaning of the Dutch regulations, for on April 2, 1917, it desired to know whether the regulations applied to neutral as well as to belligerent armed merchantmen.[31] It was not until April 14, 1917, a week after the United States had entered the war, that the Dutch Government replied. It explained that the royal decree referred to in the previous note prohibited the presence of all foreign warships and assimilated vessels in the interior waters and territorial waters of the Netherlands dominion in Europe, but that its provisions did not apply to the colonies. The Neutrality Proclamation prohibited the presence of such vessels of belligerents in the jurisdiction of the state, including the colonies and overseas possessions. Consequently, the presence of belligerent armed

---

28) *Dutch White Book—Armed Merchantmen*, p. 3; *A. J. I. L.*, Supp. XII, 242–243.
29) *Ibid.*
30) *Dutch White Book—Armed Merchantmen*, pp. 16–17; *A. J. I. L.*, Supp. XII, 243.
31) *Dutch White Book—Armed Merchantmen*, p. 17; *A. J. I. L.*, Supp. XII, 244.

merchantmen with certain exceptions was prohibited throughout the entire jurisdiction of the state, while such neutral vessels were barred from such jurisdiction only in so far as the dominion of the kingdom in Europe was concerned.[32]

II. THE RULE OF INTERNATIONAL LAW WITH RESPECT TO ARMED MERCHANTMEN

In the late Middle ages resistance to capture was not only admitted as a right, but was in fact imposed as a duty by the sovereign. As early as 1492 Maximillian issued a decree requiring resistance. This decree was extended by Charles V in 1540. The Dutch Government issued a series of such decrees as late as 1717.[33] Like decrees were issued by other sovereigns. Charles II of England in 1672 issued the following Order in Council:

> ". . . that all masters of vessels going out on any foreign voyage . . . shall before they be cleared at the Custom House or permitted to sail out of any port of this kingdom on their respective voyages give good securities . . . that they will not separate or depart from such men of war as shall be by His Majesty appointed for their convoy, nor from the rest of their company, but that they will keep together during such their voyage and mutually assist and defend each other against any enemy to the utmost of their power, in case they shall happen to be attacked, and that to this end they will take care that their respective ships and vessels shall be provided with muskets, small shot, hand grenades, and other sorts of ammunition and military provisions according to the proportion of the men they carry."[34]

The practice of arming merchantmen was still common in the 18th and early 19th century. As evidence of

---

[32] *Dutch White Book—Armed Merchantmen*, p. 17; *A. J. I. L.*, Supp. XII, 244–245.

[33] Francois, *op. cit.*, pp. 27–29, quotes many such decrees from the *Dutch Groot-Placaetboek*.

[34] Higgins in *A. J. I. L.*, VIII, 710.

this may be cited Chief Justice Marshall's statement in the case of the *Nereide* that "In point of fact, it is believed that a belligerent merchant vessel rarely sails unarmed."[35]

During the latter half of the 19th century the practice of arming merchant vessels lapsed. Several practical reasons may be assigned for this. Piracy had all but disappeared. Privateering was declared abolished by the Declaration of Paris in 1856. Thus two important reasons for arming merchantmen in the past were no longer present. A third cause for the disappearance of the practice was the development of warships into such powerful weapons that resistance from even the best armed merchant ships became less than useless. In fact, by the opening of the World War the practice of arming merchantmen, and even great mail liners, seemed to have become permanently a thing of the past. At the Second Hague Peace Conference, Ottley, the representative of the British navy, declared "The shot of the cannon is the best guaranty that one has to deal with a warship. Merchant vessels do not have guns on board."[36] And de Louter, a leading Dutch student of international law, wrote in 1910, "The capture, or making prize of an enemy vessel, takes place in a very simple manner. Combat or violence is generally not necessary to effect it; a merchantman is powerless against a modern warship."[37]

But that a change of conditions might again turn the tables was foreseen by Freeman Snow as early as 1888. "It may be reasonably expected in coming naval wars that steamers of the great mail lines will be armed so as to defend themselves from attack, rather than to seek convoy."[38] The revival of the exercise of the right of resistance to visit and search was brought about by the sudden development of the submarine, although it had

---

35) 9 *Cranch* 388.
36) Hague Peace Conference, *Reports*, Carnegie Endowment, III, 1010.
37) *International Law*, p. 344.
38) *International Law*, p. 83.

already been brought about to some extent by the increasing use of auxiliary cruisers. The practice of forming a volunteer navy was inaugurated by Prussia in a decree of July 24, 1870, and followed by Russia in 1877. Other states did not long hesitate to follow this policy. The matter was fully discussed at the Second Hague Peace Conference and at the London Naval Conference where Great Britain opposed the right to convert merchantmen into cruisers, and France, Russia, and Germany reserved to themselves the right to convert such vessels not only in their own harbors, but even on the high seas. No action was taken on the matter by either Conference.

It was the extension of this policy among the other powers, together with their attitude at the Second Peace Conference, that set the British Government in the direction of a similar policy. The new British policy was announced by Winston Churchill, First Lord of the Admiralty, in a speech in the Commons on March 26, 1913. Churchill pointed out that the sea trade of Great Britain would be especially exposed to armed merchant cruisers of the other powers, that English trade might even be driven off the seas by these hostile cruisers. The British Government could not meet the contingency by building an equal number of cruisers, as that would be too expensive. The method of meeting the situation, as then announced by Churchill, was a follows:

"... Hostile cruisers, whenever they are found, will be covered by British ships of war, but the proper reply to an armed merchantman is another armed merchantman armed in her own defense. . . .

"Although these vessels have, of course, a wholly different status from that of the regularly commissioned merchant cruisers such as those we obtain under the Cunard agreement, the Admiralty have felt that the greater part of the cost of the necessary equipment should not fall upon the owners, and we have decided, therefore, to lend the necessary guns, to supply ammunition, and to provide for the training of members of the ship's company to form gun crews. The owners on their part are paying the cost of the necessary structural conversion, which is not great. The British mercantile marine will, of course, have the protection of the Royal Navy under all possible circumstances, but it is obviously impossible to guarantee individual vessels from attack when they are scattered on their voyages all over the world. No one can pretend to view these measures without regret or without hoping that the period of retrogression all over the world which has rendered them necessary may be succeeded by days of broader international confidence than those through which we are now passing."[39]

Resistance to visit and search by every belligerent merchant vessel remained a recognized right in the writings of practically all of the authorities on international law.[40] The Institute of International Law at its meeting in Oxford in 1913, recognized the right.[41] The right is also upheld in several prize court decisions. In the case of the *Catherine Elizabeth* Sir William Scott (afterward Lord Stowell) recognized the right of belligerent, though not of neutral merchantmen, to resist capture.[42] Chief Justice Marshall took the same position in the case of the *Nereide*,[43] and later in the case of the *Atlanta*.[44]

The revival of the practice of arming merchantmen just before the opening of the World War caused somewhat of a stir among international lawyers, who thought that the practice had lapsed into desuetude. In Germany, Schramm developed the theory that the arming of

---

[39] Higgins, *A. J. I. L.*, VIII, 710.

[40] Wildman, II, 146; Hauteville, I, 184; Wheaton, Sec. 528; Twiss, II, 187; Woolsey, p. 241; Halleck, p. 296; Phillimore, III, Sec. 339; Bulmerincq, *Revue de Droit International*, XI, 568; de Boeck, Sec. 212; Fauchille, p. 76; Ferguson, II, Sec. 225; Perels, p. 175; Dupuis, p. 121; Lawrence, p. 393; Hall, p. 456; Oppenheim, II, Sec. 85; Kleen, II, 312; Fiore, p. 469.

[41] *Annuaire*, (1913), p. 644.

[42] 5 *C. Rob.* 232, (1815). In the case of the "Fanny" Lord Stowell condemned neutral goods found on board an enemy ship having a commission of war, 1 *Dodson* 443, (1815).

[43] 9 *Cranch* 388, (1815).

[44] 3 *Wheaton* 409, (1815).

merchantmen was illegal, on the ground that such a ship had no right of defense against the legitimate right of visit and search on the part of the belligerent warships.[45] With important modifications this theory was taken over by other German writers, the most conspicuous among them being Triepel.[46] The same position was taken by a leading Dutch authority, Eysinga, Leyden University professor, in a paper read before the International Law Association at The Hague in September, 1914. Eysinga feared that the policy of arming merchant vessels would have serious consequences, because of the likelihood of an armed merchant vessel using its weapons for offense as well as for defense—that is, the return to something very similar to privateering. With the abolition of privateering all valid reasons for the arming of merchantmen had passed.[47] Those writers, who shared the German view, held that just as in war on land, there is no right to use violence against the armed forces of the enemy. The merchant vessel has no more right of resistance than has the noncombatant against the soldier, and if it does resist then it must be placed in the same category as the franco-tireur in land warfare.

With the appearance of the submarine in the World War, the arming of merchantmen took an added impulse until the practice was almost universal on the side of the Allies, and in the end even the greatest neutral nation was driven to it. The submarine, though capable of great destruction, is of frail construction, and one shot from an average caliber gun will send it to the bottom. Against such a vessel the arming of a merchantman renders it comparatively safe. This was pointed out by Winston Churchill in a speech in the House of Commons:

---

[45] *Das Prisenrecht in seiner neusten Gestalt*, (Berlin, 1913), pp. 308–310. Reprinted in Senate Document No. 332, *Senate Documents*, XXXXII, 1st Session, 64th Congress.

[46] "Widerstand feindlicher Handelschiffe gegen die Aufbringung", *Zeitschrift fur Volkerrecht*, VIII, 399.

[47] "Les Navires de Commerce Armes", *Int. Law Reports* for 1913–1914, pp. 171–176. Reprinted in Senate Document No. 332, *Senate Documents*, XXXXII, 1st session, 64th Congress.

". . . The object of putting guns on a merchant ship is to compel the submarine to submerge. If a merchant ship has no guns, a submarine with a gun is able to destroy it at leisure by gun fire, and we must remember that on the surface submarines go nearly twice as fast as they do under the water. Therefore the object of putting guns on a merchant ship is to drive the submarine to abandon the use of the gun, to lose its surface speed, and to fall back on the much slower speed under water and the use of the torpedo. The torpedo, compared with the gun, is a weapon of much more limited application. The number of torpedoes which can be constructed in a given time is itself subject to certain limitations. Any trained artillerist or naval gunner can hit with a gun, but to make a submerged attack with a torpedo requires a much higher degree of skill and training."[48]

According to figures given by Lord Curzon in the same session of the House of Commons, of the armed merchantmen seventy-five per cent escaped after an attack, whereas of the unarmed merchantmen only twenty-four per cent escaped.[49]

There is only one better method of protecting merchantmen against submarines, and that is by convoy of submarine chasers. But this method requires a very large number of warships, and can thus be used only by the big sea powers. This method also requires a large number of merchant ships to go in a unit, which is not always possible, especially not in commerce with the smaller nations and to out of the way ports. It is not to be wondered at, then, that the British Government spent so much diplomatic effort to get the Dutch Government to admit armed merchantmen into its ports.

The United States recognized the right of belligerent merchantmen to resist capture, and made the admission of belligerent armed merchantmen into its ports dependent upon the defensive character of the weapons, such

---

48) February 21, 1917, quoted by Francois, *op. cit.*, p. 42.
49) Francois, *op. cit.*, pp. 42–43.

character to be determined in each case by the port officials. As evidence of the defensive character of the arms the following were to be taken into consideration: the number, caliber, character, size, and positions of the guns; the quantity of ammunition carried; whether the vessel was manned by its usual crew and officers; whether the vessel intended to clear for a port lying in its usual trade route; whether the vessel took on board food and supplies sufficient only to carry it to its port of destination; whether the cargo of the vessel consisted of commerce unsuited for the use of a ship of war in operation against an enemy, etc.[50]

The rules laid down in this circular were superseded by new rules embodied in a memorandum of March 25, 1916. The memorandum declared that the status of a belligerent armed merchantman was to be considered from two points of view, from that of a neutral when the vessel entered its ports, and from that of an enemy when the vessel is on the high seas. The status of a belligerent armed merchantman in a neutral port was to be determined from the presence on board of a "commission of war." Unless there was such a commission the presumption was that the vessel was armed for defense.[51]

The Spanish rules provided that within twenty-four hours after the arrival of a belligerent armed merchantman in one of its ports, the captain of the vessel must give to the port authorities information regarding the character of its armaments, and to make the following declarations: 1) that the vessel was exclusively a merchantman, 2) that the vessel would not be converted until it should first have returned to its home port, and 3) that the armaments were exclusively for defense. The port official then made an examination of the vessel regarding the correctness of the declaration.[52]

Norway allowed armed merchantmen to enter her

---

[50] Circular of September 19, 1914. Text in *A. J. I. L.*, Supp. IX, 121, and also in Naval War College, *International Law Topics*, 1916, 93–95.
[51] Naval War College, *International Law Topics*, 1916, 101 ff.
[52] Francois, *op. cit.*, pp. 46–47.

ports and provided for an examination to insure the truly defensive character of the ship's armament.[53] Brazil allowed armed merchantmen to enter her ports only after a written guaranty from the legation concerned that their armament had not been and would not be used for offensive purposes.[54] Chile would receive into her ports no armed merchant vessel unless she had previously received from the government concerned a communication giving the name of the vessel, the route, roll of crew, list of passengers, and cargo as well as the management and armament of the vessel, demonstrating that the vessel was in reality armed for defensive purposes.[55]

III. COMPATIBILITY OF THE DUTCH PRACTICE WITH THE RULES OF INTERNATIONAL LAW

It is quite impossible, accepting the right of belligerents to arm their merchant ships, for a neutral to insist upon the obligation to place armed merchant ships in the same category as warships. Irrespective of whether a valid distinction can be made between vessels armed for defense by individuals and those armed by governments, the right may still exist for a neutral to assimilate an armed merchantman to warships for certain purposes.

The Dutch Government in the beginning took the position that it was its duty to place armed merchant ships in the same category as warships. But later on, and particularly in the reply to the British Government in regard to the admission of the *Princess Melita,* the Dutch Government changed its position and held that it had a right to place both kinds of vessels in the same category for certain purposes, but that it was not an obligation under international law. It adopted the rule at the beginning of the war in order to insure a more strict observance of its neutrality.

The question is, then, whether a neutral has a right to

[53] *Ibid.,* pp. 46–47.
[54] "Brazilian Neutrality", by F. A. de Carvalho, *British Yearbook of International Law,* 1922–1923, p. 131.
[55] Naval War College, *International Law Topics,* 1916, p. 31.

exclude from its territorial waters armed merchantmen as well as belligerent warships. Writes an Englishman, Sanford D. Cole:

"A state has sovereign jurisdiction over its own territory, and there seems no reason to doubt that in time of peace, entry can be refused to commercial vessels. Nor does there appear to be any reason why the same right should not be exercised in time of war between other nations, provided that the neutral state does not so act as to show partiality to either belligerent. . . . A neutral is entitled to exercise absolute control over its coastal waters, . . . It seems to me that a neutral is not bound to give unconditional hospitality to a belligerent merchantman and I am the more inclined to this view because it is on the side of restricting the rights of belligerents and enlarging those of neutrals, and this on broad grounds and apart from any general interest. . . . It may exclude the belligerent merchantman altogether."[56]

Even where there are treaties of commerce existing between a neutral and a belligerent which provide for mutual privileges of commerce, this right of exclusion can not be altogether denied. Such treaties do not demand that all categories of merchantmen and under all circumstances shall be granted admission. This position was also taken in the World War by the British Government.

"The closing of specified ports in time of war and as a military measure cannot be regarded as involving an infringement of a general provision in a commercial treaty giving the contracting parties reciprocally rights of access to the other country for purposes of trade. Such action is taken as part of the military operations against the enemy; a neutral power, which is undertaking no military operations, cannot be under the necessity of similar action."[57]

---

56) "Belligerent Merchantmen in Neutral Ports", *Papers of the Grotius Society*, 1918, pp. 23–25.
57) *D. O. B.*, IV, 46.

This distinction between the right of a belligerent to make such a rule and the right of a neutral to make such a rule seems of doubtful validity. A neutral as well as a belligerent has the right to take protective measures in times of need.

From the point of view of sound policy there is much to be said for the Dutch regulation prohibiting the admission into Dutch ports of belligerent armed merchantmen. The peculiar geographical position of Holland in relation to the belligerent powers exposed her to great dangers. In the beginning of the war when the Dutch Government made the rule, it faced an entirely new situation. Just what situations the new methods of warfare might develop could not at that time be forecast. Furthermore, it safeguarded the country against any concealed aggression. It also served as the best kind of guaranty to each belligerent that the enemy was not using any part of Dutch territory as a base of naval operations.

The Dutch regulations also had the advantage of being more easily and impartially administered. The distinction between armament for offense and armament for defense is an impossible one.[58] The possession of armament encourages the possessor to attack whenever a good opportunity offers, especially against frail craft like submarines. The German Government cited cases in which British armed merchantmen had attacked German vessels. They even claimed to cite British admiralty orders to officers of armed merchantmen suggesting offense.[59] In view of these uncertainties as to the real character of armed merchantmen, as reflected in the incriminations and recriminations between the belligerents, the Dutch regulations proved to have great advantages.

---

[58] Hyde, I, 466–472, severely criticizes the United States regulation of March, 1916. "The potentiality and special adaptability of the vessel to engage in hostile operations fraught with danger to the safety of an enemy vessel of war, rather than the designs or purposes of those in control of the former, however indicative of its character, have been and should be deemed the test of the right of the opposing belligerent to attack at sight."

[59] Note to the United States Governmenth of February 10, 1916. *A. J. I. L.*, Sp. Supp. X, 315 ff.

Once having laid down this rule for the observance of its neutrality, the Dutch Government was correct in maintaining that it could not change this rule during the continuation of the war without a breech of its neutral obligations. A neutral may change its regulations only with a view to making them more and not less strict.[60]

The attitude of the Dutch Government in regard to the treatment of armed merchantmen may point the way to a much needed reform of certain phases of the laws of war. Mr. Lansing's confidential letter of January 18, 1916, to the belligerent governments is an indication that not all neutrals were entirely sure of the way in which they should meet the problem of the admission of such vessels to their ports. Mr. Lansing wrote:

"While I am fully alive to the appalling loss of life among noncombatants, regardless of age or sex, which has resulted from the present method of destroying merchant vessels without removing persons on board to places of safety, and while I view that practice as contrary to those humane principles which should control belligerents in the conduct of their naval operations, I do not feel that a belligerent should be deprived of the proper use of submarines in the interruption of enemy commerce since those instruments of war have proven their effectiveness in this particular branch of warfare on the high seas."[61]

Mr. Lansing expressed the hope that a formula might be found by which submarine warfare could be brought within the "rules of international law and the principles of humanity without destroying its efficiency in the destruction of commerce." He pointed to the changed conditions of naval warfare brought about by the advent of the submarine. A merchant vessel carrying a small caliber gun is effective for an offense against a submarine, and since pirates are no longer found on the high seas and privateering has been abolished, the arming of merchantmen can now only be explained on the ground of a pur-

---

[60] 13th Hague Convention, Preamble, Cl. 7.
[61] Text found in *A. J. I. L.*, Sp. Supp. X, 310.

pose to render merchantmen superior in force to submarines and to prevent warning and visit and search by them. "Any armament, therefore, on a merchant vessel, seemed to have the character of an offensive armament."

The nature of the formula which Mr. Lansing hoped would be acceptable to both belligerents can be gathered from the following paragraphs of his letter:

> "If a submarine is required to stop and search a merchant vessel on the high seas and, in case it is found that she is of enemy character and that conditions necessitate her destruction, to remove to a place of safety all persons on board, it would not seem just or reasonable that the submarine should be compelled, while complying with these requirements, to expose itself to almost certain destruction by the guns on board the merchant vessel.

> "It would, therefore. appear to be a reasonable and reciprocally just arrangement if it could be agreed by the opposing belligerents that submarines should be caused to adhere strictly to the rules of international law in the matter of stopping and searching merchant vessels, determining their belligerent nationality, and removing the crews and passengers to places of safety before sinking the vessels as prizes of war, and that merchant vessels of belligerent nationality should be prohibited and prevented from carrying any armament whatsoever."[62]

Nor was Mr. Lansing the only person to express the need of a change in the rules of international law because of the changed conditions of naval warfare. From the belligerent country which profited most from the arming of merchantmen there came a hearty support of the position taken by Secretary Lansing. Sir Graham Bower, an English Admiral and a writer on international law, in an article in *The Contemporary Review*[63] also pointed to the changed conditions of naval warfare and to the fact that the rules governing the conduct of such warfare were

---

[62] *A. J. I. L.*, Sp. Supp. X, 312.
[63] November, 1917, CXII, 525 ff. *A. J. I. L.*, XIII, 60 ff.

for the most part formulated during the Napoleonic wars and had since changed little. Sir Graham would absolutely prohibit the destruction of prizes. To guarantee the noncombatant character of merchant vessels these should be completely unarmed. Sequestration of prizes in neutral ports should be permitted. The right to conduct ships into port for the exercise of the right to visit and search should also be granted, with a time limit placed on the right of this exercise and demurrage be made payable to an innocent ship for retention over a given period.[64]

That the submarine will not be abandoned as an instrument of warfare is clearly indicated by the attitude of the Italian and French Governments at the Washington Conference. Neither France nor Italy would consent either to abolition or to curtailment of the construction of submarines.[65] Furthermore, the Italian delegation took the position that an armed merchantman was a warship. This position seems to have been endorsed by the French delegation. Senator Schanzer, the head of the Italian delegation, would accept the resolutions which were finally embodied in the submarine treaty only with the understanding that the term "merchant vessel" in the resolution referred solely to unarmed merchantmen.[66] It is thus still uncertain whether the treaty which eliminated submarines as commerce destroyers will amount to much in practice.[67] Unless the right to arm merchantmen is

---

[64] The following recommendation was made by the committee of the Grotius Society on the legal status of submarines: "That if the destruction of enemy merchantmen before adjudication by a Prize Court be entirely prohibited, it should be unlawful for a belligerent state or its subjects to arm merchantmen (not incorporated into its naval forces as auxiliary cruisers) with guns or other weapons for purpose of offense or defense against prospective attacks by submarines or other war vessels. . . . In our opinion it is impossible to frame any satisfactory definition of the phrase, 'armament for defensive purposes'." The committee was composed of Prof. H. Gowdy, Sir John MacDonell, Sir H. Erle Richards, and Hugh H. L. Bellot. *Transactions*, IV, 43.

[65] *Senate Documents*, No. 126, 67th Congress, 2nd Session, p. 267.

[66] *Ibid.*, No. 126, 67th Congress, 2nd Session, p. 366.

[67] See Chapter on destruction of neutral prizes for a fuller treatment of submarines at the Washington Conference.

restricted, there is no certainty that inhuman conduct will not accompany submarine warfare. Without some restriction upon the right of merchantmen to arm, visit and search as a right of the submarine will be of no value because of the peril attendant upon its exercise, and the submarine will be tempted to fire at sight upon any suspicious vessel.

CHAPTER IX

ADMISSION OF PRIZES[1]

I. ORIGIN AND BASIS OF THE REGULATION

ACCORDING to the terms of Article 10 of the Neutrality Proclamation, a prize could only be brought into Dutch territory if the prize was unnavigable, unseaworthy, or short of fuel or foodstuffs. Such prizes were obligated to leave Dutch territory as soon as the causes for entrance had been removed. In case of refusal to leave, the prize would be liberated with her officers and crew, while the crew placed on board by the belligerent making the capture, would be interned.

In the application of this Article the Netherlands Government was soon faced with the question of whether vessels captured or requisitioned by a belligerent and put into service by him or sold, were to be considered prizes. The question arose from the Portuguese requisition of a number of German vessels found in Portuguese ports, which act was among the reasons that led Germany to declare war on Portugal. The Dutch Government believed these vessels should be permitted to enter and sojourn in Dutch ports. In the beginning it had been of the opinion that this Article applied only to vessels taken to Dutch ports before condemnation and did not apply to vessels which the captor had either sold or put into service.[2]

But in considering the transit over Dutch territory of war booty and requisitioned goods[3] the Dutch Government had concluded that a neutral power can not permit the continuation on its territory of the belligerent act by which the booty or the requisitioned goods had come into

---

[1] The correspondence relating to this subject is found in the *Dutch Orange Books; Recueil;* and *British Parliamentary Papers*, Misc. No. 2 (1918) Part I; *British State Papers*, 1917–1918, pp. 474–515.

[2] *D. O. B.*, II, 34; *Récueil*, pp. 164–166.

[3] See Chapter III.

the cntrol of the belligerent. It now concluded that this principle was applicable to prize vessels, entirely aside from the provisions of Article 10 of the Proclamation of Neutrality, since these vessels were not in fact prizes.[4] Thus the Dutch Government decided to prohibit all requisitioned or condemned vessels as well as newly captured vessels from entering the territory of the Netherlands except for reason of unseaworthiness, stress of the sea, or lack of fuel or provisions, with the customary obligation to depart as soon as these conditions were removed.[5]

II. DIPLOMATIC CORRESPONDENCE WITH RESPECT TO THE REGULATION

The first cases that arose under Article 10 of the Proclamation as interpreted above came up in regard to the navigation of the Scheldt. The Dutch Government refused to allow the British to remove by way of the Scheldt some merchant vessels captured from Germany at the outbreak of the war, upon the grounds that it could not permit its territory to be used for the continuation of a hostile act. And upon the same grounds the Dutch Government later denied Germany the right to remove these same recaptured German vessels over the Scheldt, after the German occupation of Antwerp.[6] Since the Dutch Government regards the mouth of the Scheldt as part of

---

[4] As far as the writer has been able to ascertain, only one actual case of the admission of an uncondemned prize arose. Part of the crew on the German warship "Emden", after the destruction of the German warship by the British man-of-war "Sydney", escaped and boarded the British schooner "Ayesha". On Nov. 27, 1914, the schooner because of unseaworthiness and lack of fuel entered the port of Padung. The commander desired to have the schooner treated as a warship or assimilated vessel, but since he was not able to furnish evidence that he had been duly commissioned by the competent German authorities, the "Ayesha" was held to be a prize to which the provisions of Article 10 of the Proclamation were applicable. In conformity with the provisions of this Article, the schooner was allowed to take on board only such articles as were necessary to restore her to seaworthiness and make up her lack of provisions. The next day she quit the port. *D. O. B.*, I, 32; *Recueil*, pp. 177–178.

[5] *Recueil*, p. 165; *D. O. B.*, II, 34.

[6] *Recueil*, p. 170; *D. O. B.*, IV, 26–36.

Dutch territory and not as Dutch territorial waters, a fuller treatment of this controversy is given in connection with the discussion of the transit of the Scheldt.[7]

A clear interpretation and application of the rule was made by the Dutch Government in the early part of 1916. The British Government informed the Dutch Foreign Office that it intended to send certain requisitioned merchant vessels to ports in Java and asked if the Dutch Government would raise objections to the trading of these vessels with its ports. The Dutch Government replied that it had no objections to the entrance of these vessels to its ports in case they were unarmed and flew the British flag before the war. But in case these vessels were originally enemy owned and had been captured or requisitioned during the war, entrance to Dutch ports would be denied them.[8] The British Government replied that the vessels to be sent to Java were unarmed and were under the British flag at the outbreak of the war. But the British Government denied the right of the Dutch Government to refuse admission to its jurisdiction of former enemy merchant ships, whether requisitioned or duly condemned prizes. It was a universally accepted rule that ownership of property changed upon condemnation by a duly constituted Prize Court. If the Dutch Government excluded former enemy vessels from its ports upon the grounds advanced it would also have to exclude these vessels if they had been sold to a neutral subject after condemnation by a British Prize Court, and this the British Government could not seriously believe the Dutch Government meant to do. The British Government held that the correct principle to apply in treatment of these vessels was not past ownership, which is extinguished by condemnation, but present employment of the vessel. Moreover, the Dutch regulation was inconsistent with the express terms of Article 2 of the 6th Hague Convention which permits the requisitioning of enemy vessels found in port at the outbreak of the war.[9]

---

[7] See Chapter IV.
[8] *D. O. B.*, IV, 40; *British Parl. Papers*, Notes 1 and 2.
[9] *D. O. B.*, IV, 41; *British Parl. Papers*, Note 3.

On June 19 the British Government sent a note to The Hague concerning the arrival at Tandjong Priok of the *Maria,* a vessel flying the German mercantile flag, which the British believed to be a German auxiliary cruiser. The British furthermore believed the vessel to have been originally British and to have been lying at Hamburg at the outbreak of war. The British Government stated that the attitude of the Dutch Government in this matter was wrong, but that so long as it maintained this attitude it was incumbent upon the Dutch Government to ascertain the history and status of the *Maria* and to treat her according to the rule laid down. Either the Dutch Government had to revise its rule or it had to order the vessel to leave Dutch jurisdiction.[10]

The Dutch Government at once sent a cablegram to the Governor General of the Netherlands East Indies asking for information. The East Indies Government had already made an investigation of the case on its own initiative and sent in its report, which was received within a few days after the despatch of the request for information. According to this report the Indies officials also believed the *Maria* to have been originally an English vessel, namely the *Dacre Hill.* The officials were the more convinced of this since the captain of the vessel was unable to clear up certain suspicious circumstances. Orders were immediately sent to the Indies officials to request the *Maria* to leave the Indies waters at once or undergo internment.[11] The Dutch Government indicated that it would in a later note reply to the British objections to the new application of the rule laid down in Article 10 of the Proclamation of Neutrality.

This decision of the Dutch Government did not, however, satisfy the British Government. To intern the *Maria,* in case she did not leave the Indies waters, and to restore her to Germany at the close of the war, was utterly incompatible with the rule as laid down in the Dutch Aid Memoire of April 1st, and also contrary to the principle

---

10) *D. O. B.*, IV, 41–42; *British Parl. Papers*, Notes 4 and 5.
11) *D. O. B.*, IV, 42; *British Parl. Papers*, Note 6.

which was supposed to underlie the rule. To intern the vessel would be precisely a violation of the principle, since it would enable one of the belligerents to continue the hostile act by which the vessel was acquired under the protection of a neutral. The only course consistent with the rule and the principle underlying it, was to proceed to compulsory expulsion of the vessel from Dutch waters in case she refused to leave.

A second objection of the British Government to the Dutch decision eventually to intern the *Maria* was that it was contrary to the obligations of neutrality. The German vessels were able to use the Dutch ports only as a place of refuge to escape enemy capture, because of the control of the British naval forces over the seas, whereas British vessels required entrance to Dutch ports only in the course of ordinary trade operations. The rule as applied would thus allow the former British vessels captured by the Germans to use the Dutch ports and waters solely as a place of refuge while denying the former German vessels captured by the British an equivalent concession.[12]

To this protest, as well as to the original British objections to the rule, the Dutch Government made an extended reply in a note of the 1st of December, 1916. It pointed out that it had at the very beginning of the war made the decision not to allow the transportation across its territory of any goods obtained as the result of an act of war, and this rule had been applied to all goods so obtained, no matter how legitimately the goods might have been acquired under the law of war. Under this regulation the navigation of the Scheldt had been prohibited to the thirty-seven vessels captured and re-captured at Antwerp at the commencement of the war. The regulation as laid down in the case of the *Maria* was no different from the rule laid down then. The rule in respect to the ownership of captured vessels and in respect to the requisitioning of enemy vessels belongs to the law of war, whereas the rules which the neutral must apply belong to the law

---

[12] *D. O. B.*, IV, 42–43; *British Parl. Papers*, Note 7.

of neutrality. The Dutch Government did not deny entrance to its jurisdiction to a requisitioned or captured vessel after it had been sold to the subject of a neutral state and had acquired the right to fly the flag of that state. The neutral Government under whose flag the vessel flies assumes responsibility for the ownership of the vessel, and the other neutral has no longer the duty to inquire into the original status of the vessel. As regarded the internment of the *Maria,* the only sanction known to international law for the violation of the prohibition of entrance to neutral jurisdiction is internment. Furthermore, such prohibition may not exclude entrance in all cases, as for instance in case of unseaworthiness, stress of weather, or lack of fuel and provisions. The *Maria* had been granted a definite period in which to make repairs, and when on the 12th of November this period terminated, the vessel was interned. In respect to the question of the ultimate disposition of the *Maria* after the war, the Dutch Government gave the assurance that the vessel would not be restored to Germany without further consideration. If the peace terms contained no provisions for the disposition of the *Maria,* the Dutch Government would decide the matter upon a basis of strict impartiality. Furthermore, the fact that the regulation providing for internment operated unequally upon the opposing belligerents was of no concern to the neutral government so long as the regulation was logical and justified.[13]

Another incident shortly arose to cause the British Government to send another note of protest. On December 28, 1916, the British steamship *Hunstrick* entered the harbor of Sabang for the purpose of refueling. The authorities of the port ascertained that the *Hunstrick* was originally the German ship *Belgia* which had been captured by the British during the war. Upon this ground the port authorities refused to allow the vessel to add to her store of fuel, since she had ample supply to reach the

---

13) *D. O. B.,* IV, 43–44; *British Parl. Papers,* Note 8.

next British port. The vessel was ordered to leave the port, which she did.[14]

This incident led the British Government to renew its protest in a note of March 23, 1917. The British Government made special efforts to point out that it regarded the Dutch action as a violation of the provisions of the treaties of commerce and navigation in force between the two countries. Article 3 of the Treaty of October 27, 1837, provides among other things that all vessels which have been captured from the enemy and have been regularly condemned by a British Prize Court, shall be regarded as British vessels, and under Article 2 of the Convention of March 27, 1851, the Dutch Government agreed that all vessels which according to the laws of Great Britain are to be deemed British vessels should for the purpose of the Treaty of 1837, be deemed British vessels. A reservation was made by the Dutch plenipotentiary who signed the Treaty restricting its application to the European possessions of the Netherlands, but this did not affect the definition of British merchant vessels which was accepted by the Dutch Government in that treaty. In thus making a distinction between the *Hunstrick* and other British merchant ships the Dutch Government was violating a treaty engagement with Great Britain.[15]

In a note of June 13, 1917, the Dutch Government once more justified its regulations in respect to the admission of vessels whose status had been changed as the result of an act of war. The provisions of the treaties cited did not obligate either party to admit all vessels of the other under all circumstances, and the British Government itself had not hesitated to close certain of its harbors to Dutch vessels during the war. Nor could the Dutch Government subscribe to the opinion, in view of the fact that the provisions of the treaties applied only to the European territory of the Netherlands, that the British vessels should profit under the provisions of this treaty in the overseas harbors. As far as the *Hunstrick* was concerned,

---

[14] *D. O. B.*, IV, 38; *British Parl. Papers*, Note 8.
[15] *D. O. B.*, IV, 44–45; *British Parl. Papers*, Note 9.

the Dutch Government felt that the interpretation given the rule by the Indies authorities was too severe, and instructions had been sent to the Indies Government officials to henceforth permit vessels acquired by an act of war to take on fuel to the limit of their capacity, no matter how near the next port of their own country might be.[16]

The British Government was not yet convinced of the justification of the Dutch rule and in a memorandum of October 5, 1917, replied to the last Dutch note and once more set forth its objections to the regulation. The closing of certain ports in time of war as a military measure could not be regarded as a violation of the treaty, since such action was taken as part of the military operations against the enemy, while a neutral, undertaking no military operations, could not be under the necessity of similar action. The fact that the British Government had itself invoked the principle that neutral territory must not be used to facilitate the perpetuation of acts of war, in the case of the transit across Dutch territory of goods coming from the parts of Belgium occupied by the Germans, did not deprive it of the right to criticize the principle involved. Moreover, the rule laid down operated to violate and not to carry out the principle. The only way the principle could be enforced would be either to expel all such vessels from its ports or to restore them to their former owners. To intern such vessels was actually compelling the perpetuation of the act of war for the duration of the war, since the Germans could prevent recapture of the vessel by merely steaming into a Dutch port. The fact that belligerent troops and warships are permitted to take refuge within neutral territory under the rules of international law was not, in the opinion of the British Government, at all relevant since the internment of duly condemned prizes was not required by international law. The note ended in an expression of surprise that there should be associated with the name of The Hague so many peculiar and unsound views of international law as had been adopted or invented by the

---

16) *D. O. B.,* IV, 44–45; *British Parl. Papers,* Note 10.

Dutch Government during the war, and this was "bound to be a factor for consideration in deciding upon the meeting place for future international legislative conferences."[17]

An extended reply to these protests was made by the Dutch Government in a note of the 28th of February, 1918, but a few new points were brought forward. Just as the British Government had the right without treaty violation to exclude Dutch vessels from certain of its ports as a military measure, so the Dutch Government could do the same in the interest of maintaining a strict neutrality. Whatever might be the validity, from the point of international law, of a decision of a national prize court, such decision could not restrict the right of a neutral to take in respect to such vessels measures which comported with its state of neutrality. The rule was not unsound simply because it did not apply to condemned vessels which had been sold to subjects of other neutrals, since from the moment that a neutral state gives a vessel the right to fly its flag, the vessel is given a new juridical personality—the personality of a neutral vessel. For the transfer of the flag, the neutral state whose flag the vessel now flies, is alone responsible. Nor could the vessel be restored to its original owners, since that would completely set aside the consequences of the act of war, and this a neutral could in no wise do. And to compel a vessel to leave port under all circumstances would make the recapture of the vessel certain, as in the case of the *Maria*. This, too, would be contrary to the maintenance of a strict neutrality.[18]

The British Government had also demanded the internment of the crew of the *Maria* upon the ground that she had entered Tandjong Priok armed, with munitions hidden on board, and that the crew belonged to the German naval forces. An investigation failed to reveal the existence of any of the alleged facts and the Dutch Government refused to intern the crew.[19]

---

17) *D. O. B.*, IV, 46–47; *British Parl. Papers*, Note 11.
18) *D. O. B.*, IV, 47–48, Note 32; *British Parl. Papers*, Note 12.
19) *D. O. B.*, IV, 48–50; Notes 33–37.

III. COMPATIBILITY OF THE DUTCH REGULATION WITH THE RULES OF INTERNATIONAL LAW

The Dutch rule of prohibiting the admission of adjudicated prizes and requisitioned enemy vessels is novel in international law. Questions with respect to the admission of uncondemned prizes have, of course, been numerous. In the famous case of the *Appam*, a captured British merchantman brought into Newport News by a German prize crew was libelled by the original owners. The German ambassador protested the jurisdiction of the courts over the prize on the ground that under the Prussian-American Treaty of 1799 German captors had a right to sequester their prizes in American ports. The German ambassador further contended that in any event Article 21 of the 13th Hague Convention, to which the British Ambassador appealed, was not applicable since Great Britain had refused to ratify it. The United States Supreme Court restored the vessel to the original British owner, holding that the case was governed by Article 21 of the 13th Hague Convention on the grounds that its provisions limiting the right of bringing in prizes to cases of unseaworthiness, stress of weather, or want of fuel or provisions, was merely declaratory of international law.[20]

Many considerations, such as that of self-defense and the maintenance of a strict neutrality, which may be advanced to justify the prohibition of entry of warships into neutral waters, can not be advanced with the same force to justify the prohibition of entry of condemned prizes or requisitioned enemy vessels. The Dutch regulation in respect to the admission of these latter vessels directly raises the question of whether a belligerent merchantman has an unqualified right to enter and use a neutral port.

---

[20] 243 *U. S.* 124; Scott, *Cases*, pp. 857 ff. In the case of the "Farn", the United States Government allowed the privileges of a belligerent warship to be extended to an uncondemned German prize captured from the English. The vessel was being used as a tender to some German warships. The Secretary of State held that "an enemy vessel which has been captured by a belligerent cruiser becomes as between the two governments the property of the captor without the intervention of the Prize Court", *A. J. I. L.*, Sp. Supp. IX, 361–365.

It is generally admitted that a state may refuse to allow commercial intercourse on land, subject to modification by existing treaties. But in regard to intercourse by sea this right[21] is not so clear, since the sea serves as an international highway and the hospitality of all ports is a necessity if the seas are to serve effectively as such highways.[22] Though there may be some uncertainty as to whether the ordinary hospitality accorded by one nation to the ships of another is a privilege or an undoubted right, the best evidence indicates that, subject to the right of entering a port for humanitarian reasons, it is a privilege and not a right. Prohibition of entry to certain ports is not uncommon. Even during the war England prohibited entry to several of her ports.[23] In the Napoleonic Wars the United States, though not prohibiting the entry, prohibited the departure of all vessels, foreign as well as domestic, on a foreign voyage.[24]

A brief reference to navigation politics will confirm this view. Many states discriminate against foreign vessels in their ports,[25] while others absolutely exclude foreign vessels from their coastwise trade.[26] The exclusion of foreign vessels from colonial trade and shipping is a practice that was at one time almost universal,[27] and in China even today no port is open except by treaty.[28] Here is a present day international situation, to which most of the leading powers have subscribed, frankly based upon the principle that a state may close or open its ports at its own desire. A modern case of an exercise of an extraordinary power over vessels in its harbors is that of Portugal which, while technically still a neutral, requisitioned the German ships in her ports. This action of Portugal was defended "as a right which is inherent

---

21) See Fisk and Pierce, *International Commercial Policies*, Chapter VI, "Prohibitions Affecting International Trade".
22) Oppenheim, II, 417.
23) See Chapter on admission of armed merchantmen.
24) Moore, *Digest*, VII, 142 ff.
25) Fisk and Pierce, *op. cit.*, Chapter XVIII, "Navigation Politics".
26) Bowman, *The New World*, pp. 510–513.
27) Fisk and Pierce, *op. cit.*, Chapter XVIII, "Navigation Politics".
28) Bowman, *op. cit.*, pp. 510–513.

in the sovereignty of the state, and which can not be challenged by any foreign power."[29] Italy, in 1915, while still a neutral, seized German vessels in its ports. If a neutral may exercise such a drastic power as the requisitioning of foreign vessels in its ports, a neutral may exercise the lesser power of excluding altogether from its waters belligerent vessels acquired as a result of an act of war, though a question as to the reasonableness of the classification may well be raised.

The Dutch practice of excluding condemned prizes must, however, face a serious criticism. It has been a universally accepted rule that condemnation by prize courts, except in cases of extreme irregularity, gives good title.[30] The sentence of a belligerent prize court of competent jurisdiction is conclusive, and binding upon all parties and in all countries.[31] Any other rule would lead to all kinds of confusion. It is of course true that the Dutch Government did not go behind the title the court decision gives, but it nevertheless practiced an active discrimination against vessels holding such title.

Undoubtedly the real reason that impelled the Dutch Government to adopt this rule was the situation in regard to the transit of materials over Holland from Belgium to Germany.[32] Germany wished the free transit of all goods across Dutch territory but by reason of pressure from England some sharp limitations were placed upon this transit by the Dutch Government. One of the restrictions upon this transport across Holland was that no war booty or requisitioned goods could be so transported. These restrictions upon this transit over Dutch territory the German Government bitterly resented. In this, as in so many

[29] Viscount, then Sir Edward, Grey in the British House of Commons, May 14, 1916.

[30] Wright, *Enforcement of International Law Through Municipal Law in the U. S.*, pp. 132–133. Moore, *Digest*, VII, 636 ff.

[31] American Cases: "Invincible", 1 *Wheaton* 238, 261 (1816); "The Alberta", 9 *Cranch* 359 (1815); "The Estrella", 4 *Wheaton* 298, (1819); British Cases: "Hughes and Cornelius", *King's Bench*, (1682), *Spinner*, 59; "Donbree vs. Nakier" 2 *Bingham's New Cases*, 781, 795, (1836).

[32] See Chapter III.

other instances during the war, Holland was caught between the conflicting interests of a continental and a maritime belligerent power. So when the Dutch Government was led to impose these restrictions on the transport across its land, it felt logically bound, in justification to Germany, to apply the same rule to its territorial waters. If a neutral ought not to allow its territory to be used to facilitate the continuation of an act of war, it ought not to permit its territorial waters to be so used.[33] It will be remembered that the rule was formerly adopted and promulgated in view of the treatment to be accorded to the German vessels which had just been seized by Portugal, should they seek to enter Dutch ports.

The Dutch Government never fully answered the British objections that the rule as applied actually worked to violate the principle it sought to carry out. What shall the neutral do in case such a vessel enters one of her ports and refuses to leave? The Dutch Government decided that internment was the only course to pursue in that case. But as the British Government pointed out, in case of a belligerent which had been swept from the seas and which has no outlying ports to speak of, internment of the vessel may often serve its purpose as well as taking the vessel into its own ports. It is true that in most cases the peace terms will determine the ultimate disposition of the vessel, but the continental belligerent can, by taking the vessel into a neutral port and allowing it to be interned there, prevent the stronger maritime power from again acquiring use of the vessel for the duration of the war. This really amounts to sequestration as provided by Article 23 of the 13th Hague Convention, and oddly enough this phase of the question was raised by neither party.

Lastly, it ought to be noted that the Dutch regulation excluding from Dutch waters belligerent vessels acquired as a result of an act of war, is in the direction of placing neutral duties in case of naval war upon the same basis as the duties of a neutral in case of war on land.

---

[33] *D. O. B.*, II, 34, for statement by Dutch Government to this effect.

Chapter X

INTERNMENT REGULATIONS AND THEIR
ADMINISTRATION

I. Regulations with Respect to Internment

TO THE Dutch internment regulations belong first of
all the provisions of the Neutrality Proclamation.
With the exception of Article 3, which provides for the
internment of belligerent warships violating the prohibition of admission to Dutch territorial waters, the internment articles of the Proclamation are in practical correspondence with those of the 5th and 13th Hague Conventions dealing with this subject. During the early
months of the war, however, additional regulations of a
more detailed nature were issued. Thus on August 8,
1914, the Minister of War issued certain regulations for
carrying out the provisions of the first clause of Article 3
of the Proclamation.[1] Most of these regulations are
nearly identical with Chapter II of the 5th Hague Convention.

A third national internment regulation is found in the
royal decree of November 27, 1914, issued to supplement
the royal decree of March 19, 1913, and merely provides
some additional rules for the organization and work of
the Netherlands Red Cross. Article 2 in particular
charges this organization with the duty of establishing
and maintaining a Bureau of Information for the sick
and wounded, which bureau shall also serve as the
Bureau of Information for prisoners of war and interned
soldiers. This Bureau shall be charged with the extension
of aid to these persons in conformity with Articles 14 and
15 of the 5th Hague Convention.[2]

A law passed on December 31, 1914, containing penal
and disciplinary regulations with respect to military per-

---

[1] See Appendix VIII.
[2] See Appendix IX.

sons of foreign powers interned in the Netherlands, constituted the fourth national regulation with respect to internment. In general, this law placed military persons interned in the territory of the State on the same footing as far as penal and disciplinary laws and regulations were concerned, with Dutch military persons, and the internment camp for the above purposes was incorporated into the organization of the Netherlands land and sea forces. Any such persons leaving in violation of a promise, or violating a promise under which they were granted a temporary or permanent leave, were punished with a maximum of six years of military imprisonment. The above offenses were punishable even though they were committed outside of Dutch territory in Europe.[3] In a statement of interpretation of this law it was declared that the expression "interned military persons belonging to a foreign power" was to be construed in a liberal sense, to include not only foreign military persons, but also escaped prisoners of war.[4]

II. DIPLOMATIC CORRESPONDENCE WITH RESPECT TO INTERNMENT REGULATIONS

A. PERSONS

1. *Internment of Shipwrecked, Wounded or Sick, Coming from Belligerent Warships*

On the morning of September 22, 1914, three English cruisers, the *Abouker,* the *Cressy,* and the *Hogue,* were torpedoed about thirty miles from the Dutch coast by the German submarine "U-9." About 200 men of the torpedoed vessels were rescued by two Dutch vessels, the *Titan* and the *Flora.* A small number of the rescued sailors upon request were handed over to a British torpedo boat, which arrived upon the spot soon after the disaster, while the others were landed upon Dutch territory. Pending the decision of the Dutch Government as to whether internment should take place or not, the shipwrecked

---

[3] See Appendix X.
[4] Carsten, *Maatregelen,* p. 148.

sailors were placed in temporary internment. They were, however, soon released by the decision of the Government that a neutral is under no obligation to proceed to internment in case of shipwrecked, wounded, or sick brought into neutral territory by a neutral merchant vessel without having encountered a warship of the opposing belligerent and without having had communication with such warship.[5]

On June 22, 1916, twenty-two shipwrecked sailors were landed upon Dutch territory by a Dutch fishing vessel. These twenty-two, of whom twenty-one were German and one was British, were some of the survivors of the crews of belligerent warships which had had a battle in the North Sea. These were likewise freed.[6] A peculiar case was that of the survivors of the French shipwrecked torpedo boat, *Mousquet*. In the early part of the war this vessel was destroyed in a battle with the German cruiser, *Emden*, and the shipwrecked crew placed on the British merchant steamer, *Newburn*, by the commander of the *Emden*. The commander of the *Emden* entered on the journal of the *Newburn* that he granted the French sailors freedom, and when the vessel arrived at the port of Sabang the sailors were not interned.[7]

The German Government protested that in accordance with the general principles of international law the shipwrecked men of the three British vessels should have been interned. The German Government, however, did not wish to protest their liberation, but expressed the expectation that the Dutch Government would continue to press its demands with the British Government for the liberation of German citizens, subject to service in the German army, taken from Dutch vessels, an act utterly in violation of international law. The Dutch Government in reply directed attention to the provisions of the Hague Convention for the adaptation to naval war of the principles of the Geneva Convention. Article 12 of this Con-

---

[5] *Recueil*, p. 174. *D. O. B.*, II, 34.
[6] *D. O. B.*, III, 32.
[7] *Ibid.*, I, 34.

vention deals with wounded, sick, or shipwrecked, found, among others, on neutral merchant ships. In regard to these persons this Article recognizes the right of belligerent warships to demand that they be handed over. Article 14 stipulates that such persons falling into the power of the other belligerent are prisoners of war, and the Article then further stipulates what may be done with them. One of the possibilities cited is that they may be taken into a neutral port. In this event, Article 15 then further provides that the shipwrecked, sick, or wounded, who are landed at a neutral port with the consent of the local authorities, must, unless an arrangement is made to the contrary between the neutral and the belligerents, be guarded by the neutral state so as to prevent them again taking part in the operations of the war. The Convention did not take into account the possibility of sick, wounded, or shipwrecked being picked up by a neutral merchant ship not meeting a belligerent warship. A passage in the report of Professor Renault, who served as the reporter of the Commission which drafted the Convention, expressly states that if a neutral merchant vessel which has casually picked up wounded or sick, even shipwrecked men, arrives in a neutral port without having met a cruiser and without having entered into any agreement, the individuals which it disembarks do not come under the provision of Article 15, but are free.[8] The Netherlands had ratified the above Convention and was bound to conduct itself according to its provisions, regardless of the fact that Great Britain did not ratify it. The conduct of the Dutch Government was not in conflict with the provisions of Article 3 of the Proclamation. The rescued English sailors were, the moment they were taken on board the Dutch vessels, guests of the Netherlands, and they landed on Dutch territory independently of their own wills. Had they been picked up within the Dutch territorial waters as shipwrecked because of a naval encounter there, Article 3 would have been applicable.[9]

---

[8] Hague Peace Conference, *Proceedings*, I, 73.
[9] *D. O. B.*, II, 27–28.

The German Government remained dissatisfied with the Dutch position. It contended that the rescued shipwrecked persons should have been released only with its consent. Since Great Britain had not ratified the 10th Hague Convention, the ratification by Germany and the Netherlands could have no influence as against Great Britain. Only the general principles of international law were applicable to this case, and these provide that persons belonging to the armed forces of a belligerent state coming upon neutral territory must be interned. The German Government added that the retention of the shipwrecked British sailors would have placed in the hands of the Dutch Government a powerful weapon with which to compel the British Government to release the German reserves taken off Dutch vessels. The line of action of the Dutch Government in the two cases gave the German Government the impression that in respect to the two belligerents the Dutch were not measuring with the same yardstick. To this the Dutch Government replied that its position as a neutral did not permit it to ask the advice of a belligerent power as to how it was to administer its neutrality measures. It is true that Article 18 of the 10th Hague Convention states that the provisions of the Convention do not apply except between contracting powers, and then only if all the belligerents are parties to the Convention, but the Dutch Government had declared through its ratification of the Convention that it regarded the provisions as declaratory of international law, and that it would use its provisions as a guide of neutral conduct no matter who were the belligerents. The Dutch Government resented the implication that it was not administering its neutrality measures with impartiality. Only could it be said that this was the case if a different rule was adopted in an exactly similar situation.[10]

In still another note on this subject the German Government maintained that the Dutch Government could have made the release of the shipwrecked British sailors contingent upon the like release of German subjects

10) *Ibid.*, II, 28–29. Note of March 15, 1915.

illegally taken off Dutch vessels. The Dutch Government maintained in reply to this that it could no more consult Great Britain than Germany in regard to a duty imposed upon her as a neutral, and that it could not make the performance of this duty the subject of an agreement with one of the belligerents.[11]

A brief correspondence with the British Government took place over the internment by the Netherlands of survivors of the British submarine "E-17," which were brought to land by the Dutch warship *North Brabant*. The "E-17" was destroyed while submerged outside of the Dutch three-mile limit. The British Government protested the internment of its crew because of the fact that, according to the statement of its commander, the "E-17" had mistaken the *North Brabant* for a German cruiser and had precipitately plunged itself under water, in spite of a grave defect in its mechanism. The *North Brabant* was thus the immediate, though unconscious cause of the destruction of the "E-17." Furthermore, the wrecking of the "E-17" had not been the result of a naval battle. Nor had the 10th Hague Convention been ratified by Great Britain, and on grounds of Article 18 the Convention was not applicable to British shipwrecked sailors. The British note, however, placed more emphasis on the moral than on the juridical aspects of the question.[12] The Dutch Government in its reply pointed to the plain provision of Article 13 of the 10th Hague Convention to the effect that if sick, wounded, or shipwrecked persons are taken on board a neutral warship, every possible precaution must be taken that they do not again take part in the operations of the war. The fact that Great Britain had not ratified the Convention was irrelevant, since the Convention had been ratified by so many powers that it must be regarded as declaratory of international law, and so the Dutch Government regarded it. Nor did the fact that the "E-17" had become shipwrecked because of the mistaken identity of the *North Brabant* and not as a result of a

---

[11] *Ibid.*, II, 29–30. Notes of Sept. 20, 1915, and Jan. 31, 1916.
[12] *Ibid.*, II, 31. Note of Feb. 3, 1916.

naval battle make any difference. The provisions of Article 13 are stated in general terms and do not distinguish between a shipwreck caused by a naval battle and a shipwreck caused by other means.[13]

In the case of military aviators belonging to belligerents and found in danger of death in the open seas and picked up by a neutral merchantman and landed at a Dutch port the same rule was applied as in the case of shipwrecked sailors brought into Dutch territory by a neutral vessel. And by application of the same principle as applied to shipwrecked sailors brought in from the high seas by a neutral warship, belligerent military aviators were also interned.[14]

2. *Internment of Military Persons in Civilian Clothes*

In the early days of the war there were among the Belgian soldiers which crossed the Dutch frontier some who had discarded their uniforms for civilian clothes in order to facilitate their escape to Dutch territory. The Dutch Government also interned these. Whenever a person in civilian clothes was found to have upon him identification plates or marked underwear, from which it appeared that the wearer belonged to the armed forces of a belligerent, he was interned.[15]

3. *Internment of Deserters*

A considerable number of German deserters crossed the Dutch frontier from Belgium in the early days of the war, and so far as they bore evidence of belonging to or having belonged to the German armed forces, they were interned. The German Government, according to the Dutch papers, notified the Dutch Government that it would no longer reimburse the Dutch Government for the expenses incurred in the internment of German deserters, and that likewise it would no longer give aid to the de-

---

13) *Ibid.*, II, 31–32. Note of March 18, 1916.
14) *Ibid.*, II, 30. *Recueil*, pp. 145–146.
15) Carsten, *op. cit., pp.* 99–103.

pendents of these deserters left behind in Germany.[16] The German Government clearly intended the Dutch Government to understand that it no longer regarded the deserters as belonging to its armed forces. This led the Dutch Government to adopt a new rule in regard to deserters crossing its frontier. It decided to free the deserters already interned, and not to intern those crossing its frontier in the future. In the opinion of the Dutch Government, deserters, from the point of view of the neutral in whose territory they are found, have lost the character of belligerents. However, they must not be freed until after the neutral has made an independent investigation in regard to the actual circumstances under which they crossed the frontier, and as to whether they are regarded as deserters in their own country, and have been condemned as such. In conformity with the above rules many German deserters were freed.[17]

4. *Wounded Brought Over the Dutch Frontier by Neutrals and Interned*

During the fighting in the early days of the war along the Limburg frontier, several Dutch Red Cross ambulances crossed over and brought a number of wounded German and Belgian soldiers into Dutch territory, where they were interned. After an investigation into the circumstances under which these wounded soldiers were brought into Dutch territory, the Dutch Government decided that they had been wrongfully interned since they had been brought into Dutch territory without their consent, and that consequently they ought to be released. The same rule was followed in similar cases along other parts of the frontier.[18]

5. *Liberation of Invalid Military Persons Interned in Holland*

In the early part of 1915 an agreement was reached between Great Britain and Germany in regard to the ex-

---

[16] *Ibid.*, 101–102; refers to item in *De Telegraaf* of September 22, 1915.
[17] *D. O. B.*, II, 34. Recueil, p. 178.
[18] *D. O. B.*, I, 36. *Recueil*, p. 177.

change of invalid war prisoners. This agreement led the Dutch Government to propose to the Belgian, German, and British Governments that they consent to the liberation of those of their soldiers interned in Holland who had become permanently unfit for further military service. To this proposal the belligerents consented, Germany also agreeing to accept the condition imposed by the Belgian Government that the liberated Belgian prisoners should not be treated as prisoners of war upon their return to Belgium. In conformity with the above agreement a number of invalid persons interned in Holland were sent back to their home country.[19]

6. *Foreign Leaves Given to Interned Military Persons*

By analogy based upon Article 11 of the 5th Hague Convention and Article 24 of the 13th Hague Convention, the Dutch Government believed it could grant leaves outside of the country in case of special circumstances, such as serious illness of near relatives. Those desiring such permission were obliged to give their word of honor that they would return within the stated time. Although the Hague Conventions contain no provisions for liberties to interned soldiers below the rank of officers, the same privilege was extended to privates in similar circumstances.[20]

7. *Transit of Invalid Prisoners of War Across Dutch Territory*

As was mentioned above, the English and German Governments early in 1915 came to an agreement for the repatriation of all prisoners of war who had become unfit for further military service. The coöperation of the Dutch Government was asked in order that the transit might take place over Holland. The Dutch Government coöperated to the fullest extent, while the Dutch Red Cross took upon itself to provide and care for the invalid soldiers during the transit.

In the middle of February the first exchange took

---

[19] *D. O. B.*, I, 36. *Recueil*, pp. 177–178.
[20] *D. O. B.*, I, 35–36. *Recueil*, pp. 176–177.

place. The German prisoners were brought from England to Flushing on an English vessel, which also took back to England the English prisoners brought to Flushing by train. A second exchange took place in June, and this time the Dutch Government was asked to permit the transport over sea to be made on a Dutch boat. This request was also granted, and the Netherlands Red Cross under this arrangement assumed the care of the invalid soldiers on the sea voyage also. On the same basis other exchanges took place in August, October, and December of 1915, and February of 1916. The costs of the transport across Holland and also the costs of the transport on the Dutch vessel were borne by the Dutch Government at its express wish.[21] In an exchange of May, 1916, the transport at sea again took place on a British hospital ship. In exchanges on August, October, and December of 1916, the Hoek of Holland was made the point of embarkation and debarkation, and the sea transport took place on a Dutch vessel. In the last named exchange invalid German civilians, interned in England, were included.[22]

8. *Internment in Holland of British and German War Prisoners and Civilians*

A meeting was held in The Hague in June and July, 1917, of representatives of the British and German Governments to discuss different matters in regard to the internment of combatant prisoners of war and civilians. The Netherlands Minister for Foreign Affairs presided over the meeting with the assistance of the Dutch Minister at Stockholm. The discussions thus held led to a number of agreements of which only a few are of interest here. The Dutch Government declared itself ready to receive for internment within its territory 8,000 prisoners of war from each belligerent. The British and German Governments agreed to repay the costs of the internment of their respective subjects and to supply the necessary material for the building and upkeep of the internment

---

21) *D. O. B.*, I, 36–37; II, 35–36.
22) *Ibid.*, III, 28–29.

camp, for medical aid, fuel, food, and clothing for the interned, or at least not to hinder their importation into Holland. Under the agreement Holland received for internment 7,500 sick and wounded combatant prisoners of war, 6,500 officers and non-commissioned officers who had been in captivity not less than eighteen months, and 2,000 invalid civilians. They were placed in different parts of the country, and were housed some in hotels, some in reconstructed houses, and some in barracks. Since both the German and British Governments undertook to promptly return to the Netherlands any of these persons who might escape and come within their power, the persons interned under the agreement were given considerable liberty.[23]

B. Property

1. *Internment of Military Supplies Brought Upon Dutch Territory by Belligerent Soldiers*

All war supplies brought into Dutch territory by belligerent soldiers were sequestrated in a depot at Delft.[24] So far as is known only war material originally belonging to them was ever brought into Holland by any of the belligerent soldiers crossing the frontier.

2. *Internment of Warships*

The unusual regulations of the Dutch Government in regard to the treatment of warships led to many internments, the history of which is fully discussed in Chap. VII.

3. *Internment of Airships*

By royal decree of August 3, 1914, the Dutch Government forbade all airships, whether neutral or belligerent, from crossing the Dutch frontier.[25] All efforts were made to prevent them from crossing the frontier and to force them to land when above it. The Dutch territorial

---

[23] *D. O. B.*, IV, 77–87. Agreement also found in *British Parl. Papers*, Misc. No. 12 (1917, cd. 8594).
[24] Carsten, *op. cit.*, p. 115.
[25] See Chapter VI.

waters were included within the prohibited jurisdiction. All belligerent airships landing in Dutch territory were interned for the duration of the war. Hydro-airplanes were placed on the same footing as airships.[26]

4. *French and Belgian Railway Cars in Dutch Territory*

The French and Belgian railway cars in Dutch territory were differentiated into two groups: *a)* those cars which before the occupation of Belgium had crossed the Dutch frontier in the course of ordinary traffic, and *b)* those cars which had been sent across the Dutch frontier upon the fall of Antwerp in order to prevent them falling into the power of the German authorities. The Dutch Government decided that neither the cars belonging to class *a* nor those belonging to class *b* could be allowed to cross the Dutch frontier either into Germany or into German occupied territory. Under Article 53 of the 4th Hague Convention these cars could be seized by Germany, if and when these cars came under her jurisdiction. To allow these cars to be sent into either German territory or German occupied territory would be virtually surrendering the cars to German seizure at the expense of the opposing belligerents. This would not be in conformity with the maintenance of a strict and impartial neutrality. Thus although the cars were not officially interned, they were placed in quasi-internment by the prohibition on Dutch railways not to send the cars into the two specified territories.[27]

5. *Internment of War Material Brought into Dutch Territory from the High Seas*

In August, 1914, a German hydroplane while above the North Sea just outside of the Dutch waters was compelled to alight because of mechanical trouble. After having alighted it floated to shore and landed on Dutch territory where it was immediately interned by the Dutch authorities. The German Government protested this in-

---

26) *D. O. B.*, I, 35; II, 24–27.
27) *D. O. B.*, I, 37. *Recueil*, p. 180.

ternment on the ground that a hydroplane, especially one coming into Dutch territory as had this one, should be regarded as a warship or an assimilated vessel, and that this hydroplane should be permitted to repair her damages according to the provisions of Articles 5 and 6 of the Proclamation and then be allowed to depart. The Dutch Government rejected this attempt to assimilate hydroplanes to warships, contending that they were *sui generis*. The internment of the hydroplane was dictated by the general rule by virtue of which any part of the armed forces of a belligerent must be interned when found in neutral territory.[28]

From the very beginning of the war all kinds of war material was cast upon the Dutch shore. Some of it came from wrecked or destroyed warships and airplanes, but much of it was made up of torpedoes and mines, washed up by the storms, and not infrequently causing loss of life and great material damage. The explosive instruments of war were taken apart and together with all other material cast up on the Dutch shores were placed in internment.[29]

A protracted correspondence took place between the British and Dutch Governments with respect to the treatment of seaplanes and other war material salved on the high seas and brought into Dutch territory.[30] Shortly after the destruction just outside of the Dutch waters of the three English cruisers, *Cressy, Aboukir,* and *Hogue,* the English Government demanded the return of all objects of value of the three vessels which might have been cast upon the Dutch coast or found in the waters of the North Sea. The Dutch Government replied that all the objects which formed a part of the equipment of the warships were being collected by the Dutch military authorities and would be interned until the close of the war, while the objects which were the personal property of

---

[28] *D. O. B.,* II, 24–26.
[29] Carsten, *Maatregelen,* pp. 124–126.
[30] *D. O. B.,* IV, 17–21. *British Parl. Papers,* Misc. No. 4 (1918), cd. 8985.

the crews of the vessels would be handed over to the British consul at Amsterdam as soon as possible.[31]

Subsequently a number of cases arose involving the internment of seaplanes or their equipment salved on the high seas and brought into Netherlands jurisdiction. The Dutch Government followed the rule laid down in the above case. All personal property of the crews was immediately restored, but all objects which formed a part of the equipment were interned. To this internment the British Government protested at some length and with great vigor. According to the British notes the rules governing internment are not based on any one single and uniform principle largely due to the fact that the rules grew up gradually and severally and were agreed upon from different motives. Each particular case, then, should be judged according to the circumstances which characterize it. The case of seaplanes salved on the high seas and brought into neutral territory is similar to the case of shipwrecked members of belligerent forces rescued by neutral merchantmen. If such shipwrecked men are rescued by a neutral warship, they must be interned according to the 10th Hague Convention, Article 13, whereas if they are rescued by neutral merchantmen and brought into neutral harbors, they need not be interned. None of the basic reasons for the duty of neutrals to intern belligerent forces could be used in favor of rescued seaplanes. The seaplanes did not enter Dutch jurisdiction to escape capture, to take in supplies, or to undergo repairs. In fact, the seaplanes did not get into Dutch territory voluntarily and on their own account, but quite accidently, because the rescuing merchantmen might as well have taken it into an English as to a Dutch port. And lastly, in several cases at least, had the seaplanes been left at sea they might have been salved by the British Government, or by a British ship and taken into a Dutch port.[32]

---

31) *D. O. B.*, IV, 17. *British Parl. Papers*, Misc. No. 4 (1918), cd. 8985, p. 1.

32) *D. O. B.*, IV, 19–20. *British Parl. Papers*, *op cit.*, pp. 3, 4, 16, 17.

The Dutch Government justified its regulation with respect to the internment of seaplanes salvaged on the high seas and brought into Dutch jurisdiction, on the ground that to restore a shipwrecked warship, its accessories, or any other war material found on its coasts or salvaged on the high seas and brought into its ports, to the belligerent state to which they belonged, would be rendering to that belligerent a service incompatible with the observation of a strict neutrality and contrary to the principle stated in Article 6 of the 13th Hague Convention which fodbids a neutral to supply a belligerent, either directly or indirectly, with war material of any kind whatever. The Dutch Government did not deny that the different rules established by the second Hague Conference were not part of a single and absolute principle, but contended that a dominant principle did nevertheless exist, which, in conformity with the third paragraph of the preamble to the 13th Hague Convention,[33] should guide neutral states when they have to make a decision in cases not expressly provided for. This principle requires that a neutral abstain from all action which amounts to strengthening the armed forces of the belligerents. The rules prescribing internment are applications of this principle, and those which exclude it in certain cases have the character of exceptions. The case of shipwrecked men rescued on the high seas by neutral merchantmen and brought into neutral ports formed such an exception, but no such exception had been agreed upon with respect to war material brought into neutral territory under the same circumstances, and there is nothing to indicate that the powers represented at the Peace Conference regarded it as subject to the same rule as is applied in the case of shipwrecked men. In addition, a very good reason did exist for the exception just noted, and that is that in keeping with the general principle of international law which seeks as far as possible to safeguard personal liberty.

---

[33] The third paragraph of the preamble runs: " .... in cases not covered by the present convention, it is expedient to take into consideration the general principles of the law of nations."

This consideration did not arise in the case of material salved on the high seas. The principle to which the Dutch Government appealed permitted it to decide with absolute impartiality all cases not provided for in the Hague Conventions or in the deliberations of the Conferences, while the British view, on the contrary, which did not admit of the existence of any dominant principle, and which would judge each case according to the circumstances which characterized it, would lead in practice to many arbitrary decisions.[34]

III. INTERNMENT REGULATIONS OF THE GENEVA AND HAGUE CONVENTIONS

Internment is a relatively new development in international law. Internment on a large scale began only with the Franco-Prussian War, when large sections of the French Army were interned in Belgium and Switzerland.[35] The question of internment was taken up for consideration for the first time at an international conference at Brussels in 1874. The articles on internment of military forces incorporated in the Brussels Declaration were later adopted in almost identical form by the Institute of International Law meeting in Oxford in 1880, and later by the First Hague Conference which incorporated them into the Convention Respecting the Laws and Customs of War on Land. At the Second Hague Peace Conference the articles on internment were taken out of the above Convention and placed in the Convention Respecting the Rights and Duties of Neutral Powers and Persons on Land, where they appear as Chapter II.[36] With the exception of Article 13, which was added in 1907, and paragraph 2 of Article 14, which was added in 1899, the existing provisions for internment of military forces are the same as those adopted at Brussels in 1874.

Article 11 provides that a neutral which receives on its territory troops belonging to the belligerent armies shall

---

[34] *D. O. B.*, IV, 20–22, 24.
[35] Lawrence, *op. cit.*, pp. 622–623.
[36] *Reports*, Vol. 1, 339.

intern them, as far as possible, at a distance from the theater of the war; it may keep them in camps, confine them in fortresses, or in places set aside for this purpose; and it may liberate the officers on parole not to leave the neutral territory without permission. Article 12 provides that in the absence of a special convention to the contrary, the neutral shall supply the interned with the food, clothing, and relief required by humanity, which expenses shall be made good at the conclusion of peace. The question of what must be done with escaped prisoners of war, or prisoners of war brought by troops taking refuge in neutral territory is settled by Article 13. They are to be left at liberty, and if the neutral allows them to remain in its territory it may assign them a place of residence. Under Article 14 the neutral is given authority to grant passage through its territory of sick and wounded belonging to the belligerent armies, on condition that the trains carrying them shall carry neither personnel nor material of war. Should sick and wounded of one belligerent party be brought into neutral territory by the opposing belligerent party, the neutral must guard them so as to insure their not taking part in military operations again. And finally Article 15 provides for the application of the Geneva Convention to the sick and wounded interned in neutral territory.

Several articles in regard to internment are also found in the other Hague Conventions. Thus Article 14 of the 4th Hague Convention imposes upon the neutral the duty of establishing a bureau of information for the interned within its territory, while Article 16 of the same Convention confers upon such bureaus the privilege of free postage. Article 13 of the 10th Hague Convention provides that if sick, wounded, or shipwrecked persons are taken on board a neutral warship, every possible precaution must be taken that they do not again take part in the operations of the war, while Article 15 regulates the disposition of the shipwrecked, wounded, or sick, who are landed at a neutral port. Unless an arrangement is made to the contrary between the neutral and the belligerents they must be guarded by the neutral so as to prevent them from again taking part in the operations of the war. The 13th Hague Convention also contains a few provisions with regard to internment. Thus the first paragraph of Article 3 stipulates that the prize crew of a vessel which has been captured within the territorial waters of a neutral state must be interned if the prize is still within its jurisdiction, while Article 21 prescribes internment for the crew of a prize which violates the harbor regulations laid down in the article, and Article 24 prescribes the same treatment for both the belligerent warship and its crew violating the provisions of that article.

A final regulation in regard to internment is found in paragraph 3 of Article 2 of the Geneva Convention for the Amelioration of the Condition of the Wounded in the Field. Both belligerent states under this Article are authorized to make mutual agreements to send the sick and wounded of the enemy to a neutral state with its consent and on condition that it shall charge itself with their internment until the close of hostilities.

IV. COMPATIBILITY OF THE DUTCH INTERNMENT REGULATIONS WITH THE RULES OF INTERNATIONAL LAW

In the main the Dutch internment regulations followed rather closely the provisions laid down in the Gevena and Hague Conventions, and in so far as they did no comment is necessary. However much these Conventions have done to give certainty to the measures which a neutral must take in regard to internment, the provisions still lack much of completeness, and the peculiar position of Holland in relation to the theater of the war produced several situations which are not covered by these conventions. Thus the Dutch Government was confronted with the necessity of making decisions several times as to whether or not it should proceed to internment, without having any clear rules of international law to guide it. This caused the Dutch Government to proceed at times with great uncertainty, as for instance when it first interned wounded German soldiers brought into its territory by Dutch Red Cross ambulances, and then after reconsideration released them. These defects and omissions in the existing conventions may well become the subject for the consideration of future international law conferences.

A first grave defect in the conventional internment regulations became apparent when the Netherlands Government was faced with the problem of what it should do with the shipwrecked sailors brought into port from the three British warships which were torpedoed just outside of the Dutch territorial waters. Article 15 of the 10th Hague Convention, which prescribes the rules to be followed in case shipwrecked, wounded, or sick are landed at a neutral port, is phrased in indefinite terms, and leaves uncertain the important question as to whether its provisions apply to such persons which landed only by certain kinds of vessels or when landed by any kind of vessel and under any set of circumstances. However, when the Article is read in connection with the proceeding article and is regarded as a continuation of it, the natural conclusion seems to be that it is only when shipwrecked, wounded, or sick are landed at a neutral port by a belligerent that they must be interned. When, in addition to this, the passage of Renault's report is considered, in which he expressly states that if a neutral merchant vessel which has casually picked up wounded, sick or shipwrecked men arrives in a neutral port without having met a belligerent warship, the men are not to be interned, the correctness of the Dutch decision can hardly be questioned.

The case of the survivors of the French torpedo boat *Mosquet*, which were placed on board the British merchantman *Newburn* by the commander of the German cruiser *Emden* and then landed by the *Newburn* in the port of Sabang, involved the question of what must be done when shipwrecked persons are landed at a neutral port by a belligerent merchantman, but since the commander of the *Emden* expressly granted these men their freedom the grounds upon which the Dutch Government decided not to intern them remain uncertain. Probably the best judgment is that the provisions of Article 15 of the 10th Hague Convention are applicable only to ship-wrecked, wounded, or sick landed at a neutral port by a belligerent warship.

The burden of the maintenance of a strict neutrality by a state near the theater of the war is reflected in the rules adopted by the Dutch Government with respect to the internment of military persons in civilian clothes and the internment of deserters. Included among the 700,000 Belgian refugees which entered Holland there were undoubtedly many soldiers in civilian clothes and not to intern them clearly would be contrary to the purpose of Article 11 of the 5th Hague Convention.[37] But to give any kind of an examination to so many refugees in order to ascertain whether or not they bear any marks which could identify them as belonging to the belligerent armies, is no small nor easy task.

The rule adopted by the Dutch Government with respect to the internment of deserters is undoubtedly a sound one. The belligerent can hardly be expected to pay the costs of the internment of a deserter from its army, and from the point of view of the neutral and the other belligerent party there is really no sense in the internment. An actual deserter, who is regarded as such in his own country, can be counted upon not to return there, and hence need no longer be regarded as a potential soldier, or as belonging to the belligerent army. But the neutral must be in a position to assure the other belligerent that it is liberating only persons who are deserters beyond a doubt. This will in most cases require a careful investigation. The action of Germany was quite clearly a violation of the internment provisions of the 5th Hague Convention. A belligerent can not by a uni-

---

[37] The Swiss Government, however, did not believe it had an obligation to investigate whether or not persons crossing the frontier in ciivlian dress belonged to belligerent forces. Naval War College, *International Law Topics*, 1916, pp. 78–79.

lateral declaration free itself of the obligations to pay the costs of internment in a neutral state so long as that internment is in strict conformity with the provisions of the convention.

That the Netherlands Government should never have interned the German wounded brought into its territory by the Dutch Red Cross ambulances is clear. The wounded soldiers did not enter Dutch territory of their own volition, and had they been left on the field they very probably would have been picked up by their own medical or ambulance corps. They had in no way violated Dutch territory and Germany was fully within its rights in protesting the action of the Dutch Government in thus withdrawing men from its armed forces.

The correctness of the regulation of the Dutch Government relative to the internment of war material brought into Dutch territory from the high seas is open to doubt. The Dutch Government stated that the underlying principle upon which the regulation was based is that a neutral must abstain from all action which amounts to strengthening the armed forces of the belligerent, but it may very plausibly be argued that the regulation violated the principle rather than gave effect to it. The case of a seaplane brought from the high seas into a neutral port by neutral merchantmen is in many ways similar to the case of wounded persons brought into neutral territory by neutrals. It is true that in many cases the wrecked seaplanes would be lost altogether unless picked up by neutral merchant ships and brought into port by them, but from the point of view of a belligerent engaged in a desperate war internment of the seaplanes until the end of the war is not much preferable to their being totally lost. Furthermore, if the wrecked seaplanes had not been picked up by the neutral merchantmen they might have been picked up by British merchantmen, or by some neutral merchant vessel on its way to a British port. And so the regulation to intern war material brought in by neutral vessels has rather the effect of weakening the armed forces of the belligerents, and the neutral must abstain

171

from any action that has that effect just as well as it must abstain from any action that will strengthen the belligerents, unless of course some violation of its neutrality is involved. But war material brought into neutral territory from the high seas by a neutral merchantman can in no way be considered as an act on behalf of the belligerent. The war material is brought into a neutral port without its consent and it serves none of the purposes of the belligerent, unless it be the remote one of salving a particular kind of property that may have little value to the belligerent by the time it is restored. On the other hand, of course, a neutral can not be engaged in salvaging war material for any one of the belligerents, but to this it may be replied that neutrals are under no obligation to touch war material found on the high seas. Human lives are not involved and there is no great loss to humanity even if such property is totally lost.

Article 42 of the Aircraft and Radio Convention proposed by the Commission of Jurists states that "a neutral government shall use the means at its disposal to intern any belligerent military aircraft which is within its jurisdiction after having alighted for any reason whatsoever, together with its crew and the passengers, if any." Garner interprets this article to cover also aircraft and their crews brought in from the open seas.[38] The writer doubts the correctness of that interpretation. Not all belligerent military aircraft found in neutral jurisdiction are to be interned, but only those "having alighted."

---

[38] *A. J. I. L.*, XVIII, 79–80.

Chapter XI

RULES OF PREVENTION AND ABSTENTION

I. Prohibition of the Use of Wireless

THE NEUTRALITY PROCLAMATION contained no provision for the regulation of the installation and use of wireless telegraphy stations on Dutch territory.[1] By a proclamation of the Minister of War in the *Staatscourant* of August 5, 1914, the use of installations of wireless telegraphy within the kingdom was prohibited in the interest of national defense.[2] Supervision over the enforcement of the regulation was placed in the hands of the military officials and the technical service of the Royal Telegraph. In a notice of August 8, 1914, it was explained that the territorial waters were to be understood as included under the term "kingdom."[3] Although not expressly stated, the prohibition naturally did not apply to government installations.

Switzerland was the only other neutral which prohibited the use of wireless installation within its territory.[4] Many of the neutral governments resorted to the exercise of a strict censorship,[5] and the United States

---

[1] This is rather a glaring omission in view of Article 3 of the 5th Hague Convention, under which belligerents are forbidden to erect on neutral territory a wireless telegraphy station or other apparatus for the purpose of communicating with belligerent forces on land or sea, or to use any installation of this kind established by them before the war on neutral territory for purely military purposes, and which had not been opened for the service of public messages. However, Article 8 provides that a neutral power is not called upon to forbid or restrict the use on behalf of the belligerent of telegraph or telephone cables or of wireless telegraphy apparatus belonging to it or to companies or private individuals. But when a neutral power proceeds to prohibition or restriction of such installations, Article 9 provides that it must apply its measures impartially to both belligerents, and see that the same obligation is observed by companies or private individuals owning such apparatuses.
[2] See Appendix VII.
[3] *Ibid*, VII.
[4] Naval War College, *International Law Topics*, 1916, p. 69.
[5] *Ibid.*, 1916, pp. 36–38, 42–44.

173

even went so far as to take over the operation of certain wireless stations which were under suspicion.[6] The British and French Governments made several complaints that the neutrality of some of the Latin-American countries was being violated by the action of wireless stations in sending messages to German warships on the high seas.[7] All the important maritime nations took measures to dismantle wireless apparatus on belligerent merchant vessels in port.[8]

The Dutch Government by its Proclamation thus exercised over wireless installations within its territory the fullest powers provided under neutrality conventions, namely, absolute prohibition. The advantages of an absolute prohibition over restrictions are apparent. A prohibition is much easier to enforce, and moreover, is never open to the claim or even the suspicion, that the neutral's regulations are not being impartially applied.

However, the Dutch Government found that even the prohibition was difficult to enforce, as is illustrated by the two following cases of violation. The *Preussen,* a German merchantman of the Hamburg-American line, unequipped with a wireless installation, entered the harbor of Sabang on August 3, 1914. For fear that the vessel might be captured by enemy merchantmen, her owners decided to lay up the vessel in that harbor. On the 6th of August the wireless prohibition was proclaimed in the Dutch Indies. During the night of the 27th of October the government wireless station at Sabang received several calls, evidently intended for some German merchantman lying in the harbor. An investigation brought to light the existence of a wireless station on board the *Preussen.* The antennae, carefully concealed from outside view, were connected with a secret receiving apparatus in the cabin of one of the ship's officers. In the same way a wireless installation was discovered on board the *Main,* a German

---

6) *Ibid.,* 1916, p. 91; Garner, *op. cit.,* II, 411–413.
7) Garner, *op. cit.,* II, 413–414.
8) United States, Brazil, Chile, Peru, Uraguay, Sweden, Norway, and Venezuela, Naval War College, *International Law Topics,* 1916, p. 123.

merchantman, laid up since the beginning of the war in the harbor of Flushing. From all appearances the ship had been completely abandoned except for one or two guards. Suspicions of the Dutch officials were aroused when in the first days of April, 1915, a government station picked up a message in code coming from Zeebrugge, and evidently intended for some vessel in the harbor of Flushing. An investigation revealed on board the *Main* a cleverly concealed wireless apparatus. The wires were ingeniously hid by running them along masts, poles, and walls, while the dynamo was found in the engine room.[9]

II. Transit of Supplies to the Wireless Telegraph Station on the Enclave of Baarle-Hertog

Toward the end of the year 1915 the Dutch Government noticed that a wireless station had been installed in Baarle-Hertog, a Belgian enclave completely surrounded by Dutch territory. After a careful consideration of what should be its attitude toward the transit to the enclave of goods necessary for the operation of the station, the Dutch Government decided that it would have to prohibit such transit in the interest of a strict neutrality. The presence of the wireless station made of the enclave a base of operations for the Belgian army and it would be contrary to the maintenance of a strict neutrality for the Dutch Government to allow passage over its territory of materials needed by such a base of operations, which on all sides was protected against attack by neutral territory. The fact that the enclave was Belgian territory did not relieve the Dutch Government of the responsibility for the operation of the wireless station.

To enforce this regulation a military cordon was placed around the enclave and all goods that might be of service to the station were denied passage. The same kind of restrictions were made to apply to all persons going to and coming from the enclave. Such persons had to pass a Dutch military post where an investigation was

---

[9] Carsten, *op. cit.*, pp. 65–67.

made as to their identity and where they were searched for smuggled goods. These special measures were taken in addition to the general export prohibitions which applied to this territory as to all other foreign territory. A special commission, composed of Dutch and Belgian officials, passed on all requests for imports into the enclave.

The Belgian Government, in a note of April 18, 1916, protested the detention at the Dutch border of twelve barrels of oil sent from England and addressed to the mayor of Baarle-Hertog. In its reply to this protest, forwarded to the Belgian Minister at The Hague on the 6th of June, the Dutch Government explained the legal grounds upon which its measures of control were based. It was pointed out that the Second Hague Conference had recognized the importance of wireless stations from a military point of view, and in the 5th and 13th Conventions prohibited their installation by belligerents upon neutral territory. The 5th Article of the latter Convention states that the place at which a wireless station is located, which station is used by a belligerent, assumes by that fact the character of a base of military operations. The installation of the wireless station at Baarle-Hertog by the Belgian Government made of the enclave a base of operations of the Belgian army. In the opinion of the Dutch Government the maintenance of a strict neutrality obliged it to prevent any of its territory from being used in any way to favor the utilization of a base of operations of one of the belligerent parties which was completely protected from aggression by the adverse party. As a consequence it was incumbent upon the Dutch Government to prohibit the transportation to this base of operations of all articles which could be of service to the wireless station.[10]

III. BASE OF OPERATIONS

A. DEPARTURE OF VESSELS OUT OF DUTCH HARBORS

The Dutch Government was very careful to prevent its ports from being used as a base of operations. By pro-

---

[10] *D. O. B.*, II, 32–34; *Recueil*, pp. 168–170.

hibiting all belligerent warships and armed merchantmen from entering the jurisdiction of the state the enforcement of this duty was in a measure made easier, but a country situated as was Holland in the World War, needed to exercise extreme care. The Neutrality Proclamation contained several articles in regard to the matter. Article 13 forbade in state territory, the equipping, arming, or manning of vessels intended for military purposes on behalf of a belligerent. Under Article 14 it was forbidden to supply belligerent warships or assimilated vessels with arms or munitions, or to aid in any way in augmenting their crews or equipment. Without permisson from the proper local authorities, it was forbidden under Article 15, to make any repairs on belligerent warships or assimilated vessels, or to furnish them with food or coal. Under Article 16 it was forbidden to aid in the dismantling or in the repairing of prizes, except to the extent of rendering them seaworthy, and it was equally forbidden to buy or to accept, in exchange or gift, prizes or captured goods, or to guard them for others.[11]

In connection with the enforcement of Article 13 several regulations were issued. All vessels leaving Dutch territory had to be provided with a safe-conduct signed by the proper Dutch officials. Vessels not provided with a safe-conduct were subjected to a searching examination, and not until after they had furnished reasonable evidence of not seeking to violate the provisions of Article 13 were they permitted to depart. Safe-conducts were granted only to vessels flying the Dutch flag, and only after the officials were satisfied that there was no question of a sale or lease, or in case a sale or lease had taken place, that the buyer or lessee gave a written declaration that the vessel was not intended for the military purposes of a belligerent government, and that the buyer or lessee needed the ship for his own use. In case of sale the ship had to be brought under the flag of the country of which the new owner was a national before it could leave the Netherlands jurisdiction. The

---

[11] *D. O. B.*, I, p. 3; *Recueil*, p. 3.

above regulations were applied to all vessels, regardless of whether they had been provided with own motive power or not. The general rule was laid down that no Dutch ship leased to persons or companies of belligerent nationality or domiciled in a belligerent country would be permitted to leave the Netherlands jurisdiction, but in exceptional cases this rule was waived. A permanent or continuous passport was granted to all Dutch vessels carrying on a regular transport service between Dutch and foreign ports upon the owners making a declaration that during the war they would sell no vessel to foreign buyers without first informing the chief of the Marine Staff of the conditions of the sale. Over vessels flying a foreign flag only such control was exercised as was necessary for the security of the state and the enforcement of neutrality.[12]

B. SURVEILLANCE OVER BELLIGERENT COMMERCIAL AND FISHING VESSELS IN DUTCH WATERS

A very careful watch was kept over belligerent commercial and fishing vessels found in Dutch waters. Where there were grounds for suspicion the vessels were subjected to a search by the patrol boats, and in cases of doubt the vessels were brought into the nearest port there to undergo a more careful examination. When the Dutch patrol officials thus brought the *Senator Oswald,* a German fishing vessel, into the port of IJmuiden for examination, the German Government protested that under international law a neutral had no such right. The Dutch Government replied that international law imposed upon a neutral the duty to prevent its territorial waters from being used by a belligerent as a base of naval operations. For the enforcement of this obligation the Dutch Government had established a vigorous control over all belligerent vessels found in Dutch waters, and in order to exercise this control in an effective way the Dutch Government reserved to itself the right to subject to examination all vessels found in the Dutch territorial waters

---

[12] *D. O. B.,* I, 30–31.

and if the examination could not be effectually made at sea, to conduct them for that purpose to a Dutch port. No rule of international law was opposed to this measure, which was no more than an act of sovereignty necessary for the maintenance of neutrality in the territorial waters of the state.[13]

IV. CENSORSHIP OF MILITARY INFORMATION

The Dutch Government held that the maintenance of a strict neutrality imposed upon it the duty of preventing as much as possible the use of its territory for the observation of the movements of belligerent forces and the forwarding of this information for use of the adverse party. This was also made to include the movements executed by warships and aircraft outside of Dutch territory but observed from Dutch territory. For the execution of the above decision great care was taken not to permit the transmission of such news to agencies of information until after a six-hour delay. However, when there was involved a violation of Dutch territory, including the Dutch territorial waters, the immediate publication of such news by telegraph was entirely free.[14]

V. THE RAISING OF THE STEAMSHIP "GNEISENAU" AT ANTWERP

With the fall of Antwerp the Belgian authorities sent to the bottom of the Scheldt the *Gneisenau,* a German ship seized at Antwerp at the beginning of the war. When the Dutch Government learned that a Dutch firm was about to contract to raise the *Gneisenau,* it informed the contractors that they would not be permitted to transport from Dutch territory to Antwerp the equipment necessary for that purpose. The Government's decision was based upon the conviction that the act here involved the annulment in favor of one of the belligerent parties, on the field of war, of the effect of an act of war committed intention-

---

13) *D. O. B.,* I, 32; *Recueil,* p. 167.
14) *D. O. B.,* I, 32; *Recueil,* p. 168.

ally by the other belligerent party. For this reason the Dutch Government did not think that it would be compatible with the maintenance of a strict neutrality to permit the firm to put its project into execution.[15]

VI. RECRUITING OF DUTCH LABORERS FOR SERVICE IN BELLIGERENT COUNTRIES

The Central Employment Bureau at The Hague took the position at the beginning of the war that it could not permit its services to be used for the placing of laborers in any belligerent country until after it was satisfied that the employment was in no way connected with the military operations. The local employment bureaus did not deal with employment in foreign countries except through the Central Bureau. All other persons and institutions that might be approached with a view to the recruiting of laborers in belligerent countries were ordered to refuse their services for this purpose unless they were furnished guaranties of the peaceful character of the work.[16]

VII. TRANSIT OF EMPTY FREIGHT CARS ACROSS DUTCH TERRITORY

A diplomatic complaint was made by the British Government in September, 1917, that from fifty to one hundred empty freight cars were daily crossing the Dutch frontier from Belgium. According to the allegation these empty cars were sent into Holland to keep the badly congested German lines in Belgium free. The British Government urged an immediate enquiry into the alleged traffic, the existence of which if established, could not be held to be in accordance with an attitude of strict neutrality on the part of the Dutch Government. In view of the heavy transport of war materials from Germany and Belgium to the front in Flanders, the continual evacuation of empty railroad cars from Belgium into Holland was of great military assistance to Germany. By this practice

15) *D. O. B.*, I, 37; *Recueil*, p. 179.
16) *D. O. B.*, I, 38; *Recueil*, p. 182.

the Belgian railways were afforded great relief, and the dispatch of troops and war material to the Western front was greatly facilitated.[17]

The investigation instituted by the Dutch Government revealed the allegations to be without foundation. It was found that the empty cars entered Holland exclusively upon the request of the Dutch railway companies, and never at the request of the German officials, and instead of from fifty to one hundred empty cars entering Holland each day, it was found that during the preceding period of about ten months only three or four cars a day had entered Dutch territory. This number was much too small to have any such effect as that outlined in the British note.[18]

VIII. Sufficiency of the Dutch Regulations to Enforce Neutral Duties of Prevention

The Dutch regulations described above set a high standard of neutral duties of prevention. Dutch territory was greatly exposed to the danger of being used as a base of belligerent operations so that strict regulations were highly desirable. The neutral is only required to prevent such materials and articles from leaving its territory as can be used for hostile purposes as soon as they are outside of the three-mile limit. Thus a neutral is under no obligation to prevent the export of coal as contraband, but it must prevent coal from leaving its ports if it is destined to supply belligerent warships stationed outside of its territorial waters. The Dutch Government went much beyond this requirement in preventing supplies from going to the Belgian wireless stations at Baarle-Hertog, and in prohibiting equipment for raising the *Gneisenau* from leaving its territory. The strict surveillance it exercised over vessels in its waters and ports gave both parties of belligerents an effective guarantee that

---

[17] *D. O. B.*, IV, 50–51.
[18] *Ibid.*, IV, 51, Note of January 4, 1918.

Dutch territory was not being used as a base of belligerent operations. In prohibiting the use of wireless installations on its territory the Dutch Government exercised the most extreme form of regulation possible.[19]

---

[19] It may be observed here that the proposed Aircraft and Radio Regulations exceed the requirements laid down in the provisions of the 5th Hague Convention—Article 3b of which only prohibits the use of any radio-telegraphic installations established by belligerents before the war on the territory of a neutral for purely military purposes, while Article 3 of the proposed convention prohibits the erection or operation by a belligerent or its agents of radio stations within neutral jurisdiction. See *A. J. I. L.*, Sp. Supp. XVII, 123 ff. for the proposed convention.

Chapter XII

RIGHT OF ASYLUM—THE CASE OF THE KAISER

THOUGH not strictly a question of neutrality the case of the former German Emperor is so closely related to the general history of Dutch neutrality in the World War as to deserve at least a brief treatment in this study. The Allied and Associated Powers at the Paris Peace Conference resolved to try William of Hohenzollern "for a supreme offence against international morality and the sanctity of treaties." A special tribunal was to be constituted to try him, this tribunal to be composed of five judges, one appointed by each of the five great powers, namely, the United States, Great Britain, France, Italy, and Japan. The tribunal was to be "guided by the highest motives of international policy, with a view to vindicating the solemn obligations of international undertakings and the validity of international morality." The Government of the Netherlands was to be requested to surrender the ex-Emperor in order that he might be put on trial.[1]

The ex-Emperor arrived at the Dutch border village of Eysden in the early morning of November 10, 1918. He was not immediately allowed to enter Holland, but was detained for a whole day at the border pending arrangements with governmental officials as to his future status and the conditions upon which he would be admitted. Just what those conditions were has never been made public beyond the statement that his status was to be merely that of a private person, that his movements were to be closely guarded and limited to the residence assigned him by the Netherlands Government, and that this hospitality was not to be abused by political activities.[2]

[1] Treaty of Versailles, Part 7, Article 227, Naval War College, *International Law Documents*, Treaty of Peace with Germany, 1919, p. 90.

[2] Barnouw, *op. cit.*, p. 197.

183

Neutrality of the Netherlands During World War

January 16, 1920, the Netherlands Government received a note signed by M. Clemenceau, in his capacity as President of the Peace Conference, demanding the surrender of the ex-Emperor. After listing a series of "crimes," such as the "cynical violation of the neutrality of Belgium and Luxembourg, the barbarous and pitiless system of hostages, the mass deportation," "the systematic devastation of whole territories without military end, the unrestricted submarine warfare involving the inhuman abandonment of victims in the open seas," for which the ex-Emperor was held "at least morally responsible," the note went on to state that "Holland would not fulfill her international duty if she refused to associate herself with the Entente Powers, within the limit of her ability, to pursue, or at least not impede the punishment of crimes committed."[3]

The Dutch Government replied to the demand for the surrender of the ex-Kaiser in a note of January 23, addressed to the President of the Supreme Council. The Netherlands Government had been an absolute stranger to the origin of the war and had with great difficulty maintained its neutrality to the end. It found itself with regard to the facts of the war in an entirely different position from that of the Powers. It repelled with energy every suspicion of wishing to cover up, by assertion of its sovereign and moral authority, violations of the essential principles of the solidarity of nations, but it was not able to recognize an international duty of association with the Powers in this act of "high international policy." "If in the future there should be constituted by the society of nations an international jurisdiction, competent to judge in case of war deeds, qualified as crimes and submitted to its jurisdiction by statute antedating the acts committed, it would be fit for Holland to associate herself with the new regime."

The note ended in the refusal of the Netherlands Government to admit any other duty than that imposed by the laws of the Kingdom and national tradition. "Neither

---

[3] *D. O. B.*, (1919–1920), p. 12.

the constituent laws of the Kingdom which are based on the principles of the law universally recognized, nor a tradition which has made of this country, at all times, a ground of refuge for the vanquished of international conflicts, permitted the Government of the Netherlands to defer to the desire of the Powers by withdrawing from the ex-Emperor the benefit of its laws and this tradition. Law and national honor, respect for which is a sacred duty, are opposed to it."[4]

The reply of the Netherlands Government was unacceptable to the Supreme Council and a second note was despatched to the Dutch Government again demanding the surrender of the ex-Emperor. After again dwelling upon the offenses of the former German ruler and expressing surprise that the Dutch reply contained not a single word of disapproval of these crimes, the note went on to lecture the Dutch Government on its duty of using all the measures at its disposal to bring about the punishment of the ex-Emperor. The Dutch Government was reminded that the permanent presence of the ex-Emperor under a dangerously inadequate control, only a few kilometers from the German frontier, where he remained the center of an active and growing intrigue, constituted for the Powers a menace which they could not be expected to accept. Should the ex-Emperor escape it would impose a heavy responsibility upon Holland.[5]

The Dutch Government refused to yield. In a note delivered to the Allied Governments on the 5th of March, it stated that it "would be committing an act contrary to laws and justice, and incompatible with the national honor if it consented, at the request of the Powers, to violate these laws by abolishing the rights which they accord to a fugitive finding himself within the country's territory." The Dutch Government regretted that the Powers seemed to have the impression that it did not appreciate its responsibility with respect to the guarding of the ex-Emperor. "Mindful of its duties in this connection,

[4] *D. O. B.*, (1919–1920), p. 13.
[5] *D. O. B.*, (1919–1920), pp. 13–14.

the Queen's Government has, and from the beginning, borne in mind the obligations imposed by its duties, and will continue to do so, being in a position in the free exercise of Dutch sovereignty to take on the spot all necessary effective measures of precaution, and to subject the freedom of the ex-Emperor to necessary limitations."[6]

II. Compatibility with the Rules of International Law of the Refusal to Surrender the Ex-Emperor

In the absence of a treaty there is no legal obligation to surrender a person charged with crime.[7] Treaties of extradition generally stipulate as a condition that the offense for which extradition is asked be a crime by the laws of both countries, and moreover, political offenses are regularly excluded.[8]

Lansing and Scott, the American members of the Commission of Responsibilities dissented from that part of the Commission's report which recommended the trial of William II of Hohenzollern, on the ground that, according to the rules of international law, the head of a state is responsible for his acts only to his own people, that he is immune from trial in any foreign court, and that his acts are to be deemed acts of state, and as such, impressed with essentially political character. Reference was made to the opinion of Chief Justice Marshall, in the case of the *Schooner Exchange versus McFaddon*,[9] for the reasons underlying the exemption of the sovereign and the sovereign agent of a state from judicial process. A second objection of the American members was to the jurisdiction of the proposed court, which was to be an entirely new creation, and which, therefore, could not have any

---

[6] *Ibid.*, (1919–1920), pp. 14–15.
[7] Moore, *Digest*, IV, 245–267; Lawrence, pp. 258–260; Hershey, pp. 263–264; Fenwick, pp. 210–211; Hall, p. 69.
[8] Fenwick, p. 214; Hershey, pp. 267–268; Moore, *Digest*, IV, 322–355; Lawrence, pp. 262–267.
[9] 7 *Cranch* 116 (1812).

authority to try the offenses when committed. Moreover, the ex-Emperor was to be tried for an offense to which no penalty had been fixed by international law.[10]

The dissenting report of the American members of the Commission points out very effectively the legal defects in the Allied demand for the extradition of the ex-Emperor. Article 227 arraigned him for offenses which were not crimes under the common law or the legislation of any state, and in their note to the Netherlands Government of January 16, 1920, the Allied Governments stated that "in addressing this demand to the Dutch Government the Powers believe it their duty to emphasize the special character. It is their duty to insure the execution of Article 227 without allowing themselves to be stopped by arguments, because it is not a question of public accusation with juridical character as regards its basis, but an act of high international policy imposed by the universal conscience, in which legal forms have been provided solely to assure such guarantees as were never before recognized in public law."[11] This is indeed strange language to use in a note requesting the extradition of a person charged with an offense. In view of the fact that extradition treaties are very strictly interpreted and that

---

10) "Report of the Commission of Responsibilities", Pamphlet, Carnegie Endowment for International Peace, Division of International Law, No. 32, pp. 58 ff. Also in *A. J. I. L.*, XIV, 127 ff. See House and Seymour, *What Really Happened in Paris*, "The Trial of the Kaiser", by J. B. Scott, and Lansing's address in the American Bar Association *Reports*, XXXXIV, 255 ff (also reprinted in *A. J. I. L.*, XIII, 613 ff) in defense of their position.

11) Wright holds that the "trial of the Kaiser under international law by a tribunal whose jurisdiction was sanctioned by neutral states including that in which he was seeking asylum, as well as the principal belligerents, would avoid the difficulties of jurisdiction, sovereign immunities, and extradition, and would offer the greatest probability of a decision at once just and expedient." "The Legal Liability of the Kaiser", *Political Science Review*, XIII, 128.

political offenders are uniformly excepted from extradition, the legality of the Dutch Governments's refusal to surrender the ex-Emperor is beyond dispute.[12]

---

[12] The Dutch position is defended by Prof. Simons of the University of Utrecht in 46 *Clunet* 953 ff.; by Dr. Petong, a German jurist, in 47 *Clunet* 132 ff.; M. Travers, a French jurist, in the *Rev. de Droit International* (1921), p. 134; by J. B. Scott in House and Seymour, *op. cit.*; and Lansing in *A. J. I. L.*, XIII, 644 ff. Hyde, II, 847 ff. defends the position of the American members of the Commission, while Garner, in *Recent Developments in International Law*, p. 450, criticizes it. However, in the later volume Garner concludes that "the noncompliance of the Dutch Government with the allied demand was legally irreproachable." The Dutch position is criticized by Merignhac in *Rev. de Droit International*, 1920, 54.

PART III

CONTROVERSIES OVER NEUTRAL RIGHTS

CHAPTER XIII

BLOCKADE AND RETALIATION

I. BELLIGERENT MEASURES AND DUTCH PROTESTS

SEVERAL minor blockades were declared during the World War, but neither of the two leading maritime powers ever formally declared a blockade of the ports of the other. However, the governments of both these powers, Great Britain and Germany, took measures which were clearly intended to have all the effects of a blockade and were referred to as such in subsequent official documents and diplomatic correspondence. Most of these measures were declared to be retaliatory, following one upon the other, and are given in their chronological order.

A. GERMAN MINES OFF THE ENGLISH COAST.

On the 8th of August, 1914, the German Government informed the Dutch Minister at Berlin that it would probably be necessary to lay mines off the bases of operation of enemy fleets and enemy ports of embarkation and debarkation of troop transports.[1] Since the Dutch Government did not regard this action as conflicting with the provisions of the Hague Convention of 1907, relative to the laying of automatic submarine contact mines, it did not protest the action.[2]

B. BRITISH INTERFERENCE WITH DUTCH FISHING OFF THE ENGLISH COAST

The British Government, in a note of September 28, 1914, declared that the German naval authorities were "sewing mines indiscriminately on the high seas, off the North Sea Coast of Great Britain," and it had reason to

---

[1] *Dutch White Book*, "Diplomatieke Bescheiden Betreffende de Vaart in de Noordzee en het Kanaal in Verband met den Oorlogstoestand" (hereafter cited as North Sea Book), (1915), p. 3. *D. O. B.*, I, 17.

[2] *North Sea Book*, p. 1; *D. O. B.*, I, 17.

suppose that this was being done by fishing trawlers disguised as neutral vessels. In order to defend itself against this illegal action the British Government decided that all ports of the east coast of Great Britain should be closed to neutral vessels on and after October 1st, and that after the same date it would be necessary to exercise special measures of control over the waters of the North Sea contiguous to the English coast. Any neutral fishing vessel off the east coast of Great Britain, Longitude one degree east, when north of Latitude fifty-four degrees thirty minutes north, or west of Longitude two degrees thirty minutes east, when south of Latitude fifty-four degrees thirty minutes north, could not be regarded as engaged in legitimate fishing operations and would be treated as under suspicion of being engaged in mine-laying. "Any trawlers not in the exclusive employment of the German Government but illicitly laying mines in the intervals of their fishing will be sunk if caught in the act of mine-laying or, in the event of their resisting capture or search or attempting to escape, the crews being unauthorized combatants, will be liable to be treated as war criminals and shot after trial by court martial."[3]

The Dutch Government offered no objections to the general provisions of this measure, but it contended that it would be in conflict with the rules of international law if neutral vessels found in the prescribed zone after the date mentioned should be regarded otherwise than as merely under suspicion, and in case of their attempting to escape the exercise of the right of search, the vessels should be sunk and the crews treated as war criminals.[4] To this the British Government replied that it had never been their intention to treat the suspicion as confirmed in the absence of additional proof.[5]

C. BRITISH MINE-FIELDS IN THE SOUTH OF THE NORTH SEA

On October 3, 1914, the Dutch Government was informed by the British Government that the British Ad-

---

[3] *North Sea Book*, p. 3.
[4] *North Sea Book*, p. 4, Note of October 7, 1914.
[5] *Ibid.*, p. 4, Note of November 4, 1914.

miralty had established a system of mine-fields between Latitude fifty-one degrees fifteen minutes north and fifty-one degrees forty minutes north, and Longitude one degree thirty-five minutes east and three degrees east. The measure was declared necessary on military grounds as a counter measure to the German policy of mine laying and submarine warfare.[6]

D. The British Declaration of the North Sea as a Military Area

The whole of the North Sea was declared a military area by the British Government on November 3, 1914. "Within this area merchant shipping of all kinds, traders of all countries, fishing craft, and all other vessels will be exposed to the gravest dangers from the mines which it has been necessary to lay and from the warships searching vigilantly by night and day for suspicious craft." Moreover, from November 5th onwards the Admiralty "announce that all ships passing a line drawn from the northern point of the Hebrides through the Faroe Islands to Iceland do so at their own peril."[7] The Dutch Government protested this measure as contrary to international law, in accordance with which only the immediate sphere of action of belligerent military operations constitute a military area. The North Sea because of its area, could not in its entirety form such a sphere. The declaration, therefore, constituted a grave violation of the fundamental principle of the freedom of the seas, and was distinctly contrary to the spirit of the 8th Hague Convention, signed and ratified by Great Britain, which imposed on the belligerent power laying automatic contact mines the duty of taking all possible precautions for the safety of pacific navigation. Such navigation ought to be provided with a free passage. The detours made necessary by the British action were excessive and subjected Dutch commerce to great inconveniences.[8]

---

6) *Ibid.*, pp. 4–5.
7) *Ibid.*, p. 5; *Recueil*, p. 85
8) *North Sea Book*, pp. 5–6; *Recueil*, p. 87.

E. German War Zone Declaration

On February 4, 1915, came the German announcement declaring the waters surrounding Great Britain and Ireland, including the English Channel, a war zone. Because of the British misuse of neutral flags and because of the accidents of naval war, even neutral vessels would be exposed to dangers in the war zone. Navigation along the north of the Shetland Islands, the eastern part of the North Sea, in a belt of at least thirty miles in width along the Dutch Coast, would be free from danger.[9] Previous to this announcement, on February 2, 1915, the German Government warned neutral commerce to keep away from the north and west coasts of France. Numerous troops and great supplies of war material were being transported from England to France and the German Government was resolved to prevent this transportation by every method of warfare available.[10] By notes of February 4th and 9th, the German Government announced that neutral fishing along the German coasts would be subject to restrictions. The presence in these waters of British naval vessels disguised as Dutch fishing vessels was given as the justification for this measure.[11] The announcement of the War Zone Declaration was accompanied by a memorandum citing reasons in justification of the measure. Germany found itself under the necessity of taking military measures in retaliation for the illegal practices followed by England in its commercial warfare against Germany. The neutral powers in the main not only acquiesced in the measures of the British Government, but had even "contributed toward the execution of the measures adopted by England in defiance of the principle of the freedom of the seas by prohibiting the export and transit of goods destined for peaceable purposes in Germany."[12]

Responding to the German Declaration and memoran-

---

9) *North Sea Book,* p. 7.
10) *Ibid,* pp. 6–7; *Recueil,* p. 97.
11) *North Sea Book,* p. 6; *Recueil,* pp. 126–137.
12) *North Sea Book,* pp. 7–8.

dum, the Dutch Government first of all denied the charge of contributing toward, or even acquiescing in, illegal British measures. From the beginning of the war it had vigorously protested measures on the part of belligerents, which in its opinion, were contrary to international law, even where its own interests were not directly involved. It had obtained the release of some of the German subjects taken off Dutch vessels, and it had not abandoned demands for the release of still others. It had refused to give any guaranty whatsoever to the Allied Powers that goods imported from overseas would not be re-exported to Germany. Its export prohibitions were in no way due to British pressure, but solely to a desire to conserve within the country, stocks absolutely necessary for domestic use. Against the declaration by Great Britain of the North Sea as a military area the Dutch Government had pressed the same protest that it was now directing against the German decree. However, in practice the British decree had in no way affected Dutch navigation. Dutch vessels continued to follow the same route they had followed before the decree. The Dutch Government was confident that the German operations of war would affect Dutch navigation just as little. The Dutch memorandum concluded by saying that, in view of the fact that it was the inevasible duty of the belligerent to determine the nationality of a commercial vessel before proceeding to capture or destruction, the German Government would be held strictly accountable should a Dutch subject become a victim of an error on the part of the German forces.[13]

The German Government sent an *Aufzeichnung* to the Dutch Government on February 12, 1915, in which it was explained that for reasons of self preservation German submarines in the War Zone would not be able to make examination of the nationality of the merchant vessels they might meet. Under these circumstances there could no longer exist a guaranty for the safety of neutral navi-

---

[13] *North Sea Book*, pp. 8–9.

gation. Neutral commerce was again expressly warned against navigating in the waters of the War Zone and urged to take the routes prescribed by the German Marine Staff.[14]

F. British "Blockade" Order

By order in council of the 11th of March, 1915, the British Government decreed: 1) that no merchant vessel which had sailed from her port of departure after March 1, 1915, would be allowed to proceed on her voyage to any German port. Unless the vessel received a pass enabling her to proceed to some specified neutral or Allied port, goods on board such vessels would have to be discharged in a British port. 2) No merchant vessel which had sailed from any German port after the first of March would be allowed to proceed on her voyage with any goods on board laden at such port. 3) Every merchant vessel which sailed from her port of departure after the same date on her way to a port other than a German port, carrying goods with an enemy destination or which were enemy property, might be required to discharge such goods in a British or Allied port. 4) Every merchant vessel which sailed from a port other than a German port after the above date, having on board goods which were of enemy origin or were enemy property might be required to discharge such goods in a British or Allied port. All goods so discharged would be placed in the custody of the prize court. The goods in the second and fourth cases would be detained or sold under the direction of the

---

14) *Ibid.*, p. 9. "God knows I'm afraid some American boat will run on a mine somewhere in the channel of the North Sea. There's war there as there is on land in Germany. Nobody tries to get goods thru on land on the continent, and they make no complaints that commerce is stopped. Everybody tries to ply the channel and the North Sea as usual, both of which have German and English mines and torpedo craft and submarines almost as thick as batteries along the hostile camps on land. The British Government (which now issues insurance) will not insure a British boat to carry food to Holland enroute to the starving Belgians; and I hear that no government and no insurance company will write insurance for anything across the North Sea." Page Memorandum, Hendrick, *Life and Letters of Walter Hines Page*, I, 388–389.

prize court, while the goods in the first and third cases, if noncontraband and not requisitioned for the use of the British Government, would be restored by the court upon such terms as the court might deem just.

The only penalty for breach of the provisions of this order apart from confiscation of goods of enemy ownership and origin, was that a merchant vessel which had cleared for a neutral port from a British or Allied port or which had been allowed to pass having an ostensible destination to a neutral port and had proceeded to an enemy port, would if captured on any subsequent voyage, be liable to condemnation. The order stated that certain orders issued by the German Government purporting to declare the waters surrounding the United Kingdom a military area, were in violation of the usages of war, and gave the British Government an unquestionable right of retaliation.[15] The French Government issued practically the same decree on the same date.[16]

In response to this announcement the Dutch Government in a note of March 19, 1915, protested the measure as contrary to the principle established by the Declaration of Paris of 1856, in accordance with which neutral or enemy goods, with the exception of contraband of war, are not liable to capture under a neutral flag. Under the Order in Council the British Government would use restraint not only in regard to enemy private property, regardless of whether it had the character of contraband, but also in regard to neutral property in case there was a presumption of enemy destination or origin. In regard to Article 8 of the Order in Council, which indicated that there would be a relaxation of the provisions of the Order "in respect to the merchant vessels of any country which declares that no commerce intended for or originating in Germany or belonging to German subjects shall enjoy the protection of its flag,"[17] the Dutch Government declared it could not make a declaration of this nature. In

---

[15] *Recueil*, pp. 29–31; also in *A. J. I. L.*, Sp. Supp. IX, 110–112.
[16] *Recueil*, pp. 43–45.
[17] This provision is not found in the French decree.

its opinion the observance of the duties of neutrality forbade such an agreement.[18])

By order in Council of January 10, 1917, the British Government extended the provisions of the Order of March 11, 1915, to all countries at war with Great Britain.[19])

G. BRITISH SEIZURE OF THE DUTCH FISHER FLEET

In the summer of 1916, a large number of Dutch fishing vessels were brought into British ports by the British naval authorities. Presence within zones declared to be dangerous for neutral fishing by the British Government was first given as the ground for this procedure. Several fishing vessels were brought before the British Prize Court on the ground of carriage of contraband. The British Government contended that the large quantities of fish brought into Dutch harbors by Dutch fishing vessels, and from there exported to Germany, could not be regarded otherwise than as carriage of contraband. If a stop were put to the export of fish from Holland the British Government would release the Dutch fishing vessels held in its ports, whether seized for contraband carriage or for invading the danger zone. The British Government suggested that representatives of the owners of the fishing fleet come to London to form an agreement.

Responding to this the Dutch Government cited Article 7 of the 5th Hague Convention and Article 7 of the 13th Hague Convention, in which it is expressly stated that a neutral is not obliged to prevent the exportation of anything whatever on behalf of one or other of the belligerents. The declaration of a danger zone could not justify the seizure and detention of neutral vessels encountered in such a zone. Fish, being an article of food and belonging to the category of conditional contraband, could not be captured unless destined to a belligerent government or to its armed forces. The Dutch fishing vessels

---

[18]) Note to British Government, March 19, 1915, *Recueil*, pp. 33–34. Similar note to French, *Ibid.*, pp. 45–46.
[19]) *D. O. B.*, I, 5.

carried fish exclusively to Dutch ports and the fishermen had, throughout the duration of the war, scrupulously abstained from furnishing fish to belligerent warships encountered at sea. The Dutch North Sea fisheries was not a business of international transport called into being by the needs of one of the belligerents, but a national industry of ancient origin and in no way due to the state of the war. A large part of the population of the country was dependent upon this industry for its living. If the British Government was concerned about the amount of such fish sold to Germany it was free to prevent this by buying as much fish as it wanted in the open market in Holland. In conclusion the Dutch Government demanded the immediate release of all the Dutch fishing vessels detained in British ports.[20]

Not until after an agreement had been signed between the British Government and the Netherlands Ship Owners Union were the ships released or did the practice of bringing in the fishing vessels cease. In exchange for the recovery of their ships and the promise of facilities in getting supplies for their trade from overseas, England was given an option on twenty per cent of all herring caught after the Netherlands Government had bought as much as it needed for home distribution, and the export to Germany was limited to twenty per cent of the total catch.[21]

This agreement with only one of the belligerent parties evidently did not work well, for Dutch fishing was likewise molested by the German navy. The trawler *Bertha Elizabeth* was taken into the port of Cuxhaven in April, 1915, and was released only after she had disposed of her fish. The German Government refused to acknowledge the claims brought forward by the Dutch Government in behalf of the owners of the vessel.[22] Moreover, the Dutch

---

[20] *D. O. B.*, III, 20–21.

[21] *Ibid.*, III, 21. Barnouw, *op. cit.*, p. 130. This agreement was replaced by an agreement signed Nov. 9, 1918, between the Allied Powers and the Netherlands Export Society, *D. O. B.*, (1919–1920), 130–131.

[22] *D. O. B.*, III, 21–23.

fisheries were dependent upon German coal and salt for their existence. Attempts to make agreements satisfactory to both belligerents proved futile.[23]

H. British Declaration of Danger Zone in the Waters Surrounding the German Bay

On January 25, 1917, the British Government announced that "In view of the unrestricted warfare carried on by Germany at sea by means of mines and submarines not only against the Allied Powers but also against neutral shipping, and the fact that merchant ships are constantly sunk without regard to the ultimate safety of their crews, His Majesty's Government gives notice that on and after the seventh proximo the undermentioned area of the North Sea will be rendered dangerous to all shipping by operations against the enemy and it should therefore be avoided."[24]

I. Declaration of "Blockade Zones" by Germany and Austria-Hungary

The climax of these measures of reciprocal retaliation came with the announcement of the German and Austro-Hungarian Governments on January 31, 1917, that "From February 1, 1917, all sea traffic will be stopped with every available weapon and without further notice in the following blockade zones around Great Britain, France, Italy, and in the eastern Mediterranean."[25] These blockade zones were later modified and extended.[26]

Against this measure the Dutch Government brought one of the most vigorous protests of the war. The regime instituted by the declaration was declared utterly illegal: it extended the operations of war over a vast area; it even comprised the intentional attack on neutral vessels no matter what their cargo or destination, and without re-

---

[23] *Ibid.*, III, 43. See also Japikse, *op. cit.*, pp. 111–114.
[24] *A. J. I. L.*, Sp. Supp. XI, 36.
[25] *Dutch White Book*, "Diplomatieke Bescheiden Betreffende den Verscherpten Duikbootoorlog", (1917), pp. 1–4.
[26] *D. O. B.*, IV, 9–11.

gard to whether their presence in the forbidden zone was voluntary or due to circumstances beyond their control. From the point of view of international law a blockade could not be legally extended over so vast an area, and international law recognized only the confiscation and not the destruction of vessels seeking to force the blockade. The note concluded with the warning that the responsibility for the eventual destruction of Dutch vessels in the zones in question and the loss of human lives which might follow would fall on the German Government.[27]

In its protest against an attack on four Dutch vessels the Netherlands Government asserted that with respect to Dutch merchant ships the German naval forces had no other rights than those found in prize law. Direct acts of war against the merchant vessels of a friendly power were absolutely excluded so long as these vessels did not render themselves guilty of acts of war. According to established international law the exercise of the right of capture must never place in peril the lives of the crew. It went without saying that the belligerent could not escape this duty by previously declaring a part of the free seas a zone of war.[28]

Aside from the question of the legality of the blockade zones, which question remained open, differences also developed between the two governments over questions of fact. Several Dutch vessels were destroyed, according to the contention of the Dutch Government, outside of the zones. In several cases the German Government consented to submit the determination of this question of fact to a commission of inquiry, agreeing to pay damages if it was found that the vessel was not within the zones when torpedoed.[29]

---

[27] Note of Feb. 7, 1917, *Dutch White Book*, "Diplomatieke Bescheiden Betreffende den Verscherpten Duikerbootoorlog" (1917), Note to the German Government, pp. 2–3; Note to Austro-Hungarian Government, *ibid.*, p. 4.

[28] *D. O. B.*, IV, 8.

[29] Such a Commission, composed of a Dutch, a German, and a Swedish naval officer, decided that the steamship "La Campine" was sunk within, and the steam trawler "Amsteldijk" outside of the blockade zones, *D. O. B.*, IV, 8–9. German planes also attacked Dutch vessels in these zones, *D. O. B.*, I, 23; III, 15; *Recueil*, p. 123.

J. Extension of British "Blockade" Order

In consequence of the announcement by Germany of unrestricted submarine warfare, the British Government by Order in Council of February 16, 1917, declared that any vessels carrying goods with an enemy destination or of enemy origin would be liable to capture and condemnation in respect of the carriage of such goods, unless such vessels called at an appointed British or Allied port for the examination of her cargo. Goods which were found on the examination of any vessel to be goods of enemy origin or of enemy destination would be liable to condemnation.[30]

K. Waters Surrounding the German Bay Declared a Danger Zone by Germany

As a counter measure to the British decree of January 17, 1917, which declared the waters surrounding the German Bay a dangerous area, the German Government on March 6, 1918, declared that navigation in these waters would henceforth also be dangerous because of measures taken by the German naval forces against enemy navigation there.[31]

L. British Mines Within Dutch Territorial Waters

On the 30th of March, 1918, the Dutch torpedo boat "G" was sunk by a mine within the territorial waters off Terschelling, and on the 2nd of May, 1918, the *Fransnaerebout,* a Dutch marine fisher, met its destruction from the same cause in the same waters, with the loss of several lives. Many mines were fished up, all anchored within the territorial waters. The mines proved to be of British make. The Dutch Government protested against this violation of their territorial waters and demanded damages for the loss of the two vessels. The British Government denied that the mines had been planted within

---

[30] *D. O. B.,* IV, 5.
[31] *D. O. B.,* IV, 12.

the Dutch waters by British naval forces and suggested that the mines had been swept inwards by Dutch or German mine sweepers or fishing vessels. The Dutch Government rejected this explanation since the findings of its naval experts clearly indicated that the mines had been planted where they had been pulled up. The two Governments failed to reach an agreement on the facts and the matter was dropped.[32]

II. Losses of the Dutch Merchant Marine

On the ground of their presence within the blockade zones German submarines sank twenty-five Dutch steamships, four motorboats, twenty-four sailboats, and thirty-three fishing vessels. Three steamships suffered serious damages from German submarine attacks. One steamship and four fishing vessels were sunk by German torpedo boats, while a sailboat was destroyed by an attack from a hydroplane. As a result of the above attacks twenty-five lives were lost. The destruction of thirty-six steam and motorboats, three sailboats, and twenty-six fishing vessels, with a loss of nearly two hundred lives, was ascribed to mines. Many other vessels were reported missing.[33]

The explosion of mines washed up on the Dutch coast also frequently caused serious damages. The Dutch Government brought this matter to the attention of both the British and German Governments, pointing out that the mines apparently did not meet the requirements of the 8th Hague Convention, according to which anchored automatic contact mines must become harmless as soon as they break loose from their moorings. The German Government replied that notwithstanding every possible precaution there would always be some mines that were not

---

[32] *D. O. B.*, V, 34.

[33] Statistics given in Francois, *op. cit.*, pp. 259–260. Also *D. O. B.*, (1920–1921), p. 31. The German Prize Court allowed damages in the case of the steamship "Gamma" and the sailboat "Marian" on the ground that the vessels could not yet have learned of the blockade zone declaration when torpedoed, February 1, 1917.

mechanically perfect, wherefore it could not admit that its mines did not fulfill the requirements of the Convention. Moreover, this Convention was not applicable in the present war, since not all the belligerents were parties to it. The British Government also denied that its mines did not meet the requirements of the 8th Hague Convention, and like the German Government, would not admit responsibility for the damages caused by the explosion of these mines on the Dutch shores. However, the British, moved by a sense of equity and fairness, did make reparation for damages in several cases.[34]

The responsibility for the loss of several Dutch vessels, before the commencement of the unrestricted submarine warfare and outside of the blockade zones after their announcement, was in several cases run down and laid to the account of German submarines, with reclamation of damages from the German Government.[35] One of these cases, the *Tubantia,* led to a long exchange of correspondence between the Dutch and German Governments, with the final agreement to refer the dispute to an international commission of inquiry.[36] The *Tubantia* was sunk on March 16, 1916, by a torpedo No. 2033. The German Government maintained that this torpedo, which was from U-boat 13, had been launched at a British vessel on March 6, 1916, and that possibly it had remained afloat until struck by the *Tubantia.* The Commission placed responsibility for the sinking of the *Tubantia* upon the explosion of a torpedo launched by a German submarine, but left in suspense the question of whether the torpedoing took place knowingly or as the result of an error.[37]

---

34) *D. O. B.,* V, 28. Until June, 1919, more than 6,200 of these mines, washed up on the Dutch coast, had to be discharged by the Dutch coast guards. The majority of these mines were English. Barnouw, *op. cit.,* p. 129.

35) "Katwijk", *Recueil*, p. 102; *D. O. B.,* I, 18; "Rijndijk", *D. O. B.,* III, 18; "Teda", *D. O. B.,* IV, 15–16; "Geertruida", *D. O. B.,* IV, 12–13; "Bertha", *D. O. B.* (1919–1920), p. 12.

36) *D. O. B.,* II, 14–17; *Ibid.,* (1920–1921), p. 12.

37) *D. O. B.* (1921–1922), pp. 18–21; *A. J. I. L.,* XVI, 485 ff.

Blockade and Retaliation

III. ECONOMIC BLOCKADE OF HOLLAND

More and more as the war progressed the Netherlands lost its economic autonomy, until by the end of the war economic control had almost completely passed to the belligerents, with most of it resting in the hands of the Allied and Associated Powers. The peace time prosperity of Holland is largely based on the Rhine transit traffic between Rotterdam and the great German industrial hinterland, on the extensive colonial trade with the Dutch East Indies, and on the exports of her agricultural products. The war paralyzed many of Holland's industries, situated as the country was in the direct pathway between the two leading hostile powers, contiguous to one of them, and dependent on both for essential supplies. By preventing these essential supplies from reaching Holland the belligerent powers were enabled to effect a far reaching control over the economic activity and internal affairs of the country.

The extreme pressure the Allied Powers exerted upon Holland was intended to secure the cessation of exports from Holland to the Central Powers, and the control of the exportable surplus tonnage of the country for Allied use.[38] To secure these objects the belligerent parties resorted to all available methods, the advantage resting with that party which at the moment could exert the greatest pressure. Among the measures used, aside from those already mentioned, were the Trade Black Lists,[39] specific and general embargoes,[40] the refusal of bunker coal to neutral vessels unable or unwilling to meet Allied requirements, favorable insurance to all vessels engaged

---

[38] Parmalee, *Blockade and Sea Power*, p. 72.

[39] *Ibid.*, pp. 122, 130, 181, 69–90.

[40] *Ibid.*, pp. 45–48, 132–133, 150–151. British Proclamation prohibiting the export of certain commodities, Aug. 3, 1914, and British Proclamation prohibiting the export of certain articles to the Scandinavian countries and the Netherlands, October 2, 1917, Naval War College, *International Law Documents*, 1918, pp. 95–97. For U. S. export restrictions see *Ibid.*, 1918, pp. 192 ff.

in trading in Allied interests, discriminations favorable
to shipping lines engaged to meet Allied requirements,[41]
and special agreements in respect of particular commodities.[42]

Thus caught between the demands of both groups of
belligerent powers, Holland was forced to a rigorous regulation of the economic life of the country, involving a
close control over exports and imports. In the early days
of the war, licenses for agricultural products were issued
by the Agricultural Export Bureau, a branch of the Ministry of Agriculture. Only a certain percentage of the
home product could be exported; the remainder had to
be placed on the market for home consumption. The
granting of licenses for the export of commercial products
was under the supervision of committees appointed by
the Minister of Commerce. This system proved defective
and in September, 1917, the unified control of all exports
was vested in the *Nederlandsche Uitvoer Maatschappij*
(the Netherlands Export Company), which was a governmental agency.[43]

The control over imports came not from the Government but from a private organization, the *Nederlandsche
Overzee Trust Maatschappij* (Netherlands Oversea Trust
Company), popularly known as the N. O. T. As early as
September, 1914, the Dutch Government appointed a
Commission to assist and advise the Dutch importers and
exporters on how to carry on their overseas commerce
without violation of neutrality. The Commission was be-
sieged with demands for assistance. This Commission
conceived the plan of organizing a joint stock company
to which imported goods could be assigned with an adequate guarantee to the belligerent governments that these
goods would not be re-exported to their enemies. According to the statutes of the company, its purpose was
"to act as intermediary for Netherlands' merchants or

---

[41] "Official Report of the Administration of the Blockade", 1918,
War Cabinet's report, *Ibid.*, 1918, p. 94.
[42] *British Parl. Papers*, Misc. No. 2, 1916, cd. 8145. Also Salter, J., *Allied Shipping Control.*
[43] Barnouw, *op. cit.*, p. 146; Parmalee, *op. cit.*, pp. 138–139.

trading companies with a view to enable the unmolested conveyance from overseas of merchandise which has been, or may be declared absolute or conditional contraband by belligerent Powers." This wording was later changed in accordance with the modified circumstances to read, "to act as intermediary, in the fullest sense of the word, on behalf of merchants of Dutch nationality to insure so far as possible, uninterrupted import and export despite circumstances arising out of the war." The statutes also definitely declared that the company was excluded from trading on its own account. Some of the most important financial and shipping interests of the Netherlands took part in the organization of the Trust.[44]

The Executive Committee of the Trust carefully examined the character of every applicant and decided upon what conditions its services could be granted. The applicant, if an importer, was obliged to give a money guarantee that the goods imported and the products of these goods as well, would be only for domestic consumption or for re-export to the Dutch colonies, or for re-export to neutral states for consumption there. This monetary guarantee took the form either of a bank deposit or a deposit of securities, which would be forfeited in case of breach of the contract. Fees were charged to cover only the cost of administration. Guarantees generally were for specific importations, but to importers making a continuous use of the Trust a continuous guarantee was allowed. Certain goods, like wheat, meal, or flour, could not be consigned to the Trust, but were consigned directly to the Government, which had taken over the distribution of these commodities. Sir Francis Oppenheimer, Commercial Attache at the British Legation at The Hague, served as intermediary between the Trust and Allied and Associated Powers.

The Trust was a great aid in keeping Dutch industries

---

44) Most of this material is taken from G. Keller, *The N. O. T. The Netherlands Overseas Trust*, The Hague, 1915, English translation, 1917; and an article by a Dutch advocate of The Hague, Alexander Nicol Speyer, in *International Law Notes*, I, 117 ff.

going, for it gave its assistance to the importation of goods to be worked up in Holland and re-exported. Unless there was a general governmental prohibition on the export of a commodity, goods and articles manufactured from them could be re-exported to neutral countries. Even goods and their products imported from a belligerent country could be re-exported to the land of origin.

The consents of the Trust to serve as intermediary were of two kinds—one for belligerent countries and the other for neutral countries. Belligerent governments permitted exports to Holland only after a license had been obtained, and the authorities refused to grant licenses for exports to Holland unless the goods were consigned to the Trust. Thus the Dutch trader seeking to import goods from a belligerent country was compelled to use the Trust's intermediary. Consents for shipments from neutral countries were demanded by the shipping companies, for by refusing to take shipments not consigned to the Trust, the company's vessels were insured against unnecessary delay at the hands of the belligerent naval forces.[45]

The N. O. T. was of course expected to exercise a strict control over the goods imported throughout its intermediary if it was to enjoy the confidence of the belligerent governments. First of all, careful inquiries were made as to the reliability of the applicants and the nature of their trade. Secondly, a large staff of commercial experts carefully traced the fate of the goods. And lastly, the Trust retained complete control of the goods until

---

[45] See the case of the "Seguranca", an American vessel, which was detained in a British port until all the consignees had agreed to receive their goods through the N. O. T., *A. J. I. L.*, Sp. Supp. IX, 343–344. The work of the N. O. T. was aided also by certain decisions of the Dutch courts. A Dutch steamer had been permitted to leave a British port for Rotterdam only after the master had taken an oath not to deliver any part of the cargo except to persons having consents from the N. O. T. A consignee demanded delivery of the goods against documents as usual, and upon refusal of the master, brought in a claim against him in the courts on the grounds that he (consignee) as third party was in no way subject to the consequences of the voluntary acts of the master. The claim was rejected by the court. *International Law Notes*, I, 43.

they came into the actual possession of the consumer. And certain articles, like cotton, could be imported only by the consumer directly. However, it seems that in spite of all these precautions the confidence of the Trust was occasionally misused.[46]

The business of the Trust grew by leaps and bounds. To accommodate its staff it repeatedly had to acquire additional office space. Even as early as 1915 the Consent Department averaged 2,300 permits a week. Though not conducted on a profit basis the N. O. T. was able to turn over to the Netherlands Relief Committee 100,000 florins in August, 1915, and another 200,000 florins in October of the same year. New departments were constantly added, as for instance the Financial Department in 1916, which was established to examine all securities to be exported from Holland to overseas countries.

The German people viewed the Trust with great disfavor and charged it with being a tool of the British Government.[47] That it was a great aid in the enforcement of the blockade is apparent, but that it was deliberately designed to aid one of the belligerent parties to the disadvantage of the other does not follow. That one group of belligerents could profit more from it than the other was due to Allied naval supremacy and the accident of geography. On the part of Holland it was an excellent stroke of policy which enabled it to keep out of the war and to acquire supplies absolutely needed to keep its industries going and its population from starving.

German hostility to the Trust occasionally caused serious difficulties in the operation of the system. In the case of the *Lupus,* a Norwegian steamer en route to Amsterdam, the Supreme Court of Berlin condemned a cargo of pyrites consigned to the Trust. The Court was of the opinion that if the conditions had been reversed and a

---

46) See the cases of the "Noordam", Lloyd's *Cases,* VIII, 337 and of the "Oranje Nassau", Lloyd's *Cases,* IX, 189 ff.

47) German criticism of the Trust may be found in *Die Niederlandsche Uebersee Trust Gesellschaft,* by Dr. Fd. Tonnies, Jena, 1916; and *Vier Brieven over de N. O. T.* (Four letters on the N. O. T.), Amsterdam, 1916.

British warship had made the capture, the British Prize Court would have condemned the cargo on the ground of ultimate destination. On touching upon the fact that the N. O. T. was the consignee of the cargo, the Court declared that the Trust had "become entangled in obligations to such an extent that they were compelled under any circumstances to comply with the request of England to relinquish to England goods imported into Dutch ports, and to subject these goods to the jurisdiction of the English Prize Court."[48]

The Trust also became the object of distrust and dissatisfaction in Holland. The commercial interests centered at Rotterdam, because of the transit trade over the Rhine, are in close touch with Germany, while the business interests of Amsterdam, controlling the East Indian trade, were strongly pro-Ally in sentiment. The Rotterdam interests naturally found little in the Trust to approve. The Trust had become a tremendous power in the state; its president was frequently referred to as the uncrowned king of Holland.[49] Its standing with the Dutch people was not increased by the fact that its policy was dictated by the British Government. Even the Dutch Government became jealous of its power and its alleged usurpation of governmental functions.[50] By the law of 1917, establishing the Netherlands Export Company, the Dutch Government sought to place under the control of a governmental agency many of the functions hitherto exercised by the Trust.[51] The power of the Trust suffered a severe decline after the spring of 1917. The Allied declaration of a general embargo against Holland, the German threat to send no more coal, and the German

---

[48] *Entscheidungen des Oberprisengerichts in Berlin,* 1918, 377; Scott, *Cases,* Note 49, p. 1003.

[49] Japikse, *op. cit.,* p. 91.

[50] Letter of an American official at The Hague, dated August 5, 1918, quoted by Parmalee, *op. cit.,* pp. 151–152.

[51] Parmalee, *op. cit.,* pp. 151–155, 139.

declaration of unrestricted submarine warfare, all tended to strip the Trust of its former power.[52]

A feature of the Allied blockade system was the rationing of the border neutrals. As a part of this policy the Allied Governments concluded many agreements with the Trust and other trade associations in Holland. By these agreements the Allied Governments permitted restricted amounts of imports into Holland subject to the Trust guarantee of home consumption. The first of a series of these agreements was the general agreement concluded July 20, 1915, between the British Government and the Trust. Various special agreements were entered into with respect to particular commodities such as metals, rice, tires, jute, tinplate, and hides. By the agricultural agreement of November, 1916, between the British and General Trading Association and the Dutch Agricultural Export Bureau, strict limitations were placed upon the exportation of foodstuffs from Holland to the Central Powers.[53]

But Holland was dependent upon Germany as well, and in exchange for such essential imports as coal, iron, and potash, the German Government demanded a large part of the Dutch surplus of agricultural produce.[54] After the entrance of the United States into the war the Associated Powers demanded that Holland should drastically reduce these exports to Germany. Holland's refusal to accede to these demands was met by the General Em-

---

[52] How the N. O. T. was regarded by traders in other neutral countries doing business with Holland can be gathered from the following extract from Lansing's note to Page, October 21, 1915: "Arrangements have been made to create in these neutral countries special consignees, or consignment corporations, with power to refuse shipments and to determine when the state of the country's resources requires the importation of new commodities. American commercial interests are hampered by the intricacies of these arrangements, and many American citizens justly complain that their bona fide trade with neutral countries is greatly reduced as a consequence, while others assert that their neutral trade, which amounted annually to a large sum, has been entirely interrupted." *A. J. I. L.*, Sp. Supp. X, 79.

[53] Parmalee, *op. cit.*, pp. 146–151; *D. O. B.*, (1919–1920), pp. 23–26, 37 ff.

[54] *D. O. B.*, (1919–1920), pp. 41, 56–59.

bargo and finally the requisitioning of the Dutch vessels in American and British ports.

The effects of the Allied blockade on Holland needs only a brief mention in this study. Holland's transit traffic, an important national industry, was brought to a standstill. The Dutch exports from Holland to Germany were cut to less than a seventh of the annual pre-war average. The same was true of the export of herrings. The export of cattle to Germany had ceased completely by 1917.[55] In the case of thirty-eight out of forty-four leading commodities, or groups of commodities, the imports had fallen in 1918 to less than the average annual net imports during the three years from 1911 to 1913.[56] Practically no grain was imported into Holland during 1918. Holland was compelled to ration its food supply almost as rigorously as any of the belligerent countries. The national industries which depended upon foreign raw materials suffered severely, in many cases shutting down completely and causing much unemployment.[57]

The distressing conditions forced numerous new functions upon the Government. Before the war was over the Dutch Government had assumed the functions of "importer and miller and retailer of breadstuffs, of ration master of nearly all necessaries of life, of arbiter in the fixing of rents and of maximum prices for such commodities as were not placed on the distribution list, of underwriter of insurance against unemployment and war risks at sea, of controller of national shipping with power to decide to which port each ship should sail, and to requisition part of her tonnage on the home-bound voyage."[58] The national debt had practically doubled during the war and it was not until several years after the war that the Government was again able to balance its

---

55) "Official Report on the Administration of the Blockade", Naval War College, *International Law Documents*, 1918, p. 93.
56) *British Parl. Papers*, Misc. No. 8, 1918, (cd. 8989).
57) See Temperly, *History of the Peace Conference of Paris*, I, 148–153; and Bulletin of U. S. Dept. of Commerce, *Commerce and Industry of the Netherlands*, 1912, 1918.
58) Barnouw, *op. cit.*, pp. 154–155.

budget. Conditions in Holland during the latter years of the war resembled more the conditions of a belligerent than of a neutral country.[59]

IV. Rule of International Law with Respect to Blockade

Blockade in the modern sense of the term owes its origin in both principle and practice to the Dutch. Grotius in his famous work published in 1625 first laid down the principle of the blockade,[60] while the Dutch Government was the first to put it into practice when in 1630 it declared a blockade of certain ports of Flanders. Neutrals accepted the right of blockade but attempted to limit its scope. The First League of Armed Neutrality, 1780, declared that no port should be considered blockaded unless there was, "by the arrangements of the powers which attack it with vessels, stationed sufficiently near, an evident danger in attempting to enter it."[61] Holland's naval power had declined and it is therefore not surprising to find her a member of the League, an ardent champion of neutral rights. The Second League of Armed Neutrality, of which Holland was not a member, reaffirmed the declarations of its predecessor, but added the further restriction that no vessel was liable to capture unless it had been warned of the existence of the blockade by the commander of the force maintaining it and afterwards attempted to enter.[62]

With the Napoleonic Wars came an outrageous violation of the rights of neutral commerce. By the Berlin decree of 1806 Napoleon declared the British Islands to be in a state of blockade and all commerce and correspondence with them was declared prohibited. Great Britain

---

[59] For the economic and social effects of the war upon Holland see the monographs being published by the Carnegie Endowment for International Peace, *Division of Economics and History*, 1924, p. 19.

[60] *De Juris Belli ac Pacis*, Bk. III, Chap. 1, p. 5. For the early history of blockade see Westlake, II, 257–262.

[61] Hershey, pp. 66–67.

[62] Lawrence, p. 678.

replied by Orders in Council of January and November, 1807, by which neutral vessels were forbidden to trade between or even with ports in control of France or her allies, or with any port in Europe from which the British flag was excluded, without a clearance obtained in a British port. To these orders Napoleon replied with the decree from Milan, 1807, by which he declared that any vessel submitting to search by a British ship, paying duty to the British Government, or coming from or destined for a British port should be deemed a good prize.

It was not until after the Crimean War that conventional rules concerning blockade came into existence. The fourth Article of the Declaration of Paris, 1856, provided that "blockades in order to be binding, must be effective—that is to say, maintained by a force sufficient really to prevent access to the coast of the enemy." Though seeking to define the law of blockade the Declaration passed over in silence many matters in dispute.

During the American Civil War the North maintained a successful blockade on an unprecedented scale when it effectively blockaded the entire vast seaboard of the Confederacy. An important innovation was introduced into the law of blockade by the Supreme Court in the leading case of the *Springbok*. In this case the cargo of a British vessel captured enroute to Nassau was condemned on the ground that the character of the cargo was such as to indicate that its true destination was a blockaded port.[63]

With the Russo-Japanese War, 1904-1905, new practices were introduced which in effect marked a great extension of the principle of the blockade. Delimited zones of the open seas were declared strategic or military areas from which neutral commerce was excluded. In those areas mines were indiscriminately sown with the result that neutral vessels were frequently endangered.[64]

The London Naval Conference of 1908-9 attempted to draw up an extensive and definite code of rules respect-

---

[63] 5 *Wallace* 1 (1860); Evans, *Cases* (1917 ed.), pp. 405 ff.
[64] Hershey, *The International Law and Diplomacy of the Russo–Japanese War*, chapters IV–VI.

ing blockade. These rules were declared to correspond "in substance with the generally recognized principles of international law." Only the salient features of these rules can be set forth here. Only the ports and coasts belonging to or occupied by the enemy can be blockaded,[65] and to be binding a blockade must be effective.[66] The blockade must be impartially applied to the ships of all nations.[67] A blockade is not binding unless a declaration is made either by the blockading power or by the naval authorities acting in its name. The declaration must specify *a*) the date when the blockade begins, *b*) the geographical limits of the coast blockaded, and *c*) the delay to be allowed to neutral vessels for coming out.[68] Moreover, in order to be binding a blockade must be notified *a*) to neutral powers by means of a communication addressed to the government direct, or to representatives accredited to it, and *b*) to the local authorities by the officer commanding the blockading force.[69] A neutral vessel is liable to capture for breach of blockade only when it has actual or presumptive knowledge of the blockade,[70] and if a vessel approaching a blockaded port has no such knowledge of the blockade special notification must be made to the vessel by an officer of the blockading warships.[71]

Of special importance for a consideration of the legality of the practices of the World War are the remaining provisions. The seizure of neutral vessels for breach of the blockade is restricted to the area of operations of the warships detailed to render the blockade effective.[72] Access to neutral ports or coasts must not be barred by the blockading forces.[73] The doctrine of ulti-

---

65) Article 1.
66) Article 2.
67) Article 5.
68) Article 9.
69) Article 11.
70) Article 14.
71) Article 16.
72) Article 17.
73) Article 18.

mate destination is declared not applicable to blockade. Whatever may be the ulterior destination of a vessel or of her cargo, the evidence of violation of blockade is not sufficiently conclusive to authorize the seizure of the vessel if, at the time, she is on her way to a non-blockaded port.[74] A vessel is liable to capture for breach of blockade only so long as pursuit is maintained by a ship of the blockading force. "If the pursuit is abandoned, or if the blockade is raised, her capture can no longer be effected."[75] Condemnation of the vessel is made the penalty for breach of blockade. The cargo may also be condemned if it is proved that the shipper at the time of the shipment either knew or could have known of the intent to break the blockade.[76]

V. Legality of the Allied and German Blockade and Retaliatory Measures

A. Allied Blockade Measures

The French Decree and the British Order in Council bore none of the external forms of a formal declaration of blockade, nor was the word "blockade" even mentioned in either declaration. However, Grey in his note accompanying the transmission of the Order to the United States Government frankly stated that the object of the measure was to establish a blockade to prevent vessels from carrying goods to or from Germany, "and that His Majesty's Government has felt most reluctant at the moment of initiating a policy of blockade to exact from neutral ships all the penalties attaching to a breach of blockade."[77] In the *British Parliamentary Paper*, "Statement of the Measures Adopted to Intercept the Seaborne Commerce of Germany,"[78] it was stated that "no blockade of Germany was declared until March, 1915, and

---

74) Article 19.
75) Article 20.
76) Article 21.
77) *A. J. I. L.*, Sp. Supp. IX, 109–110.
78) Misc. No. 2, 1916, cd. 8145.

therefore up to that date we had to rely exclusively on the right to capture contraband," and that "the state of things produced is in effect a blockade, adapted to the condition of modern war and commerce."

The French-British measures can be regarded from several points of view, and any discussion of the legality of these measures must take all these points of view into consideration. The measures may first of all be regarded as seizure of enemy property at sea, but this would make them a violation of the provisions of the Declaration of Paris. It was on this ground that the Dutch Government lodged its protest.[79] The British Government rejected this appeal to the Declaration of Paris on the ground that goods found on neutral vessels were not confiscated but merely detained, and that goods were detained not solely because they were enemy owned but rather because they were of enemy origin or destination. "There are many cases in which proof that the goods were enemy property would afford strong evidence that they were of enemy origin or destination, and it is only in such cases that we are detaining them. Where proof of enemy ownership would afford no evidence of such origin or destination we are not in practice detaining the goods."[80]

Clearly enough, the seizure of goods which were enemy property but possessed neither enemy destination nor origin, can not be justified on the grounds of blockade, and constituted an undoubted violation of the second rule of the Declaration of Paris. The seizure of the other classes of goods can not be justified on the ground that they were merely retained and not confiscated. The rules of the Declaration of Paris were intended to guarantee neutral shipping against belligerent interference, and the rule that the neutral flag covers enemy goods is as much violated by detention as by confiscation. The Declaration of Paris is still good international law and

---

[79] Note of March 19, 1915, *Recueil*, pp. 33–34.
[80] Note to U. S. Government, July 24, 1915, *A. J. I. L.*, Sp. Supp. IX, 161.

the neutral is on good grounds in protesting its violation, even when the violation is by indirection.

Efforts were made to justify the measures as retaliation but neutrals replied that retaliation against neutrals is invalid. The validity of the British Orders in Council of March 17, 1915, was attacked on this ground in the case of the *Stigstad,* but the British Prize Court, and the Judicial Committee of the Privy Council on appeal, held that a belligerent may, if there is just cause for retaliation, interfere with the rights of neutrals to a greater degree than under the ordinary rules of international law.[81] In the case of the *Leonora* the vessel and her cargo were condemned under the Order in Council of February 16, 1917, in accordance with which vessels were made liable to capture and condemnation for carrying goods of enemy origin or destination unless they called for examination at a British port. In sustaining the decision of the British Prize Court the Judicial Committee of the Privy Council declared, "The right of retaliation is a right of the belligerent, not a concession by the neutral. It is enjoyed by law and not on sufferance," and that "in estimating the burden of the retaliation account must be taken of the gravity of the original offense which provoked it," and that "the order in council did not involve greater hazard or prejudice to the neutral trade in question than was commensurate with the gravity of the enemy outrages and the common need for their repression."[82]

The Anglo-French blockade measures can not be justified on the grounds of retaliation. One illegal act can not justify another. Moreover, a belligerent can not punish the enemy "through the sides of a neutral." There can

---

[81] Lloyd's *Cases,* V, 361; Naval War College, *International Law Decisions,* 1922, pp. 176 ff.

[82] Lloyd's *Cases,* VII, 262, 343; Naval War College, *International Law Decisions,* 1922, 184 ff; Scott, *Cases,* pp. 804 ff. Lord Stowell in the "Fox" upheld British Orders on the ground of retaliation.

be no retaliation against friends.[83] The general accept-
ance of such a doctrine would completely destroy the protection which the development of international law has
succeeded in gradually throwing about neutral trade. The
position always assumed tacitly, if not openly expressed,
by the defenders of retaliation, that the neutral has the
right of protest only against the first offender, is open to
serious objections. It is an easy matter for a belligerent
to declare that the adversary is engaging in illegal practices, and there probably never was a war in which such
accusations were not made. Each belligerent throws the
burden upon the other, and it is impossible for the neutral to establish the responsibility for the first offense,
especially under the complicated conditions of modern
warfare.[84] This position fails completely to distinguish
between neutral violations of obligations which justify
retaliation against it, and neutral failure to preserve
rights, which does not. The fact that a neutral is only
partly successful in obtaining respect for its rights is no
ground for action against it.[85]

The legality of the Anglo-French measures must
finally be discussed from the point of view of a blockade.
They differed from the previously accepted understanding of a blockade in three important particulars. In the
first place, the blockade was not maintained by a close
cordon of ships stationed along the immediate coast line,
but by a long range control over the high seas. Secondly,

---

[83] Yntema, XVII, *Michigan Law Review*, 64 ff; Borchard, *Yale
Law Review*, 1919, pp. 583 ff; Hyde, II, 665–666; Baty, *Penn. Law Review*, June, 1915, p. 717; Wright, Q., *Minn. Law Review*, V, 515–529;
Briggs, *The Doctrine of Continuous Voyage*, pp. 141 ff. Upheld by
Sir Erle Richards, *British Yearbook of International Law*, 1920–1921,
pp. 30 ff; Fleischmann, *Zeitschrift fur Volkerrecht*, IX, 158 ff; Nied-
ner, *Ibid.*, IX, 199 ff; Schoenborn, *Ibid.*, IX, 120 ff. German writers
holding retaliatory measures illegal are: Heilborn, *Zeitschrift fur
Volkerrecht*, IX, 62 ff., and Struff, *Ibid.*, IX, 220, Note 2.

[84] Sir Erle Richards offered the following solution: An international commission to inquire into the occasion of the exercise of the
right of retaliation similar to those commissions which have on frequent occasions examined the decrees pronounced by prize courts generally. *British Yearbook of International Law*, 1920–1921, p. 33.

[85] Wright, Q., *Minnesota Law Review*, V, 515 ff.

the doctrine of ultimate destination was applied, so that the import and export of goods to and from Germany by way of adjacent neutral lands was prohibited. And thirdly, the penalty for the breach of this blockade was not confiscation of ship and cargo, but sequestration, detention, or sale, at the discretion of the prize court.[86] The United States Government further protested the legality of this measure as a blockade since it was neither effective nor impartial.[87]

No serious objection can be brought against the Anglo-French blockade on the ground that it was not of the close cordon type. The introduction of mines, submarines, and airships makes it impossible for ships to be stationed in the immediate offing of the blockaded ports. Nor is this essential to an effective blockade under modern conditions.

More serious is the charge that the blockade was illegal on the ground of barring access to neutral ports. The generally accepted view of the law of blockade on this point is specifically stated in Article 18 of the Declaration of London, "The blockading forces must not bar access to neutral ports or coasts."[88] The British Government attempted to meet this objection by making a distinction between the commerce of neutral and enemy countries and that there would "be no substantial interference with trade of neutral ports except insofar as they constitute ports of access to and exit from the enemy territory."[89] The assumption underlying this statement seems to be that only that is neutral trade which has its origin or destination in a neutral country. With origin and destination "access to neutral ports" has nothing to do.

---

[86] Confiscation was made the penalty for breach by the Order in Council of February 16, 1917.

[87] See American Note of October 21, 1915, *A. J. I. L.*, Sp. Supp. X, 80 ff.

[88] American note of October 21, 1915, *A. J. I. L.*, Sp. Supp. X, 81–82.

[89] British note to the United States, July 24, 1915, *A. J. I. L.*, Sp. Supp. IX, 160.

Blockade and Retaliation

The British Government also sought to justify these measures by contending that it was merely applying old principles to new conditions. The United States prize courts in the Civil War had extended the doctrine of continuous voyage to the carriage of contraband and to blockade, and the British Government had acquiesced in it as a legitimate extension of an underlying principle to a new situation. The Allies now found themselves confronted by a somewhat similar situation and altered circumstances likewise imposed upon them the necessity of reshaping some old rules. "Adjacent to Germany are various neutral countries which afford her convenient opportunities for carrying on her trade with foreign countries. Her own territories are covered by a network of railways and waterways, which enable her commerce to pass as conveniently through ports in such neutral countries as through her own. A blockade limited to enemy ports would leave open routes by which every kind of German commerce could pass almost as easily as through ports in her own territory."[90]

In the Civil War cases the prize court extended the rule of continuous voyage or ultimate destination only to the carriage of contraband, and moreover, specifically rejected its application to a breach of blockade where the blockaded district was reached by land.[91] Some publicists regard the distinction between the rules applicable to contraband and to blockade as unsound. "If the right of a belligerent to seize contraband destined for his enemy is not allowed to be defeated by its being consigned to a neutral port, there is no logical reason why his right, in the case of blockade, to seize non-contraband

---

90) British note of July 24, 1915, *A. J. I. L.*, Sp. Supp. IX, 159.

91) "The Peterhof", 5 *Wallace* 28, 58. Woolsey declared he could find no American prize decision "in which the doctrine of continuous voyage was directly and exclusively applied as a determining factor to a pure blockade case", *A. J. I. L.*, IV, 829. However, in the "Circassion", 2 *Wallace* 135, the court seems to have applied the doctrine of continuous voyage to blockade. See Hyde, II, 666, note 3. See Briggs, *op. cit.*, Chap. IV. Briggs regards the "Springbok" case as an extension of continuous voyage to blockade.

goods with a similar destination must be defeated by the same device."[92]

To these contentions it may be replied that the rights of belligerents in regard to neutral commerce are the result of a compromise between the belligerent's demand for the right to stop all commerce with his enemy and the neutral's assertion of the right to carry on his trade unhindered with either belligerent. Maritime states have not yielded the right to intercept non-contraband goods bound for neutral ports, and international law does not recognize this right. Moreover, the right to blockade a neutral port would not be a development of existing law, but a sharp alteration. Such a right would give the belligerent an almost unlimited control over neutral trade and economic life. There is a valid reason for denying the right to seize non-contraband goods consigned to a neutral port while granting the right to capture contraband goods so consigned. All access by sea to an enemy port may be lawfully barred only when there is being waged against the port a military operation which effectually bars such access. Since such military operation can not be taken either directly or indirectly against a neutral port, the prevention of such access is unlawful. But the case of articles of a military value stands differently. Such articles the belligerent has a reasonable right to intercept, and the right to intercept such articles which would otherwise be used against it, may not be defeated merely because they are forwarded through neutral ports.[93]

The British blockade was illegal also on other grounds. There was no notification of the particular coast line invested. The blockade was ineffective since the German coasts were open to trade with the Scandinavian countries. Moreover, the blockade was not im-

---

[92] Sir Erle Richards, *British Yearbook of International Law*, 1922–1923, pp. 87 ff; Garner, *International Law and the World War*, II, Chapter 33.
[93] See Hyde, II, 668.

partially applied, for trade with German ports was open to the Scandinavian countries but not to other neutral countries.[94]

B. THE GERMAN SUBMARINE BLOCKADE

The announcement on February 4, 1915, by the German Government whereby the waters surrounding Great Britain and Ireland were declared a war zone can not be regarded as a declaration of blockade since neutral vessels were not prohibited from passing through this area. They were merely warned against the possibility of mistake on the part of the submarine commanders with respect to the nationality of their vessels. The declaration of unrestricted submarine warfare of January 31, 1917, with its later extensions, bears an entirely different character. It was the object of this measure to prevent all trade with the enemy, and, although not announced as a blockade, it was intended to have all the effects of a blockade.[95] Neutral rights were violated by the submarine warfare in several respects. It led to the destruction of neutral goods and lives on enemy vessels, and what was more serious, it led to the destruction of neutral vessels, without warning, with everything on board. Destruction may not be made the penalty for breach of blockade. Prizes may be destroyed under certain exceptional conditions, but only after all persons on board have been placed in safety. The measure was also illegal because it made no distinction between traffic solely between neutral ports and traffic destined for enemy ports. The German Government, it would seem, thought that these illegalities were covered or removed simply by declaring a "War Zone," a "Military Area," or "Destruction Zone." The mere declaration of a war zone can not create new belligerent rights. The belligerent right of military operation on the high seas can not be extended be-

---

94) American note of October 21, 1915, *A. J. I. L.*, Sp. Supp., X, 81.
95) The Dutch Government refused to recognize the measure as a blockade, but the Brazilian Government protested it as an ineffective blockade. *Brazilian Greenbook*, pp. 20, 22, 27, 42.

yond the immediate vicinity of a hostile action. Belligerents can not rid themselves of the duties imposed by the rules of war by the simple process of declaring a vast section of the high seas a war zone.[96] Such measures under the name of "barred zones," or "danger areas," constitute a grave infringement on the principle of the freedom of the seas.[97]

Attention must be briefly drawn to another feature of both the Allied and German blockades. Both parties planted mines outside of the territorial waters, whether their own or their enemies', as a means of enforcing the blockade. Occasionally these mines were found even within the territorial waters of neutrals. Moreover, many of the mines so planted failed to become harmless after breaking loose from their anchors. The terms of the Hague regulations regarding the laying of automatic contact mines are so indefinite as to give small protection from this danger to neutral trading. Mine laying as practiced in the World War constitutes a grave infringement upon the principle of the freedom of the seas and subjects the lives of neutrals and non-combatants to perilous hazards. The provisions of the Hague Convention are clearly inadequate and demand careful revision with the imposition of drastic restrictions upon belligerent mine laying in the open seas.[98]

---

[96] Several German publicists before the declaration of the blockade expressed objections to this method of warfare; Rehm, "Der Unterseebootkrieg", *Zeitschrift fur Volkerrecht*, IX, 20 ff; Heilborn, *Ibid.*, IX, 56 ff. Prominent German writers who held that the declaration of a war zone radically changed the juridical relationship were: Piloty, *Ibid.*, IX, 203 ff; Fleischmann, *Ibid.*, IX, 170 ff; and Perels in *Grenzboten*, Feb. 15, 1915, speaks of a new belligerent right, "Sperrungsrecht". See Verzijl, pp. 216–217.

[97] Similar features of the British blockade were, of course, equally illegal.

[98] Articles limiting the area within which mines might be used were proposed at the Second Hague Peace Conference, but failed to be incorporated in the Convention. The area of the use of mines was left to "the conscience, the good sense, and the consciousness of the obligations imposed by the principles of humanity", *Deuxieme Conference International de la Paix*, III, 379. For a discussion of submarine mines see Naval War College, *op. cit.*, 1914, pp. 100–138.

VI. THE FUTURE OF BLOCKADE

What effect will the experience of the World War have on the future development of the law of blockade? It does not seem as though the submarine blockade can ever be so conducted as to conform to the decent opinions of civilized mankind, to say nothing of the requirements of international law. The surface blockade, in the old sense of the term with a close cordon of warships, is no longer possible, and is bound to disappear unless some way is found of protecting the blockading warships from the attacks of submarines.[99] The belligerent can not be denied the right to prevent neutral trading with enemy ports, but neither can the belligerent be granted the right to blockade neutral ports. The Anglo-French measures in many respects resembled more a general prohibition of neutral trade with the enemy than a blockade.

The practice of rationing neutral countries is open to serious abuses. It gives the belligerent a far reaching control over the whole internal life of the country. The question of what is bona fide neutral trade is not easily settled, especially not in the case of a great trading country and colonial power like Holland. Under the guise of preventing all but bona fide neutral trade the belligerent may do permanent injury to the trade of the neutral, and to its own benefit. If the existing system of the political organization of the world is to continue, with its sharp differentiation between neutrals and belligerents in time of war, neutral trading rights must be carefully restated to safeguard them in the next conflict.

If, however, international organization should be greatly strengthened, and many of the powers now exercised by the nations under the doctrine of absolute sovereignty should be relinquished to this international

---

99) Francois is of the opinion that the long range blockade is illegal. However, he would give the belligerent the right of preëmption with respect to all non-contraband goods destined for the blockaded region, with the right, upon compensation, to destroy neutral vessels in case there is no other way to prevent the cargoes from reaching the blockaded territory, *op. cit.*, p. 217.

organization for the purpose of maintaining the peace, the blockade would become the most powerful weapon of the family of nations against a recalcitrant state. The character of the blockade would also be greatly changed, for it would then become no more than a prohibition of trade, or a boycott, against such a state, declared with internatinal sanction. In such an action the small neutral countries would have much to gain over a blockade as administered by the belligerents in the last war. In such an international boycott the small states could play an honorable part in maintaining the peace of the world, and they would likewise be freed from the indignities and curtailment of rights which they are sure to suffer under the old system.

Chapter XIV

CONTRABAND AND UNNEUTRAL SERVICE

I. Allied-Dutch Controversies

FEW questions within the field of neutral and belligerent rights have been more provocative of controversy than the questions centering about contraband. Few subjects within the field of international law have undergone more change and are more unsettled. There have been differences of opinion with respect to the unreasonableness of the distinction between conditional and absolute contraband; the destination such goods must have; the right to capture such goods when not directly enroute to the enemy country; the circumstances under which enemy destination may be assumed without further proof; and the penalties attached to the carriage of contraband. A general agreement with respect to these various questions was attempted in the Declaration of London, but with little success, as was proved by the experience of the World War.

A combination of factors caused the question of contraband to assume a new importance in the World War. Before the war was over all the great maritime powers had become belligerents. Adjacent to Germany was a group of neutral seaboard states through which Germany could import many of her supplies. The distinction between supplies intended for the armed forces and those intended for the civilian population became difficult to maintain since the military and male population were practically co-extensive. Moreover, the government strictly controlled the distribution of food. Furthermore, in modern warfare nearly all of the resources and materials of industry become essential to belligerent operations and thus become touched with the character of contraband. Belligerent regulations naturally put many difficulties in the way of the important Dutch overseas trade and transit traffic.

A. British Order in Council of August 20, 1914, and French Decree of August 25, 1914

Very shortly after the outbreak of the war several Dutch ships carrying food supplies to Amsterdam were taken into English ports. The British Government refused to release the cargoes until either their innocent destination had been clearly proved or the Dutch Government had given an express guarantee that the food supplies would be used exclusively in Holland and would not serve to release an equal quantity of foodstuffs for shipment from Holland to Germany. In justification of this measure the British Government invoked the communication of the Dutch Government in the *Staatscourant* of August 21, 1914, explaining what should be regarded as transit traffic according to Dutch commercial usage,[1] and in connection with this the information it had acquired that the German Government had completely taken over the provisioning of the country. All food supplies destined for Germany according to the British view should be regarded as destined for the use of the armed forces or a government department of the enemy state. The British Government held that, because of these facts, it might justly regard all foodstuffs destined for Rotterdam as suspect and subject to seizure unless the Dutch Government furnished the desired guarantee.[2]

On August 20, 1914, the British Government issued an Order in Council, which with some modifications and additions declared the Declaration of London to be

---

[1] According to this communication transit was regarded as the transport of: (a) goods sent with a transit-cognossement to countries situated higher upon the Rhine; (b) goods declared sent to those countries at the time the ship carrying the goods enters a Dutch port from which they can be transhipped on lighters down the Rhine or placed in entrepot; (c) goods whose destination to those countries results from documents produced upon arrival in port. *Recueil*, p. 22.

[2] *D. O. B.*, I, 10; *Recueil*, p. 22.

"adopted and put in force by His Majesty's Government as if the same had been ratified by His Majesty."[3]   On August 25, the French Government issued a decree with almost identical provisions.[4]   With the modifications laid down in Paragraph 5 of the Order the British Government reverted to the rule of continuous voyage.   Article 36 of the Declaration of London permitted the capture of conditional contraband in cases where the enemy country had no seaboard and the goods were shown to be destined for the use of the armed forces or of a department of the enemy state, but the rule laid down by the British Order provided that conditional contraband with this destination would be liable to capture regardless of the destination of the cargo or vessel.   Furthermore, Paragraph 3 of the Order laid down two new presumptions of the above destination, in addition to those found in Article 34 of the Declaration of London.   If goods were consigned to or for an agent of the enemy state or to or for a merchant or other person under the control of the authorities of the enemy state, hostile destination would also be presumed.[5]

In practice, all ships carrying conditional contraband to Holland were taken into English ports and detained until the owners of the cargoes could prove the innocent destination of their goods.   Since the British Government regarded the Dutch ports, and particularly Rotterdam, as German transit ports, and most of the goods were consigned to order, innocent destination was difficult to prove.   The Dutch Government protested the action of the British Government in each case and pressed for the release of the ship and cargo.   At the same time the Dutch Government protested the above mentioned provisions of the Order in Council, contending that it was bound, under the terms of the Rhine Convention, not to hinder the German transit traffic in any way, and that for the rest it re-

---

3) *D. O. B.*, I, 10–11; *Recueil*, pp. 23–24.
4) *D. O. B.*, I, 13–14; *Recueil*, pp. 41–42.
5) *D. O. B.*, I, 10–11; *Recueil*, pp. 23–24.

garded it as in conflict with its neutral duties to grant the guarantees demanded by the British Government.[6]

In order to provide for the great need of certain contraband articles, especially food supplies, the Dutch Government decided to import these on its own account. For the same reason it allowed Dutch traders in particular cases to have their imports consigned to the Dutch Government. But it continued to refuse guarantees of home consumption for cargoes destined for Dutch ports. Ship after ship was taken into English ports, and there detained for a shorter or longer period. Sometimes the ship was permitted to continue with its full cargo, but not infrequently the vessel was permitted to proceed only after leaving some of its cargo behind.[7]

B. British Order in Council of October 29, 1914, and French Decree of November 6, 1914

On October 5 the Dutch Government received a note from London stating that the British Government had decided, in anticipation of a new regulation shortly to be announced, to allow food supplies to proceed unhindered to consignees in Holland. The new regulation was issued on October 29 in the form of an order in council, repealing the one of August 20.[8] The new Order also declared the provisions of the Declaration of London to be in force, but subject to the exclusion of the lists of contraband and non-contraband, and to the modifications indicated by the Order itself.

In place of Article 3 of the old Order, the new Order provided that the destination referred to in Article 33 of the Declaration of London would (in addition to the presumptions laid down in Article 34) be presumed to exist if the goods were consigned to or for an agent of the enemy state. Conditional contraband would be liable to capture on board a vessel bound for a neutral port if the goods

---

[6] *D. O. B.*, I, 11; *Recueil*, p. 25.
[7] *D. O. B.*, I, 11–12; *Recueil*, p. 25.
[8] *Recueil*, pp. 26–27; *D. O. B.*, I, 12. The French decree is found in *Recueil*, pp. 42–43; *D. O. B.*, I, 14.

were consigned "to order," or if the ship's papers did not show who was the consignee of the goods, or if they indicated a consignee of the goods in territory belonging to or occupied by the enemy. Upon the owners was placed the burden of proving the innocent destination of their goods. The Dutch Government objected that in neither of the three cases designated could the enemy destination of the goods be considered established.[9]

Article 2 of the Order stipulated that where it was shown to the satisfaction of one of the principle secretaries of state that the enemy was drawing supplies for its armed forces from or through a neutral country, he might direct that in respect of ships bound for a port in that country, Article 35 of the Declaration of London would not apply. During the operation of the direction, a vessel which carried conditional contraband to a port in that country would not be immune from capture. The Dutch Government protested the legality of the Order upon the ground that international law in no way laid any restrictions upon commerce on land between belligerents and neutrals, and that moreover, a neutral vessel carrying contraband to a neutral port could not be captured. Thus the mere fact that one of the belligerents drew some of its supplies from or through a neutral country did not give the opposing belligerent the right to declare vessels carrying contraband to the ports of such neutral country subject to capture.[10]

The condition of Dutch commerce and shipping under the new regulations was practically what it was under the old. Only the establishment of the Netherlands Overseas Trust, and its recognition by the Allied Governments, brought any improvement in the situation.[11]

With respect to the new contraband lists issued by the British Government in substitution for the lists of the

---

[9] *Recueil,* pp. 27–28; *D. O. B.,* I, 12–13.

[10] *Recueil,* p. 28; *D. O. B.,* I, 12. The British Government again urged the issuance of non-exportation guarantees, but this the Dutch Government steadily refused to do.

[11] See section on N. O. T. in Chapter XIII.

Declaration of London, the Dutch Government reiterated its stand taken at the beginning of the war. It regarded this action as a backward step and as undoing the work of the London Conference. The continued extension of the contraband list could have no other effect than to render the honored rule of Paris of 1856 completely illusory.[12]

C. BRITISH ORDER IN COUNCIL OF MARCH 30, 1916; FRENCH DECREE OF APRIL 12, 1916.

This Order and Decree set aside the provisions of Article 19 of the Declaration of London in accordance with which a vessel can not be captured for breach of blockade if, at the moment, she is on her way to a non-blockaded port, regardless of the ulterior destination of the vessel or cargo. The Order also laid down as a presumption of enemy destination in addition to those laid down in the previous Order, consignment to or for a person who during the existing war had forwarded imported contraband goods to territory belonging to or occupied by the enemy.[13]

The Dutch Government, although it had regarded the new regulations as illegal, made no protest since it considered the same principles of international law to be violated as had been violated by the previous Allied regulations. Moreover, it did not think the provision setting aside Article 19 of the Declaration of London was at all applicable to ships carrying goods to Dutch ports, even though these goods were destined for Germany, since Germany was not blockaded in the sense of the Declaration of London.[14]

---

[12] *Recueil*, p. 29; *D. O. B.*, I, 13. In April, 1916, the British Government abandoned the distinction and published a single list. *A. J. I. L.*, Sp. Supp. X, 52 ff.

[13] British Order, *Recueil*, pp. 39–40; *D. O. B.*, II, 6. French Decree, *Recueil*, pp. 50–52; *D. O. B.*, II, 7.

[14] *Recueil*, p. 39; *D. O. B.*, II, 8.

D. Maritime Rights Order in Council, July 7, 1916; French Decree of July 7, 1916.

With this Order and Decree, Great Britain and France completely withdrew all previous recognition of the Declaration of London, which was declared to be no longer applicable to the greatly changed conditions of maritime warfare. The earlier orders and decrees were withdrawn—the Allied Governments would hold themselves *"uniquement a application des regles ancienment reconnues du droit international."*[15] This in practice meant that each country fell back upon its own national system as developed before the war, with certain modifications or new rules laid down in this same order and decree.

Both the British and French Governments reformulated the presumptions of hostile destination. The British Order declared that hostile destination would be presumed to exist, until the contrary was shown if the goods were consigned to or for an enemy authority, or an agent of the enemy state, or to or for a person, who during the existing hostilities, had forwarded contraband goods to an enemy authority, or an agent of the enemy state, or to or for a person in territory belonging to or occupied by the enemy, or if the goods were consigned "to order," or if the ship's papers did not show who was the real consignee of the goods.[16]

The French Decree declared that, subject to contrary proof of innocent destination, cargoes of a contraband nature found on board a ship headed for enemy territory or territory occupied by the enemy, would be subject to confiscation if the cargo was composed of articles, the importation of which into the neutral country was greater than for normal years, or if the papers accompanying the cargo did not establish the neutral country as the final and definite destination of the cargo.[17]

---

15) Memorandum accompanying the Decree, *D. O. B.*, IV, 5.
16) Paragraph (a), *D. O. B.*, III, 5.
17) Article 3, *Ibid.*, III, 6.

Only the British Order expressly set forth the principle of the continuous voyage or ultimate destination and made it applicable to contraband and blockade.[18] The reason for this is found in the fact that no British prize court had applied the principle previous to the World War whereas the French prize court, as explained in the report to the President accompanying the decree, had applied the principle in the case of the *Vrouw Houwina* in 1855.

Both regulations took over the provisions of Article 40 of the Declaration of London in accordance with which a vessel carrying contraband is liable to capture and condemnation if the contraband, reckoned either by value, weight, volume, or freight forms more than half of the cargo.[19] The French wording *"lenavire et la cargaison entiere sont sujets a confiscation"* would imply that also the innocent goods forming a part of the ship's cargo would be condemned, even though it was not the property of the owner of the vessel. However, the French Government in reply to the Dutch note of protest of August 7, 1916, stated that this was not the meaning of the provision.[20]

The British Order also provided that a neutral vessel carrying contraband with papers indicating a neutral destination, which, notwithstanding the destination shown on the papers, proceeds to an enemy port, would be liable to capture and condemnation if she were encountered before the end of her next voyage.[21]

In its protest against the British Order the Dutch Government declared the special regulations of the Order were, for the most part, merely restatements of provisions contained in the repealed orders against which it had repeatedly objected. The Dutch Government reserved the right to demand reparations for losses to Dutch interests

---

18) Paragraph (b) of the British Order.
19) Paragraph (d) of the British Order; Article 2 of the French Decree.
20) *D. O. B.*, III, 8; Note of September 1, 1916.
21) Paragraph (c).

resulting from the application of the Order.[22] The British Government replied that if the rules cited in the Order were not deemed by the Netherlands Government to be in accordance with international law they should be challenged in the prize court.[23] The Dutch Government in reply stated that it could not accept the British prize courts as the final authority in determining the legality of the provisions of the Order, and declared that this could only be decided by an international tribunal of arbitration, instituted in conformity with the treaty of arbitration between Great Britain and the Netherlands.[24]

Against the regulations of the French decree the Dutch Government made similar protest. It could not recognize the legality of the presumptions laid down in the decree, since they furnished no proof that the captured goods had an enemy destination. Moreover, the decree sanctioned the practices already followed under the previous decrees, under which the distinction between conditional and absolute contraband had been completely eliminated, and conditional contraband, according to the long established rules of international law, is subject to capture only when found on a vessel enroute to territory belonging to or occupied by the enemy, or towards his armed forces, and only in case the goods are destined for the armed forces or the government of a belligerent state. The Dutch Government reserved the right to make demands for reparations for losses resulting from the application of the decree.[25]

The French Government replied that the conditions of the present war justified the new presumptions, and that as far as the French regulations were concerned the distinction had practically lost its value. The German Government had taken over the control of all articles of service to its armies, thus all such articles were at the

---

22) *D. O. B.*, III, 7; Note of August 2, 1916.
23) *Ibid.*, III, 8; Note of August 14, 1916.
24) Note of September 22, 1916, *D. O. B.*, III, 8.
25) Note of August 7, 1916, *D. O. B.*, III, 7.

disposition of the state authorities immediately after entering German territory.[26]

II. German-Dutch Controversies

A. Contraband

The regulations issued by Germany at the beginning of the war were, even to the lists of absolute and conditional contraband, in complete conformity with the Declaration of London. However, as early as October, 1914, the German Government began adding new articles to the list of conditional contraband. When in November the German Government added rough and worked lumber to this list it notified the Dutch Government that vessels headed for neutral harbors would be permitted to proceed unmolested if provided with a declaration by the government of the state whose flag the vessel was flying, properly legalized by a diplomatic representative of Germany, guaranteeing that the vessel in question was in fact destined for the port indicated and would there discharge its cargo.[27]

The Dutch Government in reply pointed out that even the German Prize Regulations declared it to be inadmissible to hold a vessel if the place of destination and discharge were shown by the papers on board to be a neutral port. It added that it could not give the desired guarantees, since such guarantees had no basis in international law. In this connection the greater difficulties for the Dutch traders came from the importation of Swedish wood, and when in March, 1915, the Swedish Government obtained from the German Government a statement that such kinds of wood as were not considered contraband by it before the November declaration would be granted unhindered exportation, the situation was greatly relieved.[28]

---

26) *D. O. B.*, III, 8, Note of September 1, 1916.
27) *Recueil*, p. 54; *D. O. B.*, I, 15.
28) *Recueil*, p. 54; *D. O. B.*, I, 15.

Contraband and Unneutral Service

On April 18, 1915, the German Government announced certain modifications in several articles of its Prize Regulations.[29] These modifications involved practically the same departures from the Declaration of London as did the earlier British Orders and French Decrees. They laid down the same new presumptions with respect to the hostile destination of conditional contraband, made sweeping changes in the contraband lists, declared all neutral vessels carrying contraband to hostile ports under false papers liable to condemnation until the end of the war, and introduced the rule of continuous voyage with respect to contraband.[30] With respect to these modifications the Dutch Government made the same protests as it did against similar orders and decrees from the British and French Governments.[31]

A second change was made by Germany in her Prize Regulations on July 22, 1916. The modifications announced this time corresponded to the new rules laid down by the British Order of March 30, 1916, and the French Decree of April 12, 1916. The rule of continuous voyage was extended to blockade and a new presumption of hostile destination was added to those already in force.[32] The Dutch Government lodged with the German Government a brief protest of the same tenor as its protest to the Allied Governments when they announced similar new rules.[33]

B. UNNEUTRAL SERVICE

The requisition of the Dutch vessels by the Allied and Associated Governments in March, 1918, led the German Government to amend its Prize Regulations with respect to the presumptions of unneutral service. A neutral vessel was to be regarded as engaged in unneutral service when the state whose flag the vessel flies has made an

---

[29] Articles 21, 23, 27, 33, 35, and 40.
[30] *D. O. B.*, I, 15; *Recueil*, pp. 55–56.
[31] *D. O. B.*, I, 16; *Recueil*, p. 56.
[32] *D. O. B.*, III, 9.
[33] *Ibid.*, III, 9.

arrangement with the enemy for a lease of tonnage, or when the major part of the merchant fleet of the neutral state is engaged in the service of the enemy.[34]

Upon inquiry at Berlin the Dutch Government was informed that the German Government regarded the modification in the Prize Regulations as applicable to the Dutch vessels in view of the fact that after deducting the number of Dutch ships in port more than half of the Dutch tonnage had been requisitioned by the Associated Powers. The German Government also pointed out that there would be due warning before attack; and furthermore, that the difficulties from the German side would disappear in case an arrangement were made with Germany with respect to the conditions under which she was prepared to grant safe-conducts to Dutch vessels guaranteeing safe passage.[35]

The Dutch Government protested that the modification in Prize Regulations set up a presumption of unneutral service absolutely contrary to every principle of international law. The fact that the Associated Powers had requisitioned a large part of the Dutch vessels and put them into service under Dutch flags, carried no proof that the remainder of the vessels, flying under neutral flag, made itself guilty of unneutral service. Furthermore, the measure was put into effect at once, with no exceptions made in favor of ships which had set out to sea without knowledge of the measure.[36] The German Government in reply denied the illegality of the presumption laid down in the modification of its Prize Regulations, and insisted that the presumption corresponded to an existing probability.[37] The difficulty seems to have been settled in practice by the issuance of safe-conducts.[38]

---

34) Addition to Article 55; see *D. O. B.*, V, 22.
35) *Ibid.*, V, 22.
36) *Ibid.*, V, 22, Note of May 27, 1918.
37) Note of June 13, 1918, *D. O. B.*, V, 23.
38) Note of May 27, 1918, *Ibid.*, V, 22.

III. HISTORY OF THE LAW OF CONTRABAND

It was customary in the fifteenth century, and not unusual in the sixteenth century, for a belligerent to declare all trade between neutrals and the enemy prohibited. This practice was probably borrowed from ancient Rome, which imposed the death penalty upon traffic in arms with the barbarians. A precedent for the practice may also be found in the papal bulls at the time of the crusades, which forbade Christians upon penalty of slavery, to trade with the Saracens in weapons, iron, or wood. Even England issued such decrees. Sweden issued such a prohibition even as late as 1560 in the war with Russia.[39]

The United Provinces issued such decrees in the war against Spain. Such a decree was issued in 1584, reissued with modifications in 1586, 1591, and 1596. In 1599 the Government of the United Provinces returned to the earlier practice of completely prohibiting all exports to the enemy. This prohibition acquired an unusual importance from the fact that Henry IV of France commanded his subjects to submit to the prohibition for a period of six months.[40]

After 1599 a period of mitigation set in. Treaties were made in which the distinction between military supplies and other goods was laid down. In case either of the contracting powers fell into war the other power would be under obligation to prevent its subjects from transporting military supplies to the enemy. Trade in non-military supplies would be absolutely free. The treaty between England and Spain in 1604 is generally regarded as the first treaty of this kind. Holland and Sweden contracted a similar treaty in 1614. The word *contraband* was first used in the treaty of Southampton of 1625, between Holland and England. In this treaty the King of England promised to use his influence with the neutral powers to have them prohibit all trade between their subjects and

---

[39] Francois, *op. cit.*, p. 85.
[40] *Ibid.*, pp. 86–89.

Spain. Should the King fail in this attempt only the transportation of contraband goods would be prohibited.[41] By the end of the century such treaties had become quite general.[42]

The transition recorded in the above treaties is reflected in Grotius' *De Jure Belli ac Pacis*, 1625. All commodities are divided into three classes. "There are some objects," wrote Grotius, "which are of use in war alone, as arms; there are others which are useless in war, and which serve only for purposes of luxury; and there are others which can be employed both in war and peace, as money, provisions, ships, and articles of naval equipment. Of the first kind it is true . . . that he is on the side of the enemy who supplies him with the necessaries of war. The second class of objects gives rise to no dispute. With regard to the third kind, the state of the war must be considered. If seizure is necessary for defense, the necessity confers a right of arresting the goods, under the condition, however, that they shall be restored unless some sufficient reason interferes."[43]

The list of contraband articles in the treaties negotiated in the 17th and 18th centuries varies considerably. The treaties of the 18th century, however, followed the general outlines of the Peace of Utrecht, 1713. Contraband was limited to enumerated articles of a military character. Food supplies and many other articles were declared to be free except when transported to beseiged, invested, or blockaded places.[44] The First and Second

---

[41] Francois, *op. cit.*, pp. 89–90.

[42] The United Provinces had made such treaties with France, 1646; Spain, 1650; England, 1654, 1668, 1674, and 1675; Sweden, 1675; France, 1678. England had also concluded such treaties with Sweden, 1654; France, 1655; Sweden, 1661 and 1666; Spain, 1667; France, 1667; and Denmark, 1670. Such a treaty was also concluded between France and Denmark in 1663, Francois, *op. cit.*, p. 91; Hall, note p. 638; Moore, *International Law and Some Current Illusions*, p. 54. See Quigley, H. S., *The Immunity of Private Property from Capture at Sea*, pp. 7–55, for a good brief history of this subject.

[43] Lib. III, C. 1, par. 5.

[44] Moore, J. B., *International Law and Some Current Illusions*, pp. 54–55; Hall, pp. 638–643.

Armed Neutralities declared contraband to be limited to munitions of war.[45] The United States was from the beginning a leading champion among neutrals of a restricted contraband list, and, until the World War, was very successful in maintaining her position. The attitude of the United States as a belligerent may be seen from the contraband lists she issued during the war with Spain. Arms and munitions of war and machinery for their manufacture, saltpeter, military accoutrements and equipments, and horses were included in the list of absolute contraband. Under conditional contraband were listed:

> "Coal when destined for a naval station, a port of call, or a ship or ships of the enemy; materials for the construction of railways or telegraphs, and money, when such materials or money are destined for the enemies' forces; provisions, when destined for an enemy's ship or ships, or for a place that is besieged."[46]

Provisions were generally placed in the conditional contraband list. Thus the British Government regarded provisions as contraband only when they were destined for the use of the enemy's forces.[47] This was also the rule followed by British and American prize courts.[48] At the outbreak of the Russo-Japanese War in 1904, Russia extended the list of absolute contraband to include provisions. In consequence of protests made by the British and American Governments the Russian Government appointed a committee to study the question. Upon the report of this committee Russia announced that foodstuffs would be considered as contraband of war if destined for the government of the belligerent power; for its administration; for its army; for its navy; for its fortresses;

---

45) Hall, p. 646.
46) Moore, *Digest*, VII, 669.
47) Holland's *Manual of 1888;* Moore, *Digest*, VII, 668, and see letter of Lord Salisbury, *Ibid.*, VII, 685.
48) "The Jonge Margaretha", 1 *C. Rob.* 189; Mussionaire *v.* Keating", 2 *Gallison* 325; "The Commercen", 1 *Wheaton* 382.

for its naval ports; or for its purveyors. In cases where they were addressed to private individuals foodstuffs would not be considered as contraband.[49]

The whole question of contraband is dealt with in detail in the Declaration of London. Articles are divided into the three Grotian classes, each with a separate list. On the list of absolute contraband are: arms, munitions, military supplies, camp equipment, armour plates, warships, and implements, and apparatus designed exclusively for the manufacture of munitions of war, for the manufacture or repair of arms, or war material for use on land or sea. Articles exclusively used for war may be added to this list by a declaration duly notified. The conditional contraband articles were listed under fourteen general heads, namely: foodstuffs; forage and grain; clothing; gold and silver in coin or bullion, and paper money; vehicles; vessels, craft, boats, and floating docks; railway material, and telephone and telegraph materials; all aircraft and their accessories; fuel and lubricants; powder and explosives; barbed wire; horeshoes and shoeing materials; harness and saddlery; field glasses, telescopes, chronometers, and all kinds of nautical instruments. Other articles susceptible of both warlike and peaceful usage may be added to this list by declaration notified to other powers. Articles which are not susceptible of use in war may not be declared contraband. In a separate article under seventeen headings are listed a series of articles which may not be declared contraband.[50]

The Declaration declares all contraband goods liable to condemnation. In the case of absolute contraband it need only be shown that the goods are destined to territory belonging to or occupied by the enemy, or to armed **forces of the** enemy. Proof of such destination is held to be complete when the goods are documented for discharge in an enemy port, or delivery to the armed forces of the enemy, and when the vessel is to call at enemy ports only, or when she is to touch at an enemy port or

---

[49] Moore, *Digest*, VII, 686–692.
[50] Articles 22–28.

meet the armed forces of the enemy before reaching the neutral port for which the goods in question are documented. The vessel's papers are conclusive proof of her destination, unless her position is such as to give just grounds for suspicion.[51] Conditional contraband, however, is held liable to capture only when "shown to be destined for the use of the armed forces or of a government department of the enemy State, unless in this latter case the circumstances show that the goods can not be used for the purpose of the war in progress." A hostile destination is presumed "if the goods are consigned to enemy authorities, or to a contractor established in the enemy country who, as a matter of common knowledge, supplies articles of this kind to the enemy," or "if the goods are consigned to a fortified place belonging to the enemy, or other place serving as a base for the armed forces of the enemy." These presumptions, however, may be rebutted.[52]

The development of the doctrine of continuous voyage, or ultimate destination, needs also to be briefly traced. It received its first marked development as applied to the "Rule of 1756."[53] Colonial powers in the 18th century in peace time frequently reserved all trade between the mother country and the colonies to vessels of their own flag. Under stress of war this trade was sometimes opened to vessels of neutral countries. Thus France in the Seven Years War opened her colonial trade to Dutch vessels. England at once declared that neutral vessels taking advantage of this trade would be subject to capture. To evade this rule neutral vessels employed the ruse of breaking up such voyage by stopping at a neutral port. The English prize courts after 1805 did not permit this practice to nullify the rule, but confiscated the ves-

---

[51] Articles 30–32, 39.

[52] Articles 33–34.

[53] Briggs, *The Doctrine of Continuous Voyage*, gives an excellent history of the doctrine. The doctrine seems to have been applied as early as 1761, in the case of the 'Jesus" (*Burrell*, 164) in which it was applied to a case of contraband captured on the first leg of the voyage, *Ibid.*, pp. 34 ff.

sel also in these cases on the ground that the voyage between the metropolitan country and the colony was one continuous voyage. To make the deception still stronger the vessels sometimes unloaded the goods in the neutral port, only to reload them before continuing the voyage. The British prize courts condemned the vessels also in these cases,[54] although Lord Stowell condemned such vessels only when captured on the last leg of the voyage.

The analogy between reserved trading and contraband was first drawn by Lord Stowell, when he declared vessels carrying contraband cargo subject to condemnation when captured on their way to a neutral port if their ultimate destination was an enemy port. However, the ultimate destination of the vessel and not that of the cargo was considered decisive.[55] The French prize courts in the Crimean War condemned a neutral vessel captured on its way to Hamburg with a cargo of saltpetre. There were clear indications that the vessel intended to proceed with her contraband cargo to Russia after her call at Hamburg.[56]

The doctrine underwent a marked extension in the Civil War, when the United States prize courts applied it to cases in which the contraband cargo would have to be transhipped to smaller vessels in a neutral port.[57] In the case of the *Peterhof*, a vessel bound for the Mexican port of Matamoras, articles of absolute contraband were condemned on the ground of their intended overland transport to the Confederate armies.[58] Italian prize courts also applied the doctrine in the Abssynian War, 1896, in the case of the *Doelwijk*.[59] Great Britain in the Boer War followed the doctrine laid down in the American and Italian cases asserting the right to capture vessels destined for the Portuguese port of Lorenzo Marques on the Dela-

---

54) The "William", 5 *C. Rob.* 385 ff, (1806).
55) The "Immina", 5 *C. Rob.* 3, 167.
56) The "Vrouw Howina", Scott, *Cases*, pp. 995–997.
57) In the leading case of the "Springbok", 5 *Wallace* 1, (1866).
58) 5 *Wallace* 28, (1864). For a review of all these cases, see Moore, *Digest*, VII, 698–744.
59) Westlake, II, 298.

goa Bay in cases where there was ground for suspecting that they carried contraband.[60]

The questions involved in the doctrine of continuous voyage formed one of the main subjects of discussion at the London Naval Conference. The settlement arrived at by the Conference was a compromise. The doctrine was to be applied to conditional contraband only in the exceptional cases where the enemy country has no seaboard.[61] But in cases of absolute contraband the ultimate destination of the goods, irrespective of whether the carriage of the goods was direct, or would entail transshipment, or a subsequent transport by land, was to be decisive in determining liability to capture.[62]

IV. COMPATIBILITY OF THE DUTCH PROTESTS WITH THE RULES OF INTERNATIONAL LAW

It can not be contended that the action of the belligerents in departing from the contraband lists of the Declaration of London in itself constituted a violation of the principles of international law, for the Declaration itself permits additions by notification. But this does not mean that articles may be shifted from one list to the other at will. The infraction of positive international law begins as soon as articles having no, or only a remote, relation to war, are placed on the conditional contraband list, or when articles susceptible of both peaceful and warlike usage are placed on the list of absolute contraband, or when the distinction between conditional and absolute contraband is abolished.

The importance for neutral trade of limiting the definition of contraband can hardly be over emphasized. Unless there is a limit placed on the articles which may be declared contraband by belligerents, every security which neutral trade has so far enjoyed under the rules of international law will disappear. The rule that free ships

---

60) Moore, *Digest*, VII, 739 ff.
61) Article 36.
62) Article 30.

make free goods and the rule that blockades to be legal must be effectively maintained are important safeguards of neutral rights, but if the right to capture contraband is not properly limited, these two rules become absolutely worthless.[63] In fact one British writer frankly states that the Allied blockade can be justified on the basis of the logical extension of the law of contraband, and that any attempt to justify it on any other basis is futile.[64]

The swollen contraband lists issued by the belligerents during the war left few articles of lawful trade. Many of the articles placed on the contraband lists had only a remote connection with war. And indeed some of the articles found on the list of absolute contraband may be said to have a predominantly peaceful usage.[65] The development of modern warfare, and particularly chemical warfare, undoubtedly justifies a great extension of the contraband lists, but under recognized practice belligerents may not use contraband to carry on a blockade of neutral ports.

The consolidation of conditional and absolute contraband lists is also open to grave implications. The Allied Powers justified this action not on the ground of the nature of the goods but on the ground that the conditions of modern warfare made the distinction useless. So large a part of the enemy population was taking part, directly or indirectly, in the war, that no real distinction could any longer be drawn between the armed forces of the enemy and the civilian population, and the enemy government had taken control of practically all the articles in the list of conditional contraband so that they were all available for government use as soon as they entered Ger-

---

[63] See Moore *International Law and Some Current Illusions*, pp. 48 ff. Nippold in *Development of International Law After the World War*, regards the provisions with respect to contraband in the Declaration of London as a backward step, since they made possible an elastic interpretation of the conception of contraband in the practice of war. Nippold views as the goal of a regulation of contraband the defining and delimitation of its meaning, p. 39.

[64] Sir Erle Richards, *British Yearbook of International Law*, 1922–1923, p. 2.

[65] As, for instance, albumen, diamonds, soap, and starch.

man territory. If the distinction between combatants and non-combatants can no longer be maintained with respect to contraband, what justification is there for demanding that the distinction be maintained with respect to warfare? If the distinction can not be logically maintained in one field, it can not very logically be maintained in another. But if this distinction be not maintained, war will again revert to primitive methods and lapse into savagery.[66]

The Dutch protests against the application of the doctrine of continuous voyage were not well founded. Four of the leading naval powers had already applied the principle to contraband before the World War. Italy had applied as late as 1911 in the Italo-Turkish War.[67] None of these countries made a distinction between its application to absolute and conditional contraband. In view of this it can not well be held that the Declaration of London was declaratory of international law in this respect.

Most of the objections brought against the application of the doctrine of continuous voyage in the World War attach more particularly to "speculative seizure" and search in port, the new presumptions laid down with respect to the hostile destination of conditional contraband and the shifting of the burden of proof from the belligerent captor to the owner of the goods. The presumptions laid down in the Declaration of London were so vague as to afford little enough protection to neutral trade, but the extensions of the presumptions in the last war were so sweeping as to make them practically impossible to rebutt. The prize courts of Great Britain and of Germany, almost without exception, held all ports of belligerent countries to be bases of military supplies. In the case of the *Maria,* decided by the Imperial German

---

66) Borchard, E. M., in *Proceedings* of the American Society of International Law, 1923, pp. 61 ff, severely criticizes the abandonment of conditional contraband: "Nor does the allegation that the entire hostile population is at war, never possible of realization, or that the enemy country controls or rations the food supply, change the legal situation in any degree".

67) Verzijl, *op. cit.*, p. 240. The case of the "Doelwijk".

Prize Court, Belfast and Dublin were held to be military bases.[68] All the protection which conditional contraband had previously enjoyed were swept away. A recent student of the subject justly concludes that the "real problem raised by the doctrine of continuous voyage is whether it can continue to exist without gravely imperiling international maritime law."[69]

The difficulties placed in the way of Dutch commerce by prize court decisions can be gathered from the citation of some cases. In the case of the *Nieuwe Amsterdam* the French Conseil des Prises held that Amsterdam and Rotterdam *"au point de l'application de guerre, etre assimiles a des ports ennemis puisque, en vertu de la convention pour la navigation du Rhin du October, 1868, les marchandises chargees a bord des navires qui y touchent peuvent transiter librement sur le Rhin et pouvant donc entre en territoire ennemi."*[70] This same abuse of the presumptions is found in the German decisions. In the case of the *Batavier V*[71] a cargo of small articles of food supplies, such as eggs, condensed milk, onions, cheese, and herring, were condemned on the ground that London, the port of destination, was the great English base of supplies, and that the articles, subject to rebutting evidence, would have to be considered as destined for the armed forces of the enemy. The shippers appealed in vain to the fact that the captured articles were destined for sale in the open markets of England, and that the British Government was not in the practice of buying these supplies of small articles directly in the open market. This appeal

---

[68] *A. J. I. L.*, X, 927. See Chapter XVII.

[69] Briggs, *op. cit.*, p. 218. Briggs concludes further that there "appears no solution short of a rule of international law forbidding neutrals to trade at all with any belligerent. And such a rule would be contingent upon the development of an international civic sense, or feeling of mutual obligation on the part of the nations to refrain from trading with belligerents—a feeling which does not now exist. Otherwise the doctrine of continuous voyage will in the future play havoc with neutral rights when the belligerents are the big powers, and it will remain quiescent when the belligerents are the smaller nations and the Powers are neutral", p. 219.

[70] *D. O. B.*, I, 130.

[71] *Ibid.*, I, 115; Appeal, *Ibid.*, III, 50 ff.

was rejected on the ground that on account of the great dearth of tonnage the purveyors of the British Government would frequently be compelled to buy these articles in the open market. Only such facts as under ordinary conditions would explicitly exclude the possibility of the use of these commodities for hostile use would be considered as rebutting evidence.

The extension of contraband lists, the enlargement of the classes of presumptions of enemy destination, together with the doctrine of continuous voyage, may under certain conditions make neutral commerce practically impossible. A general and concise agreement with respect to these questions is an obvious need. However, it is doubtful whether even such a general agreement, no matter how fairly made, or how explicitly drawn, would not be abused so long as prize law is administered by national courts.

CHAPTER XV

VISIT AND SEARCH

DURING the World War the belligerents began the practice of taking neutral vessels into port for examination. Previous to this it had always been the practice when neutral vessels were encountered on the high seas to subject them to visit and search on the spot. The United States Government strenuously protested this new practice. It readily admitted "the full right of a belligerent to visit and search on the high seas the vessels of American citizens or other neutral vessels carrying American goods and to detain them when there is sufficient evidence to justify a belief that contraband articles are in their cargoes," but it could not "without protest permit American ships or American cargoes to be taken into British ports and there detained for the purpose of searching generally for evidence of contraband, or upon presumptions created by special municipal enactments which are clearly at variance with international law and practice."[1]

The Dutch Government does not seem to have taken so decided a position. It seems rather to have left open the question of the legality of sending neutral vessels in for search. Some correspondence with respect to this question passed between Germany and the Netherlands in the case of the *Bertha Elizabeth*. This vessel, a Dutch fishing trawler, was seized in the North Sea by a German submarine and after an examination of its papers was sent into Cuxhaven. The captain was ordered to dispose of the cargo of fish. After a few days the vessel was re-

---

[1] *A. J. I. L.*, Sp. Supp. IX, 58–59. Later the United States Government contended that search in port was not necessary to establish the nature and character of a vessel's trade. "The facilities for boarding and inspection of modern ships are in fact greater than in former times". Note to British Government of October 21, 1915, *A. J. I. L.*, Sp. Supp. X, 76.

leased, without anything suspicious having been found.[2]
The owner presented a claim to the Hamburg Prize Court
for loss of time. The Hamburg Prize Court and also the
Upper Prize Court at Berlin declared that it was incom-
petent to take cognizance of the claim since the vessel had
not been "brought in" in the sense of the German prize
regulations, but had only been conducted into Cuxhaven
for examination, and whether a vessel is "brought in" or
not depends upon the *Willensrichtung* of the commander.[3]

The Dutch Government then presented the claim on
behalf of the owner to the German Government. The
Dutch Government asserted that whenever a neutral vessel was conducted into a belligerent port for examination
and if this examination did not produce anything to
justify the confiscation of the vessel or the cargo, the
losses occasioned by this action ought to be reimbursed.[4]
In response the German Government declared that urgent
military interests might make it necessary to examine all
vessels found at a given moment in certain waters in
order to establish their character. Interests of this kind
had made it necessary to examine the *Bertha Elizabeth.*
The German Government refused to recognize a responsibility to indemnify in cases where, as in the present
case, a vessel had been brought into port for examination
because of military reasons.[5]

The British practice of bringing vessels into port for
visit was the cause of a very unusual prize case involving
two Dutch vessels, the *Elve* and the *Bernisse.* While enroute from the French Senegal to Rotterdam with cargoes
of ground nuts consigned to the Netherlands Overseas
Trust these two vessels were stopped by a British cruiser
for visit and search. After an examination of the ships'
papers prize crews were placed on the vessels with orders

---

[2] *D. O. B.*, III, 21–22.
[3] Decision in the lower court, July 3, 1915; in the upper court,
Nov. 25, 1915. Both decisions found in *D. O. B.*, III, 48–49.
[4] *Ibid.*, III, 22.
[5] *Ibid.*, III, 23.

to take them to Kirkwall. In spite of the protests of the Dutch captains the vessels were taken into the German blockade zone, where on May 23, 1917, they were attacked without warning by a German submarine. As a result of the attack the *Elve* was sunk while the *Bernisse*, though struck by a torpedo, was towed into Kirkwall with the help of British warships.[6]

On October 26th the Dutch Government, through its minister at London, presented a claim of damages in behalf of the owners of the vessels. In the opinion of the Dutch Government there was no reason for conducting the ships in question to a British port. The two neutral vessels were loaded with goods consigned to the Netherlands Overseas Trust, in possession of French export licenses, on their way from a French to a Dutch port, and with their papers in perfect order. Under these circumstances the whole responsibility for the damages flowing out of the arrest rested with the British Government, regardless of the cause which occasioned the loss. This responsibility was the more incontestable since the British authorities knew in advance that the arrest would occasion not only a loss of time but would also make it necessary for these vessels to pass through the danger zones, where they would be exposed to attacks from German submarines.[7]

The British Government in response not only denied all liability for the damages but expressed surprise at the action of the Dutch Government in presenting the claims. The British warships were performing a perfectly legitimate act in sending the neutral vessels into port for examination, and had it not been for the unjustifiable attack of the German submarines, the sending in of these vessels would have caused no loss to the owners, except the slight delay caused by such diversion and examination. Moreover, the British Government, at some inconvenience to itself, made arrangements whereby neutral vessels whose

---

[6] *Dutch White Book*, "Opbrenging van de Nederlandsche Schepen 'Elve' en 'Bernisse' ".
[7] *Dutch White Book*, p. 2.

owners were prepared to accept certain reasonable conditions might be examined at certain points outside the danger zone. The vessels in question had made no attempt to obtain these facilities, but had preferred to run such risks as might be incurred in case they should be ordered to proceed to a British port for examination. If the owners of the vessels were still of the opinion that they had a justifiable claim against the British Government, they could present it before the British Prize Court.[8]

The Dutch Government stated in reply that not for a moment had it lost sight of the fact that the two vessels had been the object of an attack by the German naval forces. From the beginning of the submarine warfare the Dutch Government had not ceased its energetic protests against all attacks of this kind, and had the *Elve* and the *Bernisse* been the victims of this kind of an attack while being conducted to a British port in the course of a legal seizure the Dutch Government would not have thought of holding the British Government responsible for the loss caused by the German attack. But this case involved an illegal seizure. The Dutch Government desired most emphatically to contest the British point of view that a belligerent has in every case the right to send in a neutral vessel, and if it does not exercise this right it is an act of pure beneficence on its part. In the opinion of the Dutch Government the right to send in a vessel is inadmissible in cases where—as was the case of the *Elve* and the *Bernisse*—the papers on board the vessel, as well as the circumstances under which the vessel was sailing, clearly proved that the vessel was not engaged in the transport of contraband goods. The Dutch Government further pointed out that British as well as American prize courts in cases of illegal seizure admitted the responsibility of the captor for all losses suffered from any cause whatever, even those due to *force majeure* or accident. For these reasons the Dutch Government would not cease to press the claim of its subject in this case.[9] Both Govern-

---

[8] *Ibid.*, pp. 12–13.
[9] *Dutch White Book*, p. 13.

ments held to their positions.[10] and in the meanwhile the Dutch owners presented their claims of damages before the British prize courts.

The British prize court's decision turned on the interpretation of the Order in Council of February 16, 1917. This Order declared that "a vessel which is encountered at sea on her way to or from a port in any neutral country affording means of access to the enemy territory without calling at a port in British or Allied territory shall, until the contrary is established, be deemed to be carrying goods with an enemy destination, or of enemy origin, and shall be brought in for examination and, if necessary, for adjudication before the Prize Court."[11] The defendants pleaded this Order as justification for their act. The court, however, held that the Order had no application to a vessel which sailed from a British or Allied port, and that as no other reasonable ground for sending in the vessel had been suggested, the Crown was in the position of a wrongdoer and could not excuse itself from returning the vessels to their owners by the plea that it was unable to do so by reason of the wrongful or criminal act of the German submarines.[12]

Search in port is undoubtedly a departure from the rules of international law of the past; and yet it can not be held to be an illogical development of formal prize law. Under modern conditions of ocean transportation and naval warfare the exercise of the right of visit and search on the high seas is frequently impossible. The practice is, however, open to serious criticism, for under it vessels are no longer sent into port on the grounds of the results of the search at sea, but merely on a suspicion which can only be verified by evidence to be searched for in port. Such a practice must necessarily involve frequent hardships and injustices to neutral vessels.

The decision of the German prize court in the case of

---

10) *Ibid.*, p. 14.
11) See Chapter XIII.
12) 1920. Decision given in Naval War College, *International Law Decisions*, 1923, pp. 121 ff. Also in *A. J. I. L.*, XV, 478 ff; Lloyd's *Cases*, IX, 243 ff.; Judicial Committee Appeal, *Ibid.*, IX, 256 ff.

the *Bertha Elizabeth* is obviously on shifty ground, as well as the position of the German Government itself with respect to this case. The distinctions which the prize court made are so vague as to be utterly worthless and if there exists an obligation to indemnify in cases of illegal seizure and detention, this obligation ought to be all the more absolute in cases where a vessel has been brought into port under circumstances which do not even justify sending her in. Interpretations such as these render even the plainest safeguards of international law illusory.

II. Interference with Mail and Official Communication

The British Government early in the war began the practice of seizing mail found on neutral vessels. Dutch vessels in particular became the victim of this practice.[13] The Dutch Government protested this action as a violation of Article 1 of the 11th Hague Convention, in accordance with which all postal correspondence, with the exception of correspondence destined for or proceeding from a blockaded port, is inviolable.[14] The British Government replied to this protest that the seizure of the mail on board the Dutch vessels was not a violation, since the seizure took place within the British territorial waters, where, in the opinion of the British Government, the provisions of the 11th Hague Convention did not apply. Vessels entering British territorial waters are completely subject to British sovereign rights.[15]

The Dutch Government refused to accept this point of view. The 11th Hague Convention guaranteed the in-

---

[13] Twenty-one sacks of mail were taken off the Dutch vessel the "Titan" on Nov. 19, 1915; four from the "Noordam" on Dec. 5, 1915; two hundred from the "Frisia", Dec. 9, 1915; thirty-nine from the "Rotterdam" on Dec. 13, 1915, of which eighteen came from Constantinople, ten from Sophia, and eleven from Berlin, *Recueil*, p. 60.

[14] *Recueil*, pp. 60–61; *Dutch White Book*, "Diplomatieke Bescheiden Betreffende de in Beslagneming door de Britsche Autoriteiten van over zee vervoerde Brievenposten", referred to as *D. W. B.—Mail*.

[15] *W. W. B.—Mail*, p. 1.

violability of postal correspondence at sea, without making an exception of the case where the vessel carrying mail touches at a belligerent port or passes through the territorial waters of a belligerent. The Convention, in order to prevent evasion of its provisions expressly states that in case the ship is detained, the correspondence must be forwarded by the captor with the least possible delay.[16]

The Dutch Government did not contend that parcel post packages shared the inviolability guaranteed postal correspondence by the Hague Convention, and it never protested their seizure on this ground. But it did hold that stocks, coupons, and other valuable papers did come under the term "postal correspondence," and that therefore they could not be seized under any pretext. It protested the action of the British Government in seizing these papers sent out by Dutch owners to different parts of the world and neither forwarding them to their destination nor returning them to the sender.[17]

Although the Dutch Government did not protest the seizure of parcel post on the ground of the inviolability of postal correspondence, it did protest that the British authorities seized many packages which contained only non-contraband articles, or contained only conditional contraband articles without proof of enemy destination.[18] To this the British Government replied that these articles of parcel post were seized on grounds of evidence of enemy origin or destination in pursuance of the Order in Council of March 11, 1915, which provided for the seizure of all goods coming from or destined for enemy territory.[19] The Dutch Government refused to accept the legality of the provisions of this Order.[20]

---

[16] *D. W. B.—Mail*, p. 22; *Recueil*, pp. 61–63.
[17] Note to the British Government, April 11, 1916; *Recueil*, pp. 69–72.
[18] *Recueil*, pp. 75–76; *D. O. B.*, II, 98.
[19] See Chapter XIII.
[20] *Recueil*, pp. 77–78; *D. O. B.*, II, 9.

III. INTERFERENCE WITH OFFICIAL CORRESPONDENCE

On May 31, 1918, the British Government informed the Dutch minister at The Hague that after the expiration of four weeks, mail addressed to a foreign government, or a representative of a foreign government in a third state, would no longer be permitted to pass over Great Britain free from censorship. Proof that the official mail of foreign governments was being used to transmit important personal business communications from and to Germany was the reason given for the action.[21]

In a note of August 7, 1918, protesting this action the Dutch Government challenged the statement of the British Government that it had no obligation to facilitate the interchange of diplomatic correspondence except that passing to and from between the heads of diplomatic missions in London and their respective governments. The Dutch Government contended that a state had the right to an unobstructed communication with its diplomatic representatives not only with respect to the state to which they were accredited but equally with respect to third states over whose territory the letters may be transmitted. Nor could the Dutch Government accept the implication that the Dutch official mail was being misused. The Dutch diplomatic and consular agents in foreign countries were under strict orders not to allow the Dutch official seal to be used for other than Dutch interests.

Beyond acknowledging the receipt of this note the British Government did not reply. The action of the British Government in refusing unhindered passage of official correspondence across its territory was not in conformity with the principle of the inviolability of diplomatic correspondence.[22] If this principle does not apply to official correspondence across a third country, countries with no seaboard would enjoy very little immunity of diplomatic correspondence.

---

[21] *D. O. B.*, V, 35.

[22] Oppenheim, I, par. 405, expressly declares diplomatic correspondence, even through third states, inviolable. For numerous cases in which the U. S. has upheld this principle see Moore, *Digest*, IV, 710 ff.

IV. USE OF NEUTRAL FLAG

The use of a neutral flag by belligerent merchantmen is a practice that places obstacles in the way of the exercise of the right of visit and search by the adversary. Previous to the World War it was generally regarded as not an unfair practice for a belligerent merchant vessel to hoist a neutral flag in order to escape capture. The practice in the World War led to serious consequences because of the unrestricted submarine warfare of the German Government. The Dutch Government protested the use of its flag by British merchantmen. It regarded the use of its flag without its consent as an abuse, which in war has grave consequences, since it throws doubts on the character of neutral vessels properly carrying their own flag. The Dutch Government contended that in the absence of international regulations governing this practice each state is alone competent to establish the conditions under which its flag may be used.[23]

The use of a neutral flag by belligerent merchantmen as a *ruse de guerre* is a practice which has been generally accepted for so many years that the Dutch protest against it in the World War bears little force. The British Government was also in a position to reply that under the express provisions of the British merchant shipping act of 1894 it allowed foreign nations to use the British flag to escape capture.[24] And so long as belligerent warships observe the rules of international law with respect to the duty of visit and search before proceeding to capture or destruction the practice entails no serious consequences for neutral vessels.

---

23) *Dutch North Sea White Book*, p. 10. The U. S. also objected to the general use of its flag by British vessels, but did not declare the practice illegal as did the Netherlands, *A. J. I. L.*, Sp. Supp. IX, 55.
24) *Dutch North Sea White Book*, pp. 9–10; *Recueil*, p. 100.

Chapter XVI

NEUTRAL CONVOY[1]

I. Diplomatic Correspondence with Respect to the Sending of Convoy

VISIT and search was a peculiarly difficult problem during the World War, and one which caused much bitter diplomatic controversy between neutral and belligerent governments. Under the changed conditions of modern commerce, the exercise of belligerent search practically forces neutral commerce from the seas. The tremendously increased mercantile tonnage of the present is being carried by vessels of constantly increasing tonnage. These great vessels can not be quickly searched at sea, but must be taken into belligerent ports for the exercise of the right of search.[2] The long delays which this entails is ruinous to shippers, many of whom found it cheaper to lay up their vessels in port than to expose them to the hazards of belligerent action.

Commerce between Holland and her colonies had all but ceased by the early months of 1918. The requisitioning in the spring of that year by the British and American Governments of the Dutch vessels found in their ports was one of the last of a series of belligerent actions, all instrumental in driving Dutch commerce from the seas. Thus when in the spring of 1918 the Dutch Government was confronted with the urgent need of sending several cargoes of military supplies and government goods to the

---

[1] The diplomatic correspondence with respect to the convoy is found in the *Dutch White Book*, "Diplomatieke Bescheiden Betreffende de Uitzending van een Convooi naar Nederlandsch Indië". Algemeene Landsdrukkerij. The Hague, 1918. Also in *British Parliamentary Papers*, Misc. No. 13 (1918), cd. 9028. Also in *British State Papers*, 1917–1918, III, 533.
[2] The United States Government, however, contended that it was not necessary to take the vessels into port for search. Note to the British Government of October 21, 1915, *A. J. I. L.*, Sp. Supp. X, 76.

Netherlands East Indies, it had to find some solution to this increasingly difficult problem. There were also several government officials, together with their families, waiting to be transported to the colonies. The Minister of Marine decided that the best way out of the difficulty was the sending of a convoy. It was hoped that a convoy would serve the double purpose of rendering the transportation reasonably free from danger and, by reason of freedom from visit and search whether on the high sea or in belligerent harbors, of guaranteeing a direct and unde-layed passage.

In the latter part of April, the Dutch Government informed the Governments of Japan, France, Great Britain, and the United States on the one side, and Germany and Austro-Hungary on the opposing side of the belligerents of its intention to send this convoy. The Dutch note stated that the convoy would be composed of the following: first, the man-of-war, *Hertog Hendrik,* accompanied by a collier; secondly, a Dutch merchant ship transformed into a man-of-war according to the rules of the 7th Hague Convention of 1907, for the transport of military men to the Dutch East Indies, and having military supplies as cargo; and thirdly, a requisitioned Dutch merchant ship, under convoy of the man-of-war, *Hertog Hendrik,* "for the transport of government passengers with their families and having for cargo exclusively goods of the Netherlands Government destined for the Government of the Dutch East Indies.[3]

The note further stated that the loading of all goods and the embarkation of all passengers would be effected under strict governmental supervision, that the passengers and their luggage would be subjected to a strict examination, that no private correspondence would be carried, and that the ships would carry no mail of any kind. With respect to the government goods it was declared that the usual manifest would be produced, with certificates of origin issued by the inspector of import duties.[4]

---

[3] *Dutch White Book,* p. 1.
[4] *Dutch White Book,* Note 1. *British Parl. Papers,* Note 3.

The Japanese Government in acknowledging the note of the Dutch Government merely stated that the proper Japanese marine authorities had been informed of the route of the convoy. The German Government requested to be informed of the names of the vessels that would compose the convoy and the date of departure, in order that this information might be sent to the German naval forces on the high seas. The German Government further insisted that the convoy would not be guaranteed immunity unless it remained outside of the forbidden war zones. The Dutch Government replied that it was the intention to have the convoy remain clear of the forbidden zones.[5]

Great Britain, as the chief naval power, was naturally more concerned with the proposed convoy than any of the other belligerents. Without awaiting the official notification of the proposed convoy, it despatched a note to the Dutch Government stating that it could not recognize the right of convoy and that it would "exercise the belligerents' right of visit and search of merchant vessels should the Netherlands Government carry out their proposal."[6] Not until after six weeks had elapsed and a second note had been sent, did the Dutch Government receive any further word from the British Government with respect to the proposed convoy. A note received on June 3 vigorously reasserted that the right of visit and search would not be abandoned, that Great Britain had never conceded the claim of immunity of ships under neutral convoy and that it could not possibly accede to the Dutch demand.[7]

But later that same day the Minister of Blockade, Lord Robert Cecil, handed the Dutch minister at London a lengthy confidential memorandum of a different tenor. The British Government regretted the discourteous and

---

[5] *Dutch White Book*, p. 1. The Governments of Denmark, Norway, and Spain gave permission for the passage of the convoy through their waters. The Governments of France, the United States, and Austria-Hungary made no reply to the Dutch note.

[6] *Dutch White Book*, p. 3, Note 2; *Brit. Parl. Papers*, Note 2.

[7] *Dutch White Book*, p. 3, Note 4; *Brit. Parl. Papers*, Note 10.

imprudent course of the Netherlands Government, and while still refusing to recognize the right of neutral convoy, it would, nevertheless, because of its friendly disposition toward the Netherlands, go out of its way to save the susceptibilities of the Dutch Government. The British Government was, on the whole, satisfied from the published Dutch reports that the Dutch Government proposed to give the belligerent practically the same guarantees and means of control that they could obtain by exercising the right of search. However, the British Government wanted it clearly understood that it did not in any way abandon the fundamental principle that the "repression of contraband and the enforcement of blockade lie, by international law, with the belligerent alone, and not with the neutral . . .," that the right of visit and search would be waived in this particular case only as an act of courtesy, and that it must not be treated as a precedent for similar concessions in the future.[8]

The memorandum then laid down the conditions on which the proposed convoy would be allowed to make its journey without interference from the British Government. These conditions were substantially the same as those put forward by the Dutch Government, and were as follows:

> "A. A detailed list of all passengers sailing in the convoy, to be furnished to His Majesty's Government, none but Dutch Government officials and their families being allowed to proceed.

> "B. Full particulars of the cargo on board any merchant vessel sailing in the convoy to be supplied in the same way as is now done by the Netherlands Overseas Trust in respect of ships under their control.

> "C. The Netherlands Government to give a formal guarantee that no goods shipped in the convoy are either wholly or in part of enemy origin.

---

[8] *Dutch White Book*, pp. 4–5; *Brit. Parl. Papers*, Note 11.

"D. The ships sailing under the Dutch Naval flag, including the converted liner, not to carry any civilian passengers nor any goods or articles other than war-like stores destined for the colonial authorities or forces, of which the complete lists should be furnished.

"E. No mails, correspondence, private papers, printed matter or parcels to be carried by any ship in the convoy (except official despatches of the Dutch Government).

"F. The convoy not to sail until the above stipulated particulars and undertakings have been furnished and have been found satisfactory by the British authorities."[9]

The Dutch Government, in reply, expressed its pleasure at the mutual agreement as to the mode of carrying out the plans for the convoy and declared that it was fully aware that the British Government did not recognize the right of convoy, but that this point of international law could be left out of account in this case of a very special sort of convoy serving exclusively in the transportation of government passengers and government goods from a mother country to her colonies. A complete list of passengers and full particulars concerning the cargo was being prepared and would be sent to all the foreign legations concerned as soon as possible.[10]

In reply, the British Government again reminded the Dutch Government that the conditions under which the convoy would be allowed to sail included the proviso that the British authorities must be satisfied as to the particular persons and goods to be shipped and in order to accomplish this it was essential that British experts in London should examine in detail the lists and documents furnished. Until these conditions had been fulfilled the convoy would not be allowed to sail.[11]

---

[9] *Dutch White Book*, p. 5, Note 5; *British Parl. Papers*, Note 11, Enclosure 2.
[10] *Dutch White Book*, p. 5, Note 6; *British Parl. Papers*, Note 13.
[11] *Dutch White Book*, p. 5, Note 7.

It had originally been intended to have the convoy sail on June 15, but due to several delays it did not sail until more than two weeks later. The convoy was to be composed of four vessels: the man-of-war, *Hertog Hendrick;* the auxiliary cruiser, the *Tabanan;* the merchant cruiser, the *Noordam;* and the collier, the *Bengkalis.* On June 14th, the manifest for the *Noordam* was ready and the next day this manifest covering the merchandise was sent to the legations concerned. The passenger list, both military and civil, was opened to inspection on the same day.[12] On the 17th a list of the goods on board the *Tabanan* and the *Bengkalis* was sent to the same legations.

The date for the departure of the convoy had in the meantime been set for the 19th, but on the 18th the British Government presented a note at the Dutch Foreign Office again reminding the Dutch Government that the British were waiving the right of visit only on certain conditions, that one of the conditions was that no goods of enemy origin should be carried by the convoy, and that before the convoy would be allowed to proceed they must be satisfied that certain dye-stuffs and chemicals of German origin, which formed part of the convoy, could not be furnished from other than German sources.[13] The British Government pointed out that it was merely maintaining the position taken in a note to the Dutch Government on June 23, 1916. In that note the British Government took the position that as regards

"Netherlands Government goods (to be sent to the East Indian Colonies) of enemy origin, His Majesty's Government are prepared to waive their wish that shipments should be made only through the N. O. T. (Netherlands Overseas Trust) provided that the Netherlands Government will adopt and put in force the same safe-guards as if the goods had been shipped through the agency of the Trust and will ensure that such goods will not be shipped

12) *Ibid.*, p. 5, Note 8.
13) *Dutch White Book*, p. 6, Notes 9 and 10.

in excess of normal quantities and will only be shipped in case they can not be procured elsewhere."[14]

The Dutch Government in a note sent on the following day contended that the dye-stuffs could not be placed in the category of "goods of enemy origin," since in regard to these materials for a long time there had existed a special arrangement between the Netherlands and Great Britain.[15] Under this arrangement concluded by the two Governments by an exchange of notes in June, 1916, dye-stuffs could be imported into the East Indies without restriction, up to a maximum amount equal to the normal pre-war importations. The Dutch Government itself undertook the purchase of the dye-stuffs directly from the German dye manufacturers, the materials were consigned to the governor general of the Dutch East Indies, and the materials were sold directly by the colonial authorities to the Javanese color printers.[16] By this method the re-exportation of the dye-stuffs was made practically impossible. The Dutch Government insisted that the British note of April 28, 1918, had made no change in this arrangement.[17]

On June 19, the British minister at The Hague presented another memorandum to the Dutch Minister for Foreign Affairs to the effect that the convoy must not sail before the British Government had received some more definite information in regard to passengers, cargo, and mails to be sent by the convoy.[18] In forwarding this information,[19] the Dutch Government took occasion to state that the departure of the convoy was not dependent upon the permission of any belligerent government, but that it would, nevertheless, hold up the departure of the

---

14) *Ibid.*, p. 6, Note 11. In April, 1918, the British requested information as to the amount of dye-stuffs procurable from countries other than the Central Powers. The Dutch furnished this information on July 23, *Dutch White Book*, p. 2.
15) *Ibid*, p. 6, Note 12.
16) *Ibid.*, pp. 6–7, Notes 13 and 14.
17) *Dutch White Book*, p. 6, Note 12.
18) *Ibid.*, pp. 8–9, Note 15.
19) *Ibid.*, pp. 8–9, Note 16.

convoy until all differences between the two countries had been cleared up.[20]

All efforts to reach an agreement satisfactory to the British authorities were unavailing. The British Government insisted that the right of visit would not be foregone unless all the German dyes were excluded from the cargo, and an explicit assurance was given to the effect that none of the remaining goods of the cargo were of enemy origin or owed more than twenty-five per cent of their value to enemy labor or materials.[21] In a reply to this note, the Dutch Government gave the required assurance that with the exception of the dye-stuffs none of the merchandise on board ships of the convoy came from countries at war with Great Britain, nor owed more than twenty-five per cent of its value to the labor or materials of such countries. In regard to the dye-stuffs the Dutch Government offered to hold up the distribution of the dye-stuffs after their arrival in India until such time as the difference of opinion with respect to the applicability of the arrangement of 1916 should be cleared up.[22] The British Government refused to accept the proposition of the Dutch Government and insisted upon the unloading of the dye-stuffs as a condition to the waiving of the right of search.[23] The British Government took the position that "the original arrangement by which dyes of German origin were allowed to go to the Netherlands East Indies was contained in Clause 18G of the Netherlands Overseas Trust agreement, which specifically lays down that the passage of goods of enemy origin required for factories, industries, or public services in the Dutch Colonies would be allowed so long as the goods in question were not procurable from other sources." One of the definite conditions accepted by the Dutch Government in regard to the convoy was that no goods shipped would be either wholly or in part of enemy origin.[24]

---

20) *Ibid.*, p. 2.
21) *Ibid.*, p. 9, Note 17.
22) *Dutch White Book*, p. 9, Note 18.
23) *Ibid.*, p. 9, Note 19.
24) *Ibid.*, p. 9, Note 20.

Upon receipt of these notes the Dutch Government decided to remove the dye-stuffs from the cargo before allowing the convoy to depart.[25]

When now the convoy was about ready to depart the British raised new objections. They objected to a passenger on board the *Noordam* whom the British suspected of being a propagandist in the service of Germany. The real objection, however, seems to have been that this man was "fanatically Mohammedan in his opinions" and "likely a dangerous firebrand in the Muzelman question."[26] Another British objection was to certain parts of wireless installation found on board the *Tabanan* which were partly of German origin.[27] The Dutch Government replied that it could not consent to the British demand that this passenger be not allowed to proceed. The passenger in question was an official in the Dutch East Indian Government, and the Dutch Government, from a thorough investigation into the case, was convinced that the British charges against him were unfounded. In regard to the parts of wireless apparatus, the Dutch Government replied that these were destined for the East Indian army and navy, were urgently needed by them and, like most of the Dutch military supplies, were partly of German and partly of Dutch origin.[28]

On July 4th the Dutch Government received word from the British Government that it had withdrawn the last named objection, and immediately upon receipt of this message the convoy sailed.[29]

---

[25] Marine Minister Rambonnett bitterly opposed this concession, and when the Dutch ministry decided to make it in spite of his objections, he handed in his resignation to the Queen June 20. The Queen accepted his resignation on the 27th, but on the 29th named him as her Adjutant Extraordinary. Japikse, *Holland im Weltkrieg*, p. 173.

[26] *Dutch White Book*, p. 10, Notes 21 and 22.

[27] *Dutch White Book*, p. 9, Note 19.

[28] *Ibid.*, p. 10, Note 23.

[29] *Ibid.*, p. 3.

Neutrality of the Netherlands During World War

II. The Rule of International Law with Respect to Neutral Convoys

A. History of Neutral Convoys Before the World War[30]

From the time of the Consolato Del Mare until the middle of the 17th century the belligerent right of visit and search seems to have gone unquestioned. The right of exemption from search of its merchantmen sailing under convoy was first asserted by Sweden in the Anglo-Dutch War of 1653. The Swedish Government announced the decision to send out its merchantmen under convoy by men-of-war whose commanders would be ordered to resist by force any attempt of a belligerent warship to visit and search any of the vessels under its convoy. Because of the short duration of the war no case of attempted search or of forceful resistance to search arose. At the close of this war a treaty was concluded between the Dutch United Provinces and England which contained the provision that the warships of either state would grant protection to all ships belonging to the other state which were making the same voyage or going in the same direction. Shortly after when England and Spain were at war, the Dutch Government claimed exemption from search for her merchantmen, and though this right was not admitted by the British, an English squadron commander did waive the right of search to a convoy under Admiral de Ruyter. In the negotiations for a new treaty between these two powers in 1657 the Dutch again attempted to include a provision for the exemption from visit and search of all vessels under convoy. The argument for the right of convoy, used by the Dutch representative, was very much the same as that used by the Dutch Government in its controversy with the British Government dur-

---

[30] For the history of neutral convoys see: Hugh H. L. Bellot, *Journal of Comparative Legislation*, XVIII, 260 ff; *International Law Situations*, Naval War College, 1911, Chapter II; and Rolin, *Le Droit Moderne de la Guèrre*, Chapitre III. Most treatises on interational law contain a short historical account of the subject. See especially Lawrence, *Principles of International Law*, pp. 669–674.

ing the World War. The Dutch representative argued that the convoy gave a better security to the belligerent government than could be obtained in any other way. However, the new treaty failed of negotiation.[31]

The English apparently suspected the Dutch of seeking to use the right of convoy to win a monopoly of the carrying trade. If the Dutch could resist English search at sea by means of strong convoys, much of the carrying trade might be attracted to the Dutch ships.[32] For a long time Holland, herself, when a belligerent, denied to neutrals exemption from search,[33] but later, in 1781, granted to neutral vessels exemption from search if under convoy of warships of their own flag, upon declaration of the commander of the convoy that the ships carried no contraband and were not engaged in unneutral service.[34] And when Dutch commanders resisted visit and search by English cruisers of merchantmen under their convoy, the Dutch Government supported their action.[35]

The doctrine of convoy found increasing favor with the continental states. In the latter part of the 18th century, the right of neutral convoy was inserted as an agreement in many treaties. In accordance with these treaty agreements the word of the commander of the convoy was to be accepted and the vessels under convoy were to be free from visit and search. Such agreements were found in a number of treaties, as follows: United States and Holland, 1780; Russia and Denmark, 1782; United States and Sweden, 1783; United States and Prussia, 1785; Russia and Two Sicilies, 1787; United States and Morocco, 1787; Russia and Portugal, 1787; United States and Tunis, 1787; United States and France, 1800.[36] The Convention

---

31) Bellot, *op. cit.*, 260 ff.
32) Letter of Secretary Thurloe at The Hague, *Thurloe State Papers*, IV, 203. Quoted by Bellot, *op. cit.*
33) Declaration of war against France, 1689.
34) Lawrence, *Principles of International Law*, p. 670.
35) In 1762 and 1780, Bellot, *op. cit.*
36) Malloy, *Treaties of United States*, pp. 328, 725, 903, 1046, 1091; Lawrence, *op. cit.*, p. 670; Bellot, *op. cit.*; Naval War College, *International Law Situations*, 1911, pp. 39–42.

of Armed Neutrality of 1800 also contained a provision asserting the right of neutral convoy.[37]

Great Britain steadily opposed any claim to exemption of the right of visit and search and continued to exercise this belligerent right. In 1798 a fleet of Swedish merchantmen under convoy resisted visit and were captured by a British squadron in the English Channel. The vessels were all condemned by Lord Stowell in his judgment in the case of *The Maria.* In this great decision Lord Stowell held: first, "That the right of visiting and searching merchant ships upon the high seas, whatever be the ships, whatever be the cargoes, whatever be the destination, is an incontestable right of the lawfully commissioned cruisers of a belligerent nation;" secondly, "That the authority of the sovereign of the neutral country being interposed in any manner of mere force can not legally vary the rights of a lawfully commissioned belligerent cruiser;" and thirdly, "That the penalty for the violent contravention of this right is the confiscation of the property so withheld from visitation and search."[38] In the spring of 1800 a Danish convoy of six merchantmen, under protection of the Danish frigate *Freya,* resisted visit and search by the British and all were seized and captured as prize. However, the vessels were released and compensation was made when the King of Denmark agreed to suspend convoys.[39]

However, in 1801, in a treaty with Russia, Great Britain for the first time since Cromwell and the last time until the Declaration of London recognized the right of exemption from visit and search of neutral vessels under convoy. Under this treaty privateers were wholly excluded from the right to visit and search, and in cases of neutral vessels under convoy of a warship, search could only be made if there were reasons for suspicion after examination of the papers on board the convoying vessel. And even then the search could only be made jointly by

---

[37] Scott, *Armed Neutralities of 1780 and 1800.* Appendix, p. 646.
[38] 1 *C. Rob.,* 340 ff. (1799); Scott, *Cases,* pp. 1003–1008.
[39] Bellot, *op. cit.*

both commanders. This convention, which had also been acceded to by Denmark and Sweden, was annulled in 1807.[40]

During the course of the 19th century no notable controversies arose over the question of convoy. The continental countries generally favored the right of neutral convoy while Great Britain as strenuously opposed it. Nothing was said about convoy in the Declaration of Paris. In several treaties made between the United States and other countries there were provisions as to visit and search. The treaty made with Brazil in 1828 provided that the stipulations in the treaty relative to the visiting and examining of vessels shall apply only to those which sail without convoy; and when said vessel shall be under convoy the verbal declaration of the commander of the convoy, on his word of honor, that the vessels under his protection belong to the nation whose flag he flies, and when they are bound to an enemy's port that they have no contraband on board, shall be sufficient.[41] Treaties with Colombia, 1846, and 1871, contained the same provision.[42] The treaty with Haiti of 1864, which was terminated in 1905, contains a similar but more detailed provision.[43] The United States throughout the 19th century claimed the right of exemption of visitation of her merchantmen when under convoy of her warships, and herself recognized the right during the Civil War.[44] However, the United States recognized the rule only so far as it applied to merchant vessels proceeding under convoy to ports not blockaded.[45]

Japan also recognized the right of neutral convoy and applied it in the Chino-Japanese War, 1894, and again in the Russo-Japanese War in 1904.[46] Russia also recog-

---

[40] C. de Martens, *Recueil*, VII, 263; Lawrence, p. 671; Bellot, *op. cit.*

[41] Malloy, *op. cit.*, I, 140.

[42] Naval War College, *International Law Situations*, 1911, 40.

[43] Malloy, *op. cit.*, I, 928.

[44] Moore, *Digest*, VII, 1204.

[45] *Ibid.*, VII, 493, Letter of Mr. Seward, August 12, 1861, to Dutch Minister.

[46] Naval War College, *op. cit.*, 1905, p. 197.

nized the right in her prize regulations of March 27, 1895.[47] Italy has recognized this right in treaties with Central and South American states and the Italian Mercantile Code has long contained a regulation to this effect.[48] Spain, in the Spanish-American War, 1898, also recognized the right of exemption from visit and search of neutral vessels under convoy of national warships.[49] And even Great Britain, though opposing the doctrine in practice, waived the right of visit and search of neutral vessels under national convoy in the Crimean War.[50]

At the London Naval Conference, 1908-1909, Great Britain finally consented to adopt the position of the continental states. The British and German memoranda alone of all the memoranda submitted to the Conference on the question of convoy maintained that under the existing rules the neutral vessel under convoy of its own flag was not exempt from visitation.[51] The provisions in regard to convoy which were in the end incorporated into the Declaration begin by laying down the principle that "neutral vessels under convoy of their national flag are exempt from search."[52] The commander of a belligerent warship may request of the commander of the convoy a written statement of all information as to the character of the vessels and their cargoes, which could be obtained by visit and search." If the commander of the warship is not satisfied with the statement, he communicates his

---

[47] Moore, *Digest*, VII, 493; Naval War College, *International Law Situations*, 1911, p. 39.

[48] Scott, *Declaration of London*, p. 51; Naval War College, *International Law Situations*, 1911, p. 38.

[49] Naval War College, *International Law Situations*, 1911, pp. 38–40.

[50] Hershey, Note p. 519; *Parl. Blue Book*, Misc. No. 4 (1909), p. 25.

[51] Scott, *Declaration of London*, pp. 49–52.

[52] Article 61: "Neutral vesels under convoy of their national flag are exempt from search. The commander of a convoy gives, in writing, at the request of the commander of a belligerent warship, all information as to the character of the vessels and their cargoes, which could be obtained by visit and search." Scott, p. 127.

suspicions to the commander of the convoy and it then becomes the duty of the commander of the convoy to conduct an investigation, but the latter need not permit the presence of the belligerent at the investigation. The commander of the convoy must furnish the officer of the warship a copy of the report of the results of the investigation. If the commander of the convoy is of the opinion that the facts justify the capture of one or more vessels, he must withdraw his protection from such vessel or vessels, and allow them to be seized by the belligerent cruiser.[53] In case of differences arising between the two commanders the belligerent officer can do no more than make his protest and leave the settlement of the difficulty to diplomacy.[54]

The Dutch convoy to the East Indies is the only case of a neutral convoy during the World War. At the conference of the three Scandinavian powers in February, 1915, the possibility of convoying Scandinavian merchantmen was considered and the principle of the right of neutral convoy espoused, but the policy was never put into actual practice.[55] Germany, in 1915, proposed to the United States that they convoy their merchantships traversing the English seat of maritime war but the United States Government ignored the proposal.[56] However, the action of the United States, in 1917, of placing armed guards on merchantships partakes somewhat of the nature of a convoy.

---

[53] Article 62: "If the commander of a belligerent warship has reason to suspect that the confidence of the commander of the convoy has been abused, he communicates his suspicions to him. In such a case it is for the commander of the convoy alone to conduct an investigation. He must record the result of such investigation in a report, of which a copy is furnished to the officer of the warship. If, in the opinion of the commander of the convoy, the facts thus stated justify the capture of one or more vessels, the protection of the convoy must be withdrawn from such vessels." Scott, p. 127.

[54] See Report of the British Delegates, Scott, *Declaration of London*, p. 250, and "The General Report of the Conference", Naval War College, *International Law Topics*, 1909, pp. 141–143.

[55] *Norse Yellow Book*, p. 22.

[56] *A. J. I. L.*, Sp. Supp. IX, 95, Note of February 16, 1915.

B. RULE OF INTERNATIONAL LAW AT THE TIME OF THE WORLD WAR

The general historical trend as reflected in practice and the increasing number of treaties recognizing the right up to the World War was clearly in the direction of the recognition of the right of neutral convoy. This general trend culminating in Articles 61 and 62 of the Declaration of London has already been reviewed, but owing to the fact that the Declaration of London was never ratified the question was never really settled.

Turning to the publicists one discovers that the continental writers generally uphold the right of neutral convoy while the English and also the early American writers generally deny the right. Among the more recent English and American writers are found many who uphold the right,[57] and some who deny it.[58]

The leading British decision on neutral convoy, *The Maria,* has already been cited. English writers often refer to the dissenting opinion of Justice Story in *The Nereide* as confirming the decision of Lord Stowell in *The Maria.* In this opinion Justice Story said, "The law deems the sailing under convoy as an act per se inconsistent with neutrality, as a premeditated act to oppose, if practicable, the right of search, and therefore attributes to such preliminary act the full effect of resistance."[59] But the decision in *The Nereide* rests upon the right of a neutral to place his goods on board an enemy armed merchantman, and not upon the right of neutral convoy, so that Justice Story's statement could have a bearing only on enemy convoy and with reference to that it was merely *obiter dicta.*

---

[57] Among those who contend that neutral convoy exempts the convoyed vessel from visitation and search are: Halleck, p. 615; Woolsey, pp. 363–364; Westlake, II, 300–301; Lawrence, pp. 669–672; Oppenheim, II, 535–536; Borchard's *Fiore,* pp. 685–686; Hershey, pp. 518–519; Fenwick, pp. 550–551; Hyde, II, 457–458; Bluntschli, par. 824–825; Heffter, par. 170; Masse, II, 271; Rolin, Book 3, Chapter 7; Calvo, I, 206. The Institute of International Law twice declared in favor of the principle, *Annuaire,* 1882, p. 48; 1913, p. 181.

[58] Kent, I, 162; Dana's Wheaton, Note 242; Hall, pp. 723–730; Holland, pp. 2 and 4; Phillimore, par. 338.

[59] 9 *Cranch* 440.

III. Compatibility of the Dutch Convoy with the Rule of International Law

From a "positivist" point of view it can not be said that the right of neutral convoy had been definitely established at the time of the World War, owing to the failure of the ratification of the Declaration of London. And the diplomatic controversy between Holland and Great Britain did not press the legal question involved after the first note. But assuming that Articles 61 and 62 of the Declaration were merely declaratory of international law, an examination of the compatibility of the demanded right of the convoy with the provisions of the Declaration may be both profitable and interesting.

According to the report of the committee which drafted these articles, the underlying principle upon which the articles are based is that the neutral government undertakes the responsibility of protecting those belligerent rights which the belligerent heretofore secured by the exercise of visit and search on the high seas. The neutral, therefore, assumes responsibility for the supervision of the vessels it undertakes to convoy. In the words of the drafting committee, "the neutral government undertakes to afford the belligerents every guaranty that the vessels convoyed shall not take advantage of the protection accorded to them in order to do anything inconsistent with their neutrality, as, for example, to carry contraband, render unneutral service to the belligerent, or attempt to break blockade. There is need, therefore, that a genuine supervision should be exercised from the outset over the vessels which are to be convoyed; and that supervision must be continued throughout the voyage."[60]

The Dutch Government on its own initiative undertook to give all the guarantees laid down in the committee's report,[61] but as might be expected, this did not remove all possibilities of controversy. It only served to

---

[60] Scott, *Declaration of London*, p. 178.
[61] *Dutch White Book*, Note 1, p. 3.

center the controversy about the character of the persons and the goods to be placed on board the convoyed vessels.

It is doubtful whether the status of neutral convoy under international law has been at all changed as a result of the practice of the World War. Great Britain waived the right of search only on the understanding that it was an exceptional concession which could not be treated as a precedent for similar concessions in the future. And it ought to be especially noted that the Dutch convoy was of an unusual character. It was in no sense an ordinary commercial convoy but a government convoy from the metropolitan country to its colonial government in eminent need of military and other governmental material. So that even if the Dutch convoy should set a precedent for the future, it would set a precedent only for a convoy very restricted in its nature.

IV. DUTCH CONVOY AS AN EXAMPLE OF A SOLUTION OF THE PROBLEM OF VISIT AND SEARCH UNDER MODERN CONDITIONS

Though some modification of the right of search is imperative, it is very questionable whether the method employed in the Dutch convoy is a solution of this perplexing problem as one American writer asserts that it is.[62] In the first place, it is to be noted that the Dutch convoy was not in any sense a commercial or merchant convoy. It was a government convoy and concerned a governmental relationship between a mother country and its colonial government in pressing need of supplies. It may well be doubted whether the British would have waived the right of search had it been an ordinary merchant convoy. Nor is this all. There are very sharp practical limitations on the use of convoy. The expense of supervision on the part of the neutral government, the different rates of speed of the vessels in the convoy, the cost of the convoy to the government which furnishes the

---

[62] Graham, *A. J. I. L.*, XVII, 704.

convoying warships –all make the convoy impracticable because of its expense. In fact, the difficulty with which the Dutch Government could get bunker coal prevented it from even considering an ordinary merchant convoy.[63] The extra costs to the Dutch Government entailed in the sending of the convoy was 1,907,500 florins, or about $763,000.[64]

The effect of the World War on neutral convoy can best be summed up in the words of Dr. J. H. W. Verzyl, a leading Dutch authority on international law:

"It would appear as if convoy in the old meaning of the term in prize-law, has lapsed into permanent disuse. With the uncertainty of the comprehension of the contraband concept in relation to the standards of enemy destination, and the complexity of modern commerce the remedy will often appear worse than the disorder—the neutral state can not assume responsibility for the innocent character of the cargo, and conceivably differences in understanding might arise between the commander of the convoy and the commander of the belligerent warship, which might lead to dangerous conflicts."[65]

---

63) See statement of Dutch Minister of Marine in First Chamber of the States–General, *British Parl. Papers*, Note 4.

64) *Dutch White Book*, p. 11.

65) *Het Prijsrecht tegenover Neutralen in den Wereldoorlog van 1914*, p. 316. Hyde, II, 628, suggests governmental guarantees of cargoes. It is doubtful whether neutral governments will assume this responsibility.

CHAPTER XVII

DESTRUCTION OF NEUTRAL PRIZES

I. Diplomatic Controversy over the Legality of the Destruction of Neutral Prizes

ON MARCH 25, 1915, while in the English Channel enroute from Valence to London with a cargo of oranges, a Dutch vessel, the *Medea*, was stopped for search by a German submarine.[1] After the inspection of the ship's papers the crew of the *Medea* was given ten minutes to quit the vessel. The vessel was then torpedoed.

This destruction of the vessel was vigorously protested by the Dutch Government in a note of April 3, 1915. It held that the destruction of a neutral prize was an act which international law had never sanctioned. Even under the provisions of the Declaration of London, the destruction of the *Medea* was illegal, since the conditions under which Article 49 of the Declaration permits destruction of a neutral prize were not present. To fall under the exception of Article 49 the neutral vessel must be subject to confiscation, and Article 50 imposes on the capturing vessel the duty to place in security, before destruction, all persons found on board the captured vessel. The capturing vessel in the case of the *Medea* had not acted in conformity with these rules. The crew of the *Medea* had not been placed in security. Those placed on board the lifeboats were abandoned by the submarine shortly after the destruction of the vessel, and they were not in safety until picked up several hours later by a boat accidentally encountered on the high seas. Moreover,

---

[1] The "Medea" was the second Dutch prize to be sunk. The "Maria", enroute from Portland, Oregon, to Belfast with a cargo of wheat was sunk September 21, 1914, by the German cruiser "Karlruhe". However, the destruction of the "Maria" was not made the subject of a formal diplomatic protest. *D. O. B.*, I, 18–19.

neither the nature of the cargo, the character of its consignees, nor the place of destination rendered the vessel subject to confiscation. Oranges could not reasonably be considered useful for feeding an army, since they contained so little nutritive substance. Nothing in the ship's papers indicated that either the armed forces, the British Government, or their agents were the consignees of the cargo; to the contrary, the publicity of the consignees supported the supposition that the oranges were simply destined for the consumption of the civil population. The fact that the place of destination was London did not offer a valid ground for capture. So vast a commercial center could not be considered as a "base of operations," a "base of supplies," or a "fortified place," and hence the goods could not be considered contraband.[2]

The German Government replied in a note of April 22, 1915, that the protest was utterly unfounded. The lifeboats in which the crews embarked were kept in tow until an English vessel was sighted, and were released only with the accord of the Dutch captain. The German Government insisted that oranges were useful for the alimentation of an army. From a number of reports which it had received it was apparent that the British Government was provisioning its troops with fruits and fruit juice. Evidence of this had also been found in the trenches captured from the British. As to the enemy destination of the oranges the German Government contended that for the commander of a warship international law recognized a presumption of enemy destination when it was consigned to a fortified place of the enemy, which at the same time served as a base of operations and supplies for its armed forces. This presumption exists no matter who the consignees may be.[3] Independent of the fact that it was necessary to consider London as a fortified place, since its maritime approaches were defended by mines and batteries, and that it has to the south of it a

2) *D. O. B.*, II, 19–20; *Recueil*, pp. 106–110.
3) Declaration of London, Article 34.

string of forts, and to the north a string of redoubts and batteries, London with its docks, arsenals, and warehouses formed an important base of operations and supplies. It was notorious that the British Government continually utilized the economic forces of this center of commerce to an extraordinary degree in the interests of the army.

In answering the principal charge of the Dutch Government—that is, the illegality of the destruction of the *Medea*—the German Government insisted that the Declaration of London did form a part of international law. All the delegates at the London Conference, including those of the Netherlands, agreed in the Preliminary Provision that "the rules contained in the following chapters correspond in substance with the generally recognized principles of international law." Moreover, the recent history of maritime war counts many cases of the destruction of neutral prizes, so that under certain conditions the legality of this method of warfare ought to be considered as established by international practice. Article 113 of the German prize regulations sanctioned this practice in the terms used by the Declaration of London. At the beginning of the war the German prize regulations were communicated to all neutral states without one protesting against the provisions of this Article. The conditions demanded by the Declaration of London as the exception under which neutral prizes may be destroyed, were clearly present in the case of the *Medea*. The German submarine found itself in proximity to the English coast, such that any attempt to bring the prize into a German port would lead to certain loss of the warship and would force the complete abandonment of the purpose of its operations.

The German Government refused to accept the contention that the Declaration of London permitted the destruction of a neutral prize only in case the commander of the warship has obtained convincing proof that the vessel and its cargo are really subject to confiscation. Such a requirement would impose on the commander an impossible task. In most cases, and particularly in cases involving conditional contraband, absolute proof that the vessel and its cargo are subject to confiscation is obtained only in the course of the proceedings before the prize court, but under the conditions in which the right of visit and search is usually exercised the commander must be satisfied with a more or less summary examination. The commander of the vessel acts at his own risk, with the understanding that his action may bring on his government an obligation to pay damages if proof overthrowing the presumption is brought before the prize court.

The incident in its entirety would be submitted for examination before the German prize court in conformity with Article 51 of the Declaration of London and of the first and second articles of the German prize court regulations. In these proceedings the proprietors of the vessel and of the cargo would have an opportunity, in conformity with Article 34, clause 3, of the Declaration of London, to prove that the cargo was of pacific destination, and that in consequence it had not the character of contraband. If this was not proved, the German Government, following the principles of international law, would not be obliged to pay damages; if, on the contrary, this was proved, the German Government would recognize the obligation to pay a just indemnity to the proprietors of the vessel and of the cargo.[4]

The divergence in the opinions of the two Governments in regard to the legality of the destruction of a neutral prize and the facts in the case of the *Medea*, was not removed in the further exchange of notes that took place. In the note of June 4, 1915, the Dutch Government repelled the contention that the provisions in the Declaration of London with regard to the destruction of neutral prizes were declaratory of established international law. The provisions of the Declaration as an indivisible whole constituted a work of compromise and mutual concessions. Thus not all of the provisions taken separately could be considered as a part of recognized and estab-

---

[4] *D. O. B.*, I, 20–21; *Recueil*, pp. 110–114.

lished international law. With regard to the question of the destruction of neutral prizes the Dutch Government wished especially to remind the German Government that in their different memoranda presented at the Conference of London, Spain, Great Britain, Japan, and the Netherlands formally pronounced themselves against the legality of such destruction. Moreover, it was the expectation of the signatory powers that the application of the Declaration would be placed under the control of the International prize court, which, however, had not been established. The Dutch Government was not unaware of the fact that there had been several cases of the destruction of neutral prizes in recent wars, but it was unable to concede that the repetition of illegal acts could clothe an international practice with the character of legality.

There was as much lack of agreement on the facts of the case as on the principles of law. The Dutch Government still maintained that the commander of the submarine had not satisfied that provision of the Declaration of London which requires a belligerent vessel to place the crew in a place of safety before destroying a neutral prize. According to the statements of the officers of the *Medea* the lifeboats had been abandoned by the submarine when, except for a small fishing vessel, there was not a single vessel on the horizon.[5] In a later note of July 31, 1915, the German Government attempted to show that the disagreement in regard to the facts was more apparent than real. The submarine officials had misunderstood a cry from the lifeboats as a request to have the boats released. That the Dutch crew in the lifeboats did not see the vessels sighted by the submarine officers was only natural, because of their lower elevation.[6]

In its next note, that of October 16, 1915, the Dutch Government shifted its attack. While still maintaining that the destruction of neutral prizes under any conditions was illegal it now asserted that, even assuming

---

[5] *D. O. B.*, I, 21–22; *Recueil*, pp. 114–116.
[6] *D. O. B.*, I, 22; *Recueil*, pp. 116–117.

that the destruction of neutral prizes is permissable under the conditions stated in the Declaration of London, the submarine could not avail itself of this right because it could not satisfy the provision of the Declaration which requires that before the vessel is destroyed all persons on board must be placed in safety. In the case of the *Medea* the persons on board had not been placed in security, but had been abandoned in small boats in the open sea far from succor. The commander of the submarine had not taken the trouble to notify the fishing vessel of the presence of the long-boats in distress. The Dutch Government could explain this line of conduct only on the supposition that the submarine commander was guided by anxiety for the safety of his own vessel and that in view of this safety it was impossible for him to tow the long-boats any farther or to notify the fishing vessel. But if a submarine is obliged in view of its own safety, to abandon the crew of a torpedoed vessel in a rough sea, far from assistance, it is evident that a submarine is not able to fulfill the conditions of Article 50 of the Declaration of London.[7]

The German Prize Court at Hamburg declared the destruction of the *Medea* illegal.[8] The Imperial Commissioner, however, took the case on appeal to the Superior Prize Court at Berlin which found the capture and destruction legal.[9] The Dutch Government in a note of September 19, 1916, protested the decision of the upper prize court as contrary to international law and proposed the submission to international arbitration of the question of whether, according to the provisions of the Declaration of London, the *Medea* was subject to confiscation.[10]

The proposal to submit the difference to arbitration was rejected by the German Government in its note of November, 1916. The German Government was not in principle opposed to submitting the decisions of its prize

---

7) *D. O. B.*, I, 23; *Recueil*, pp. 117–118.
8) *D. O. B.*, I, 102 ff gives the decision of the court.
9) *Ibid.*, II, 55 ff gives the decision of the higher court.
10) *D. O. B.*, III, 11–12.

courts to an international jurisdiction for review, but under the existing circumstances it could not alone consent to submit the decisions of its prize courts to such a review. Such consent would place Germany in an unfavorable position over against its enemies in maritime warfare. If it submitted the decision in the case of the *Medea* to an international tribunal, it would have to accede to all similar demands of other neutral powers in similar cases.[11]

During the course of the war some twelve Dutch vessels were destroyed, all by German forces, for carrying contraband of war.[12] Damages were awarded only in two cases, and then on the ground that the vessels were not subject to confiscation. In no case was there a loss of life.[13]

II. The Rule of International Law with Respect to the Destruction of Neutral Prizes

The question of the legality of the destruction of neutral prizes first arose in the Russo-Japanese War. During this war Russia sank seven neutral prizes—four British, two German, and one Danish. The British Government protested the destruction of the British vessels

---

[11] *D. O. B.*, III, 12–13.

[12] The following Dutch prizes were destroyed: the "Maria", Sept. 2, 1914, with a cargo of wheat, *D. O. B.*, I, 19, prize decision, *Ibid.*, I, 124 ff and III, 47 ff; the "Medea", *Ibid.*, I, 102 ff and II, 55 ff; the "Elzina Helena", April 3, 1914, with a cargo of lumber, *Ibid.*, II, 11 ff, prize decision, *Ibid.*, IV, 147; the "Berkelstroom", April 24, 1916, with a cargo of food supplies, *Ibid.*, II, 11 and III, 13, prize decision, *Ibid.*, IV, 148 and V, 60; the "Dina", July 5, 1916, Francois, p. 144; the "Zeeland", Aug. 1, 1916, with a cargo of coal, *Ibid.*, p. 144; the "Zeearend", Sept. 1, 1916, with a cargo of food supplies, *Ibid*, 144; the tankship "Antwerpen", Sept. 12, 1916, prize decision, *D. O. B.*, IV, 154; the "Blommersdijk", Oct. 28, 1916, with a cargo of grain and food supplies, *Ibid.*, III, 13, prize decision, *Ibid.*, IV, 164, appeal to higher court, *Ibid.*, V, 84; the "Dolfin", Nov. 16, 1916, Francois, p. 144; the "Kediri", Nov. 30, 1916, with a cargo of copper and food supplies, *Ibid.*, 144; and the "Atlas", Jan. 10, 1918, with a cargo of ground nuts, *Ibid*, p. 144.

[13] The "Berkelstroom", *D. O. B.*, IV, 148 and V, 60; and the "Blommersdijk", *Ibid.*, IV, 164 and V, 84.

and demanded an indemnity which Russia refused to pay. The Russian prize court awarded damages in the cases of the two German vessels, the Danish vessel, and one of the British vessels. The damages were awarded, however, not because the destruction of neutral prizes was illegal but because these vessels were not liable to condemnation. Russia also refused to submit the question to the Hague Arbitration Court.[14]

The question was brought before the Second Hague Peace Conference where the British, Japanese, and American delegates favored the absolute prohibition of the destruction of neutral prizes. This position was opposed by the Russian and German delegates who, however, were willing to waive their objections if belligerents should be permitted to bring their prizes into neutral ports. The optional character of Article 23 of the 13th Hague Convention, which allows neutrals to receive neutral prizes in their ports, was unsatisfactory to Germany and Russia.[15]

At the London Naval Conference, where the question was again raised, Great Britain, the Netherlands, Austria-Hungary, and Japan desired the absolute prohibition; while Germany, Russia, the United States, Spain, and France wished to make exceptions in certain cases.[16] In the articles finally agreed upon, destruction of a neutral prize is allowed as an exception if taking her into port "would involve danger to the safety of the warship or to the success of the operations in which she is engaged." Before the prize is destroyed "all persons on board must be placed in safety, and all the ship's papers and other documents which the interested parties consider relevant for the purpose of deciding on the validity of the capture must be taken on board the warship." The first question to be decided by the prize court is whether the exceptional necessity prescribed really existed. If the captor fails to establish this exceptional necessity he must compensate

---

[14] Lawrence, *op. cit.*, p. 485; Francois, *op. cit.*, p. 126.
[15] *Acts*, III, 899–902; 1048–1102.
[16] *Proceedings*, pp. 99 ff.

the parties interested and the question of whether the capture itself was valid may not be opened. If the act of destruction has been held to be invalid, the captor must pay compensation to the parties interested in place of the restitution to which they would have been entitled. Likewise, "if neutral goods liable to condemnation have been destroyed with the vessel, the owner of such goods is entitled to compensation."[17]

The earliest English prize court decision dealing strictly with the question of the destruction of neutral prizes is the decision of Dr. Lushington in the case of the *Leucade*, handed down in 1855.[18]   References are frequently made to the decisions of Lord Stowell in the cases of the *Zee Star*,[19] the *Felicity*,[20] and the *Actaeon*.[21] None of these cases, however, involved the question of neutral vessels carrying contraband.   In the *Zee Star* Lord Stowell granted demurrage to the claimants for the delay in restoring a ship and cargo which was restored by consent.   The cases of the last two vessels involved the destruction of enemy ships sailing under a British license,[22] and so whatever was said in these cases regarding the destruction of neutral prizes is merely dicta. However, in the *Leucade* Lushington definitely held that "if the captor doubt his power to bring a neutral vessel to adjudication, it is his duty under ordinary circumstances to release her."

The Supreme Prize Court of Russia in the case of the *Knight Commander*, the leading case of the seven neutral prizes destroyed by Russia in the Russo-Japanese War, maintained that the provisions of the Russian prize regulations which permit destruction under certain conditions, were not contrary to the principles of international law.   The Court stated that "the absolute prohibition of

---

[17] Articles 49–53.
[18] Roscoe's *Prize Cases*, pp. 473 ff.   See Scott, *Cases*, note p. 783.
[19] 4 *C. Rob.* 71 (1815).
[20] 2 *Dobson* 385.
[21] 2 *Dobson* 48; Scott, *Cases*, pp. 780 ff.
[22] Moore, *Digest*, VII, 522.

the destruction of a neutral vessel, notwithstanding the most glaring violations of neutrality on her part, would be equivalent to completely depriving the belligerent under certain circumstances of the right to prevent the delivery to the enemy even of ammunition, which can not be right, while as compared with the other belligerent, more favorably circumstanced, it would be quite unjust."[23]

The prize regulations of many countries permitted the destruction of neutral prizes in exceptional cases. Thus destruction was permitted before the World War by the codes of Russia,[24] the United States,[25] France,[26] Japan,[27] Germany,[28] and Turkey.[29] The United States Naval Code of 1900 was revoked in 1904, but the official report which recommended the revocation of this code, stated that Article 50 was in harmony with general usage and that hence the withdrawal of this Article made no change in the United States' position in this respect.[30]

The conditions under which destruction was permitted by these codes varied somewhat, but the conditions most generally included were: lack of a prize crew; imminent danger of recapture; danger to the warship or risk to the success of the undertaking in which she is at the time engaged.

The Institute of International Law in its meeting in 1881 and 1882 rejected the legality of the destruction of neutral prize.[31] The "Manual of the Law of Maritime Law" adopted by the meeting at Oxford in 1913 recognized the legality of the destruction of enemy prizes, but was silent on the destruction of neutral prizes. The

---

23) Hurst and Bray, *Russian and Japanese Prize Cases*, I, 54, 357; Scott, *Cases*, pp. 793 ff.
24) Russian Regulations, 1895, Art. 22; Instructions, 1900, sec. 40.
25) United States Naval War Code, 1900–1904, Articles 46, 47, 50.
26) Instructions for Navy, 1870; Moore, *Digest*, VII, 526.
27) Regulations, 1904, Articles 91 and 92.
28) German Prize Rules, 1909, Articles 113, 116, 118, and 129.
29) Regulations, 1912, Chapter 1, Articles 4 and 5.
30) Naval War College, *op. cit.*, 1903, p. 89.
31) Incorrectly reported in *Annuaire*, VI, 114, but corrected in *Annuaire*, IX, 228. Francois, p. 125.

writers of international law were about equally divided on the question.[32]

The Dutch Government was the only neutral government during the World War which took an absolute stand against the legality of the destruction of neutral prizes. The three Scandinavian Governments took the position that the provisions of the Declaration of London were declaratory of international law. Diplomatic protests were made in several cases, not against the legality of the destruction of neutral prize, however, but against the failure to place the crew in safety.[33] The Spanish Government took a similar position, protesting only, though energetically, the manner in which some Spanish vessels had been destroyed by German submarines.[34]

The position of the United States was different from

---

[32] Destruction of neutral prizes was held illegal by these English writers: Baty, *Britain and Sea Law*, p. 2; Hall, pp. 762–763; Twiss, *Ann.*, I. D. I., VI, 154; Bentwick, mentioned by Garner, *A. J. I. L.*, X, 20; Phillimore, III, 541; Bowles, *Sea Law and Sea Power*, pp. 152, 192. English writers regarding it as legal were: Holland, Moore, *Digest*, VII, 521; Walker, p. 152; Barclay, *Problems*, p. 102; Westlake, II, 309–312; and since 1909, Lawrence, pp. 485–486; Higgins in edition of Hall, 1916, p. 810; and Oppenheim, II, 547–549. American writers denying the right were: Woolsey, p. 350; Kent, I, 111–112; Taylor, p. 573; and Wheaton, Atlay, par. 359; while Dana, *Dana's Wheaton*, Note 186; Moore, *Digest*, VII, par. 1212; Wilson, 8th ed., p. 342; and Hershey, pp. 520–522 upheld it. Most continental writers acknowledged the right of destruction: Fiore, par. 1878; Bluntschli, par. 672; de Martens, III, 298; Gessner, par. 672; Bulmerincq, *Annuaire, I. D. I.*, VI, 154; *Rev. de Droit Int.*, XI, 647; Rivier, II, 350; Perels, *Annuaire I. D. I.*, IV, 154; Schramm, p. 338; Wehberg, p. 296; and Fauchille, *Rev. Gen.*, 1918, p. 77, all acknowledged this right as does Calvo, II, par. 3019, the South American. Continental writers denying the right are: Kleen, II, 350; de Boek, par. 281; and Nys, III, 706. Among Dutch writers den Beer Portugael, *Annuaire I. D. I.*, VI, 154, vigorously rejected the right to destroy a neutral prize under any conditions, whereas other writers like Struycken in *Van Onzen Tijd*, mentioned by Francois, p. 125; Ferguson, II, par. 243; de Louter, II, 476; and Verzijl, *Het Prijsrecht*, p. 329, regard it as doubtful or recognize it under very restricted conditions.

[33] *Norwegian Yellow Book*, Cases of the "Svein Jarl" and "Belbridge", Press Communication of the Norwegian Minister for Foreign Affairs, October, 1916, on the position of the Norwegian Government cited by Francois, pp. 146–147.

[34] Press Communication of Spanish Government in *Le Temps*, December 30, 1916, quoted by Francois, p. 148.

that of the other neutrals by reason of the Prussian-American Treaties of 1785, 1799, and 1828. Article 13 of the treaty of 1785, the provisions of which were continued in the treaties of 1799 and 1828, provides that contraband belonging to the subjects or citizens of either party can not be confiscated by the other in any case, but may only be detained or used in consideration of payment of the full value of the same. "But in the case supposed of a vessel stopped for articles of contraband, if the master of the vessel stopped will deliver the goods supposed to be of contraband nature, he shall be permitted to do it, and the vessel shall not in that case be carried into any port, nor further detained, but shall be allowed to proceed on her voyage."[35]

The United States Government protested the destruction of the *William P. Frye* as a violation of these treaties, and demanded that the German Government make full reparation for the destruction of the vessel.[36] The German Government recognized the binding effect of the stipulations of the treaties but insisted upon leaving to the prize court the determination of the amount of indemnity that should be paid.[37] The United States Government contended that its claim was for an "indemnity for a violation of a treaty in distinction from an indemnity in accordance with the treaty, and therefore is a matter for adjustment by direct diplomatic discussion between the two Governments and in is in no way dependent upon the action of a German Prize Court."[38]

The United States Government did not contend that the destruction of neutral prize was contrary to the rules of international law. In fact, the German Government stated in its note of July 30, 1915, that "It is not disputed by the American Government that, according to general principles of international law, a belligerent is authorized in sinking neutral vessels under almost any conditions

35) Malloy, *Treaties*, II, 1481–1491.
36) *A. J. I. L.*, Sp. Supp. IX, 180–186.
37) *Ibid.*, Sp. Supp. IX, 181–182.
38) *Ibid.*, Sp. Supp. IX, 188.

for carrying contraband,"[39] and this statement was left uncontradicted by the American Government in its succeeding notes. The American Government in its note of April 28, 1915, stated that it did not regard the Declaration of London as in force, and therefore refused to discuss its meaning and effect.[40] However, in the Russo-Japanese War, Secretary of State Hay, in a telegram to Ambassador Choate in London, stated with respect to the sinking of the *Knight Commander* that the American Government could not say that "in case of imperative necessity" a prize might not be lawfully destroyed by a belligerent captor.[41] In the new Naval Instructions of 1917 the United States permitted destruction of neutral prize, though under sharply restricted conditions.[42]

III. Compatibility of the Position of the Dutch Government with Respect to the Rules of International Law

The foregoing review of the prize court decisions, prize regulations, the opinions of writers, and the practice of belligerents in recent wars does not support the absolute position taken by the Netherlands Government on the illegality of the destruction of neutral prizes.[43] But assuming that there is a right to destroy in exceptional cases and subject to certain conditions, two important questions still remain open: namely, (1) may the right to destroy "as an exception" be reduced to a rule as it was by Germany during the World War, and (2) was the German practice in conformity with this rule?

That "exceptional necessity" may recur repeatedly in the same naval campaign is obvious. The phrase "as an exception" can not be held to mean that destruction of

---

39) *Ibid.*, Sp. Supp. IX, 189.
40) *Ibid.*, Sp. Supp. IX, 183.
41) Moore, *Digest*, VII, 520.
42) Article 96.
43) Hyde, writing after the war, holds "that the destruction of neutral prizes under the exceptional circumstances specified, is far from wrongful". II, 503.

neutral prize is to take place unfrequently. Destruction of neutral prize may take place just as frequently as the exceptional cases arise. Destruction is not rendered illegal by the fact that it is engaged in as a regular practice. Unfortunately, however, under modern conditions of naval warfare there is an inevitable extension of the class of exceptions. Modern warships carry crews only sufficiently large enough to efficiently execute their manoeuvers, so that rarely can they afford to detach a crew to man a prize. There will also be a strong temptation to destroy a prize rather than to interrupt operations by taking a prize into port. For belligerents having few ports into which prizes may be brought the temptation to destroy is almost irresistible. This is especially true when submarines are used. The German submarine commanders found their own ports blockaded and the ports of neutrals closed to their prizes, and they were forced, therefore, to choose between freeing their prizes or destroying them. The submarine seldom carries a sufficiently large crew to be able to spare a prize crew Moreover, because of its power to navigate unseen beneath the surface of the water, the submarine can get to places inaccessible to other warships, and from which it is impossible to bring back a prize.[44]

But can the submarine exercise the right of destruction in conformity with the requirements of international law to provide for the safety of all on board before destruction? The German Government never denied that the obligation to provide for the safety of the prize crew was paramount to the right to destroy; but there was much difference of opinion between the German and neutral governments as to what constituted safety and whether safety had actually been provided in particular cases.[45] The deck of a submarine or small boats in an

---

[44] See Garner, *A. J. I. L.*, X, 40; Francois, *op. cit.*, pp. 23–26.

[45] See above. See *A. J. I. L.*, Sp. Supp. X, 169–170 for the case of the American bark 'Normandie" which, although carrying contraband, "was permitted to continue her voyage unhindered, as it was impossible to guarantee that the crew would be surely rescued in the small boats if the ship were sunk".

open sea afford only a precarious safety. Yet these are objections only to the manner in which the destruction takes place in particular instances, and does not militate against the right of submarines to destroy neutral prizes. If the right to destroy neutral prizes is conceded, submarines as well as other warships may avail themselves of this right. It is not impossible for submarines to provide for the safety of the persons on board as required by international law.

The use of submarines as a weapon of naval warfare was one of the leading questions discussed at the Washington Conference. Great Britain took the position that their use ought to be completely prohibited. This position was most vigorously opposed by France. The outcome of the discussions was a treaty signed on February 6, 1922, by the British Empire, the United States, France, Italy, and Japan. The first article of this treaty contains a formal statement of the customary rules regulating visit and search and the destruction of merchantmen, and declares that belligerent submarines are not under any circumstances exempt from these universal rules. Article 2 invites all other civilized powers to express their assent to this statement of established law. The third Article declares that "any person in the service of any power" violating any of these rules shall be liable to trial and punishment " as if for an act of piracy." He may be brought to trial before the civil or military authorities of any power within whose jurisdiction he may happen to be, and superior orders will be no defence. In Article 4 the five signatory powers recognize the practical impossibility of using submarines as commerce destroyers without violating the requirements of law for the protection of the lives of neutrals and non-combatants. They accordingly agree between themselves never to use submarines as commerce destroyers and invite other powers to join in this agreement.[46]

---

46) "A Treaty between the United States of America, the British Empire, France, Italy, and Japan, in Relation to the Use of Submarines and Noxious Gases in Warfare", *International Conciliation*, No. 72, pp. 29 ff.

Destruction of Neutral Prizes

The provisions of this treaty are so sweeping as to be of doubtful value. Not every destruction of neutral prizes by the German submarines was accompanied by ruthlessness. Nor does the treaty take into account the possible development of the submarine which may render it as capable of observing the requirements of international law as any other warship. The experience of the war has shown the submarine to be a powerful weapon and it is too much to expect that it will not be used in a general war, whenever either or both groups of belligerents are reduced to extremity. Such sweeping prohibitions as are embodied in the treaty only invite further illegalities. The provision taking away "superior orders" as a defence is also a measure of doubtful wisdom.[47]

As a result of the practice in the World War the provisions of the Declaration of London with respect to the destruction of neutral prizes may be said to have become an established part of international law. Experience in the World War indicates, however, that the requirements as to the safety which must be provided for the survivors of the crews ought to be given greater definiteness. Much would also be gained if greater precision were given to the conditions under which a captor may destroy a prize.[48]

---

[47] See article on "Submarine at the Washington Conference" in *British Yearbook of International Law*, 1923–1924, pp. 150 ff, and "Changing Methods of Submarine Warfare", by Admiral Sims, in *Current History*, September, 1923.

[48] K. Jansma, an Amsterdam lawyer, suggested the following plan before the Grotius Society as a means of avoiding the destruction of neutral merchantmen: In case the captor can not take the prize to one of his own ports, he should send it to some one of its own ports, there to await the decision of the prize court; if condemned, the vessel will be delivered to the captor at the conclusion of the war; and all belligerents to bind themselves to observe this undertaking and not to recapture a vessel which was thusly captured and sent home. Grotius *Transactions*, IV, 3 ff. The objections to this scheme are obvious. See the suggestion of the British Admiral Sir Graham Bower in *Contemporary Review*, CVII. See Chapter on "Armed Merchantmen".

CHAPTER XVIII

ANGARY—THE REQUISITIONING OF DUTCH VESSELS

I. British Requisitioning of Vessels Chiefly British Owned But Flying the Dutch Flag

THE CONTROVERSY between the Dutch and Allied Governments over the requisitioning of Dutch vessels began in May, 1917, when the British Government decided to requisition a number of vessels which were really British owned, or chiefly British owned, but were sailing under foreign neutral flags. About fourteen Dutch vessels were affected by this decision. The British Government gave as the reason for this action that it could not allow ships which were valuable British property to run the risk of being hopelessly sunk at sight, owing to the fact that, being under neutral flags, they were precluded from being armed.[1]

The Dutch Government protested this measure as an act of despoliation menacing the vital interests of the entire nation. The Dutch people themselves were in dire need of this tonnage. The act constituted a direct blow at the rights of the Netherlanders, for the Dutch Government had the exclusive right of requisitioning vessels flying the Dutch flag. The only case in which international law recognizes the right of a belligerent to requisition a neutral vessel is that of absolute necessity. Relative tonnage needs certainly formed no exception to this principle. Every state in time of war as well as in time of peace, is obliged to respect the flag of a friendly state. By virtue of this principle it is the flag alone, and not

---

[1] *British White Book*, "Correspondence between the British and Netherlands governments regarding the requisitioning by the British Government of British owned, or chiefly British owned, ships under neutral flags. May 1917–February, 1918". *British Parl. Papers*, Misc. No. 5 1918), Note of May 22, 1917, *D. O. B.*, IV, 60.

the ownership of the vessel, which determines the status of the vessel under international law. These vessels belonged in their entirety to Dutch corporations no matter what be the nationality of the stockholders of these corporations.[2]

In reply the British Government stated that it did not base its right to requisition these ships upon their being actually British owned or controlled, but upon the general right of a belligerent to requisition neutral property in case of necessity. The necessity in the present case was clear. Germany was attempting to cut off all British overseas communications by means of submarines. The British Government had received information that the German authorities intended to seize or sink all British owned vessels, regardless of the flag which they fly. The British Government hoped that the requisitioning of these vessels would cause no inconvenience to the Dutch Government. Negotiations were proceeding with the object of ensuring the Netherlands a sufficient supply of tonnage for the requirements of the country.[3]

It was not until January 24, 1918, some six months after the above British note, that the Dutch Government replied. It strongly repelled the idea implied in the British note that the failure of the Dutch Government to secure a cessation of the illegal destruction of Dutch vessels by the German submarines stopped it from protesting a much lesser injury to the Dutch shipping from the side of the British. The fact that the submarine warfare had a much more disastrous effect upon Dutch commerce than the requisition in question was not a juridical argument to justify the requisition. The only justification the British might advance in defence of their action would

---

2) *D. O. B.*, IV, 61. The Dutch Government put forth the same arguments in its protest against the British Prize Court decision in the case of the "Hamborn". The vessel belonged to a Dutch corporation, of which the majority stockholders were Germans. It was condemned as good prize under the terms of the Order in Council of October 20, 1915, declaring Article 57 of the Declaration of London as no longer in force in the British prize courts. *Recueil*, pp. 34 ff. Decision found in Lloyd's *Cases*, VII, 54 ff and 67.

3) *D. O. B.*, IV, 61; *British White Book*, Note 5.

be a belligerent's right under international law to requisition vessels flying the flag of a neutral. If this was a right, then the conditions permitting the resort to such an action must be shown to be present. This right, formerly recognized in the case where a military operation necessitated the immediate use of neutral vessels lying in a belligerent port, has been strongly contested up to the present. Article 456 of the Queen's Regulations of 1899 demonstrated that the British Government did not admit this right with respect to British vessels in case of a war in which Great Britain would be neutral.[4]

In a brief note of March 15, 1918, the British Government stated that it did not think that Article 456 of the Queen's Regulations of 1899 had any bearing on the case, since it dealt solely with coercing a neutral ship to take part in hostile action. The British Government pointed to the right to requisition railway rolling stock as a more proper analogy. This right, it pointed out, is recognized in the Hague Land War Convention.[5]

In a final note of April 15, 1918, the Dutch Government pointed out that if the British Government based its right to requisition the Dutch vessels upon an analogy to the right to requisition railway rolling stock as recognized in Article 19 of the 5th Hague Convention, then it ought logically to recognize the right of neutral governments to requisition an equal amount of British tonnage, for this same article also states that "a Neutral may likewise in case of necessity retain and utilize to an equal extent material coming from the territory of the belligerent Power."[6]

II. Requisition of Dutch Vessels by the Associated Governments

Concerning the events leading to the requisitioning by the United States and British Governments of the Dutch

---

4) *D. O. B.*, IV, 62–63; *British White Book*, Note 4.
5) *D. O. B.*, IV, 63; *British White Book*, Note 5.
6) *D. O. B.*, IV, 63.

vessels in their ports, the respective governments issued conflicting reports. With the entrance of the United States into the War the position of the Dutch Government became more difficult than ever. The United States had the unquestionable right to prohibit exports. In so far as it was yet possible for the Netherlands Government to obtain supplies from the remaining neutral countries or from the Dutch colonies, there was still the practical difficulty of obtaining the bunker coal necessary for transporting the supplies to Holland.

Since the negotiations between the Netherlands Government and the individual Associated Governments produced no results, a general conference between representatives of the Dutch Government and representatives of the United States, British, French, and Italian Governments was agreed upon to meet in London in the latter part of 1917. According to the statement of the Dutch Government the purpose of the negotiations was not to arrive at a definitive agreement, since none of the representatives had the power to conclude such an agreement, but to arrive at some sort of proposal which could later be made the basis for a definitive agreement.[7]

The discussion proceeded upon two fundamental propositions, namely, (1) that the Associated Governments should facilitate the importations into Holland of foodstuffs and other commodities required to maintain her economic life, and (2) that Holland should restore her merchant marine to a normal condition of activity. A tentative agreement was finally drawn up and forwarded to the Dutch Government for consideration.[8]

While the negotiations were still going on, the Dutch Government declared itself ready in anticipation of a definitive agreement to grant the owners of the vessels detained in American ports permission to charter their

---

[7] The Dutch side of the case is presented in three reports of the Minister for Foreign Affairs to the Dutch States–General on March 11, March 30, and June 21, 1918. All three reports are separately printed as *White Books*.

[8] Report of the Dutch Minister for Foreign Affairs, March 11, 1918.

vessels for a voyage outside of the submarine danger zones. However, these vessels were not to be used to transport goods to Holland, since the Associated Governments refused to release the vessels for this use until a definitive agreement had been signed. Because of the fear of experiencing difficulties with the crews it was at the last minute decided to put the vessels into service without the coöperation of the owners. The maximum duration of the voyages was to be ninety days, with the understanding that for a limited number of vessels the duration of the voyage would be so limited that there would be sufficient tonnage at the disposal of the Netherlands at the moment the definitive agreement should come into existence. Six vessels lying in American ports already laden were excepted from this arrangement. Two of these, the *Samarinda,* laden with rice, and the *Zeelandia,* laden with a mixed cargo, would be permitted to start out on their voyage for Holland if in exchange for them two ships would leave Holland for the United States.[9]

The Dutch Government did not feel that it could proceed to a definitive agreement without first having consulted the German Government. In the first place the restrictions which the agreement with the Associated Governments would place on Dutch exports might lead Germany to refuse the export to Holland of such indispensable goods as coal. In the second place, Germany could, by closing the free channel in the North Sea, make it impossible to carry out the agreement. The German Government naturally refused to coöperate in increasing the tonnage in overseas countries.

The further statement by the Dutch Government of the cause of the breakdown of the negotiations between itself and the Associated Powers is so important that it is quoted verbatim:

"This attitude made it impossible for the Dutch Government to make any proposals to the Associated Governments. On dividing the tonnage, . . .

9) *Ibid.*

it has taken into account that the whole fleet would be in navigation. Moreover, it was not to be thought of that the Associated Governments would allow a ship to leave for the Netherlands, even with German guaranty of the free return, if the Dutch fleet had to be laid up, and even with an Associated Government guaranty of uninterrupted return would not be able to sail. Negotiations with the German Government give good grounds for the expectation that it will be found prepared to revise its attitude so far that it will not oppose the sailing of a vessel lying in Holland provided this is in exchange for a vessel lying on the other side of the ocean.

"If it is in the meantime taken into consideration that there is here 298,476 tons suitable for the trans-Atlantic service apart from some passenger vessels which do not come into consideration for this service which will undoubtedly have to serve for Dutch supplies, then it is clear that even with this revised attitude, an agreement would only be able to be reached which could not by any means be called satisfactory. Owing to the system of exchange the tonnage for Holland, especially for supplies from the Indies, would be extremely limited. Germany stated that she had to object upon principle against any limitation of export which was obviously directed against that country and on the basis of such a limitation imposed would not be willing to enter into negotiations with regard to a new economic arrangement. The Government has found in this a reason to give notice that it would not make any proposal in this matter which contained a compulsory limitation of Dutch exports."[10]

The difficulties in the way of speedily reaching a definitive agreement led the Dutch Government to ask the Associated Governments to furnish it with 100,000 tons of foodstuffs in anticipation of such an agreement. This the United States Government, in agreement with

---

[10] Report of Dutch Minister for Foreign Affairs, March 11, 1918.

the other Associated Governments, consented to do if the Dutch Government, from its side, would act as if the definitive agreement already existed. The Dutch Government was at the time, March 11, 1918, investigating whether it could proceed to such a transaction.[11]

The point of view of the United States Government is given in a statement by the President on the day the Dutch vessels were taken over. It charged the Dutch Government with a failure to put even the *modus vivendi* into operation. One difficulty after another had been raised by the Dutch to postpone the chartering of the Dutch vessels in accordance with the temporary agreement. The Dutch Government never formally expressed the reasons for these delays but the United States Government was well aware that it was due to the Dutch shipowners, who feared lest their ships should be destroyed by German submarines. Definite action on the proposed general agreement had been awaited for even a longer time. Events "had served to demonstrate conclusively that we have been attempting to negotiate where the essential basis for an agreement, namely, the meeting of free wills, is absent. Even were an agreement concluded, there is lacking that power of independent action which alone can assure performance."[12]

For these reasons the United States Government concluded that there was no alternative left but to proceed to the requisitioning of the vessels, an exercise of its indisputable sovereign rights. Dutch colonial trade would be facilitated and ships might at once be sent from Holland to obtain foodstuffs. These ships would be freely bunkered and would be immune from detention. Ample compensation would be paid to the Dutch owners of the requisitioned ships, and suitable provision would be made to meet the possibility of ships being lost through enemy action.[13]

The British account of the events leading up to the

---

11) *Ibid.*

12) "Official United States Bulletin", No. 263, p. 1; Naval War College, *op. cit.*, 1918, pp. 167 ff.

13) *Ibid*, 1918, pp. 167 ff.

requisitioning, as stated in a note to the Dutch Government on March 21. 1918, adds some details not mentioned in the President's statement. Circumstances had been so altered since the original agreement had been proposed that its conditions were no longer adequate. The condition that the Dutch shipping was not to be used in the danger zone was no longer acceptable, and might at any time have been made still less so by the extension of the submarine zone by Germany. The Associated Governments therefore proposed that in its altered form the agreement should come into force immediately. To this the Dutch Government would not consent except on condition that the shipping would not be employed for the carriage of war material. This condition was wholly unacceptable to the Associated Governments, with the result that they decided upon immediate requisitioning.[14]

The Dutch Government denied the correctness of the recital of facts as given by the President's statement and the British note. The agreement drawn up in London was not an arrangement which had only to be ratified, but only a basis on which the Netherlands Government would make proposals. The *modus vivendi* had to a large extent been put into effect. The slowness in doing so was in large degree attributable to the fact that for some unknown reason the telegrams exchanged between the shipowners and their agents in the United States either did not pass or only passed with great delay. On March 7th the Associated Governments suddenly made a new proposal, in which they insisted that the Dutch ships should be used also in the danger zone. This condition was unacceptable from the point of view of neutrality unless it were guaranteed that the ships would not be employed for the transport either of troops or of war supplies and that they would not be armed. These restrictions on the free use of the Dutch ships the Associated Governments could not accept.[15]

---

[14] *British Parl. Papers*, Misc. No. 11, 1918.
[15] Statement of the Minister for Foreign Affairs to the States-General, March 30, 1918. Also note to British Government, March 31, 1918, *British Parl. Papers*, Misc. No. 11, 1918.

Complaint was also made by the Dutch Government of innumerable difficulties Dutch ships had experienced in American and Allied ports. These ships, after having entered overseas ports in good faith, were indefinitely detained under different pretexts,—pretexts frequently not connected with the ship or its cargo. New regulations, not existing at the moment the ships had entered port, had been imposed by the United States Government. Dutch ships were being detained at Halifax, Gibraltar, Free Town, and Singapore. These ships had complied with all the formalities required, some even had sailed to those ports in execution of specific agreements with the British Government or for service of the Belgian Relief Commission. Much as its people needed supplies, the Dutch Government was loath to send any of its ships overseas to Allied ports to secure them, for in the light of past experiences it had no guarantee that these ships would not also for some reason or other be detained, and then owing to the necessities of war, seized like the others.[16]

The Dutch Government regarded the act just as offensive from the juridical point of view. It could in no way agree to the interpretation given by the Associated Governments to the right of angary, "an ancient rule unearthed for the occasion and adapted to entirely new conditions in order to excuse seizure en masse by a belligerent of the merchant fleet of a neutral country."[17] The so-called right of angary had lapsed into desuetude. It had been exercised only once in the 19th century, notably by Germany in 1870, and then only in a very restricted form. It applied only to cases of immediate military necessity, and not to a general economic need as in the present form. The modern law of both war and neutrality demand that the war be carried on by the belligerents with their own means and not with those of neutrals.[18]

---

16) *Ibid.*
17) *Ibid.*
18 Note to British Government, March 31, 1918, *Dutch White Book* of June 21, 1918.

The appeal to the right of sovereignty as a justification for the act was equally rejected by the Dutch Government. The sovereign right of a state to seize the property of others for the public good, in case of immediate need, regardless of the nationality of the owner, did not extend to ocean going vessels flying a foreign flag. Such an extension would be in violation of the respect due the flag and would hardly accord with the sacred principle of the freedom of the seas. If the freedom of access to belligerent ports is accorded in good faith to neutral ships, their freedom to leave is a natural consequence. The seizure of these ships by surprise is a violation of this good faith. No appeal to the general right of sovereignty could justify such an act of violence, especially not when applied to ships detained for many months against their will in ports which they had entered in good faith.[19]

The United States Government relied upon the right of angary to justify its action in requisitioning the Dutch vessels in its ports.[20] The British Government in its first notes also relied on this ancient rule, but it later based its right of requisitioning upon the general right of sovereignty over all persons and property within its jurisdiction. All property within the jurisdiction of a sovereign state, irrespective of ownership, and neutral property within belligerent jurisdiction is, in the absence of special treaty stipulations, as liable to requisition in case of emergency as the property of subjects. Vessels calling at a foreign port are, in the absence of special treaty provisions, fully subject to the local jurisdiction.[21]

III. History of the Law of Angary

The modern right of angary is derived from the Roman law, where almost without exception it was ap-

---

[19] Note to British Government, May 31, 1918, *Dutch White Book* of June 21, 1918.
[20] President's statement, *op. cit.* Note to Dutch Government, April 14, 1918, *Dutch White Book* of June 21, 1918.
[21] Note of April 22, 1918, *Ibid.*

plied to requisitions of land transport only. In the Middle Ages the term was used frequently to denote requisitions of vehicles and horses for purposes of military transport. During this time the term was not generally applied to requisitions of ships, although the English sovereigns from the 12th century on seem frequently to have requisitioned all shipping, no matter where found and irrespective of nationality.[22]

With the 17th century writers on international law, discussion of the nature and legality of requisitioning foreign shipping begins. One school of authorities, to which such writers as Grotius and Puffendorf belonged, held it to rest on the law of necessity, but that necessity must be very great to justify it. A second school considered the right to rest merely on the general right of sovereignty.[23] Many treaties were concluded in the 17th century with respect to the requisition of neutral shipping in time of war. Such a treaty was made in 1654 between Cromwell and the United Provinces. This treaty admitted the right in cases of "extraordinary necessity" and upon just compensation. Most of the treaties of this century absolutely prohibited such requisitions.[24]

The right of angary, still frequently exercised in the first half of the 18th century, began to fall into disuse towards its close, although revived by Napoleon in 1798 when he requisitioned a large number of neutral vessels for the transport of the Egyptian expedition. The reason for this decline was probably the large number of treaties made providing for the immunity of neutral ships.[25] Very few cases of the exercise of the right occurred in the

---

[22] This brief history of the law of angary is largely based on "Angary", by C. L. Bullock, *British Yearbook of International Law*, 1922–1923, 99 ff; and Harley, "The Law of Angary", *A. J. I. L.*, XIII, 265 ff.

[23] Bullock, *op. cit.*, pp. 99 ff.

[24] *Ibid.*, pp. 99 ff. Harley, *op. cit.*, makes the statement that all seventeenth century treaties specifically denied the right.

[25] Bullock, *op. cit.* Such treaties were made between Austria and Spain, 1725; Russia and Denmark, 1782; the United States and Prussia, 1785; France and Russia, 1787; and the United States and the Netherlands, 1783–1795.

19th century. The only case very generally known is the sinking of the seven English colliers in the Seine by the Germans in 1870 to prevent the passage of French gunboats.

The World War witnessed a revival of the law of angary. Besides the requisitioning of the Dutch vessels by the United States and Great Britain, several other countries resorted to the right. Italy in November, 1915, while still a neutral, requisitioned thirty-four German vessels in her ports. The German Government made no protest.[26] In February, 1916, the Portuguese Government requisitioned seventy-two German vessels in her territorial waters. The German Government protested this action as a breach of the treaty of 1908 between Germany and Portugal. This treaty admitted the right of requisitioning ships, subject, however, to advance payment of compensation, the amount to be determined by the bi-lateral decision of the two governments.[27] In May, 1917, the Brazilian Government requisitioned forty-two German vessels in Brazilian waters.[28] In August, 1918, the Spanish Government took over about ninety German vessels in its ports, but this was probably more in the nature of reprisal than of angary.[29]

A large number of treaties with respect to angary were made in the 19th century. The German exercise of the right in 1870 in particular caused a whole new group of such treaties to be made. Modern treaties involving the right of angary have been classified by a recent writer as follows:

Seventeenth century......3 unfavorable
Eighteenth century ....7 unfavorable, 1 favorable.
Nineteenth century
    Before 1870................1 unfavorable, 12 favorable.
    After 1870................1 unfavorable, 16 favorable.
Twentieth century..........1 unfavorable, 2 favorable.
By favorable is meant if adequate indemnity is paid.[30]

---

26) Garner, *op. cit.*, I, 175 ff.
27) *Revue General de Droit International Publique*, XXIII, 268 ff.
28) Garner, *op. cit.*, I, 175.
29) Harley, *op. cit.*
30) Harley, *op. cit.*

The tenor of these treaties is a general recognition of the right of angary. The purpose of these treaties is to place the neutral in a better position as regards indemnity or compensation.[31]

The opinion of the writers on international law has been classified by the same writer as follows:

Favorable ....Before 1870.... 8, After 1870....42[32]
Favorable with
qualifications ....Before 1870.... 1, After 1870.... 7
Unfavorable ....Before 1870....16, After 1870....16

IV. COMPATIBILITY OF THE REQUISITIONING WITH THE RULES OF INTERNATIONAL LAW

Stripped of all accretions the right of angary is seen to be merely a special application of the right of sovereignty. A state has an unquestionable control over all property within its jurisdiction. Whenever there is an urgent necessity for the use of such property for the public good the State has an undoubted right to requisition it, subject to just compensation.

This still leaves open the question under what circumstances the right of requisition may be exercised. The American and British need was hardly greater or more immediate than the Dutch need for it. The Dutch Government may not have been on very good ground when it insisted that the right to requisition could only be exercised in case of immediate, strategic military neces-

---

31) *Ibid.*, p. 273.
32) *Ibid*, p. 275. Among the leading modern authorities recognizing the right are: Hall, 4th ed., pp. 690, 765; Calvo, (1885), I, 47; Bonfils, (7th ed.), secs. 328 and 1490; Geffcken, (1889), pp. 771–778; Halleck, (4th ed.), I, 519 n; De Louter, (1910), II, 412; Oppenheim, (1912), II, 446; Perels, (1903), II, 221–222; Wehberg, (1915), p. 510; Phillimore, (3rd ed.), III, 46–49; Westlake, (2nd ed.), II, 154; Albrecht, *Requisitionem von Neutralen Privateigentum*, (1912), p. 61; Basdevant, *Rev. Gen. de Droit Int. Publique*, XXIX, 268–279; den Beer Portugael, *Het Int. Maritiem Recht*, (1888), p. 413. The two leading opponents of the right are Kleen, *Lois et Usages de la Neutralité*, II, 68; and Lawrence, pp. 627–628. The Institute of International Law in 1898 declared the right suppressed, *Annuaire*, XVII, 57, 255, 284.

sity. But on the other hand not every public necessity can warrant such drastic interference with foreign property under its jurisdiction.

There is still the further question of whether foreign vessels temporarily in port stand on the same footing in this respect as does foreign property on land. Any conception of the freedom of the seas must provide for a certain freedom in the use of ports for trading and other purposes, and also a certain immunity from local control. The public necessity required to justify the requisition of foreign vessels in port must be far greater than for the requisition of foreign property on land.

Many of the Dutch grievances pertained not so much to the final act of requisitioning itself as to the treatment of Dutch vessels in overseas ports before the requisition. The imposition of new port regulations, stricter than those which obtained when the vessel entered, the detention of vessels for months against the will of the owners, rendered the final action particularly irritating.

If the right of requisitioning foreign vessels in ports rests upon the general right of sovereignty, as the British Government finally contended, then the right can not belong to belligerents alone but may be exercised by neutrals as well. Yet when Chile and Argentina requested that they be allowed to requisition idle tonnage in their ports in order to meet their tonnage needs the British Government raised the objection that such procedure would be in violation of the conventional rules relative to the transfer of flag.[33] The revival of the right of angary in the World War points to the need of a definite re-statement of the law. The conditions under which the right may be exercised and the rights of the owner in particular need elaboration.

---

[33] Garner, J. W., *Recent Developments in International Law,* pp. 801–802.

PART IV

CONCLUSION

CHAPTER XIX

GENERAL ESTIMATE OF THE DUTCH NEUTRALITY REGULATIONS

THE PROVISIONS of the Netherlands Neutrality Proclamation, as was observed at the beginning of this study, closely followed the provisions of the 5th and 13th Hague Conventions. In fact, many of the articles of the Proclamation were almost exact reproductions of corresponding articles in the Hague conventions. The provisions of the Hague conventions and of the Dutch Proclamation were found to be inadequate and it was found necessary to issue additional regulations such as the decrees regulating internment, airflight, and radio. The Hague conventions with respect to neutrality were regarded by the Dutch Government as of binding force, even though they had not been ratified by all the belligerent powers.

The Dutch neutrality regulations fully measured up to the standard of neutrality set by the Hague conventions, and in many cases even went beyond that high standard, as for instance in the cases of the prohibition of the use of wireless installations on Dutch territory, the prohibition of the admission of belligerent warships and armed merchantmen to Dutch waters, and the very careful surveillance of all ships in its waters. Some of these measures, however, partook more of the nature of military measures imposed in the interest of national security than of the nature of neutrality measures. Only on this ground can the differential character of some of these measures be explained. This does not mean that one regulation for the domestic jurisdiction and another for the colonial jurisdiction is incompatible with the rules of international law. Propinquity to the seat of war, it is true, creates no additional neutral duties, and as long as the neutral power's regulations are not above the minimum set by international law, such a differential

311

is, of course, clearly illegal. But with respect to regulations which exceed this standard a differential regulation may be justified.

The frequency with which the Government resorted to an absolute prohibition is a significant feature of the Dutch regulations. This is a sound policy both from the point of view of the neutral power itself and of the belligerent powers as well. An absolute prohibition is more easily administered and much less likely to lead to violation of neutral territory. To the belligerent it gives the best guarantee that the neutral is not administering a complex regulation to the advantage of its enemy. Both parties of belligerents, for example, had practically an absolute guarantee that Dutch ports were not being used as a base of operations or supplies for the navy of the other. For a country geographically situated near the seat of the war as was Holland this was a matter of great importance. In thus placing the enforcement of its neutral duties in its ports and territorial waters on the same basis as the enforcement of its neutral duties on land, the Dutch Government took a long stride forward in the direction of an absolute neutrality.

In general the Netherlands adhered quite strictly to its traditional continental point of view. This accounts in part for the more frequent diplomatic controversies with Great Britain than with Germany or any of the other Allied Powers.

The Dutch regulations with respect to certain phases of neutral duties have a singular importance, for they indicate a veritable evolution of neutral duties along the lines of fundamental principles previously established. Out of the diplomatic controversies with respect to the Dutch regulations concerning aircraft, radio, internment of both property and belligerent persons coming upon neutral territory, the treatment of prisoners of war interned on its territory by mutual agreement of the belligerents, the non-admission of warships, belligerent armed merchantmen, and prizes, have come clearer conceptions of neutral duties under modern conditions of warfare. These will form a useful working basis for the recodification of the laws of neutrality on land which is so urgently needed.

In its refusal to surrender the former Emperor of Germany for trial and punishment, the adherence of the Dutch Government to its honored traditional view of the right of asylum prevented an act for which international society had not yet laid the necessary legal basis nor provided the proper judicial machinery.

The experiences of the Netherlands clearly indicate that if very many of the belligerent practices with respect to interference with neutral trade are to stand as precedents for the future, neutral rights will have suffered a tremendous diminution. The extent of neutral rights in any war depends quite largely on the strength of neutral opinion. It is significant that during the last year and a half of the World War there remained not even a single first class power to champion the rights of neutrals. Whether or not this will be the usual condition of future wars can not, of course, be predicted and does not matter. A power can not well as a neutral protest a practice which it itself is engaged in as a belligerent. The World War may be said to have set a new high mark with respect to belligerent rights, as it also in many respects set a high mark for neutral duties.

This extreme interference with neutral rights was frequently justified by the belligerents on the ground of retaliation against the enemy. Retaliatory measures once begun have no end. But this was not all. The belligerents in the World War even pressed the novel doctrine that neutrals were delinquent under international law if they failed to enforce a proper respect for their rights at sea. Stated differently, it was contended that if a neutral failed to secure respect for its rights from one belligerent, it was estopped from protesting an injury to its rights from the other belligerent.[1]

In the controversy with the Netherlands Government over the non-admission of belligerent armed merchantmen into Dutch ports the British Government went even further than this. The Dutch Government had stated that having laid down the rule of non-admission at the beginning of the war it could not change this rule during the war to the advantage of either belligerent. The British Government, however, considered that the Dutch Government "could rightly neglect this rule on the ground that the Second Hague Peace Conference only laid it down on the supposition that the belligerents would conduct war in a manner conforming to international law."[2]

The Dutch Government replied to this in the only manner possible. Neither the Hague conventions nor general international law contained a single rule, nor the records of the Second Hague Peace Conference even an indication "that a neutral state should alter its neutrality regulations in favor of one belligerent party because of the manner in which his opponent conducts war. As for the fact that warlike operations of one belligerent injure the rights and interests of the neutral, it is for the neutral to decide without any intervention on the part of the other belligerent, whether the fact gives him cause to depart from the state of neutrality which he has announced."[3] To this position the Netherlands Government adhered throughout all the diplomatic controversies over its neutral rights and duties.

As a seaboard neutral adjacent to a powerful continental belligerent the Netherlands was faced with many

---

[1] See Chapter XIII for the British and German contentions along this line. The British Government note of April 24, 1916, *A. J. I. L.*, Sp. Supp. X, 137, and the German Government note of February 16, 1915, *A. J. I. L.*, Sp. Supp. IX, 90 ff, put forth a similar contention to the U. S. Government. See comment on this by Q. Wright in the *Minnesota Law Review*, V, 525–528.

[2] Note of September 8, 1917, *Dutch White Book—Armed Merchantmen*, pp. 14–15.

[3] Note of October 22, 1917, *Dutch White Book—Armed Merchantmen*, p. 15.

difficult problems in relation to its import and export trade. To meet these problems the Dutch Government had to set up a far reaching control over the economic life of the country. By a system of non-export guarantees, Holland secured the consent of the belligerents in control of the seas to import necessary contraband goods from overseas. The administrative machinery set up to exercise the required control over the goods imported will be of great value to neutrals similarly situated in future wars. It is certain that maritime belligerents in the future will insist upon such guaranties as were given by the Netherlands Overseas Trust. A problem the neutral government will here face is whether it shall itself exercise these powers, or permit a non-governmental organization such as the Trust to exercise this unusual control over the economic life of the country. The advantages of having a non-governmental body furnishing the non-export guarantees under the present conception of neutrality are apparent. Whether the Dutch East Indian convoy, which in fact partook less of the nature of a neutral convoy in the old sense than a certification of goods before shipping, will serve as an equally valuable precedent is doubtful.

The whole question of the future of neutrality is uncertain. It will depend in large part on the development of the League of Nations. The basic idea underlying the League of Nations is that neutrality is no longer permissible. If the provisions of Article 16 of the Covenant become a working principle, neutrality to a large extent will have to disappear. The whole history of neutrality, and in particular the history of neutrality during the World War, would indicate that neutrality is a makeshift, based upon expediency, made possible only by the unstable condition of international society.

There are those who believe that the older system, with its sharp differentiation between neutrals and belligerents, not only offers fewer hazards but that it would also tend to localize conflicts, if only the fundamental principles of neutrality were more rigorously applied in

practice.[4]   Under the present conception a non-belliger-
ent remains a true neutral if his nationals stimulate both
belligerent parties with equitable assiduity. Such a conception of neutrality would involve a marked increase in
the responsibilities which the neutral government would
have to assume over the acts of its subjects. Even assuming that a neutral government can exercise this restraint, may not such neutrality be fully as burdensome
as the limited belligerency which might be necessary in
fulfillment of a member state's obligations under the provisions of the Covenant of the League of Nations? Furthermore, such neutrality is completely divorced from
justice. Such neutrality may easily work to the advantage of the aggressor in international conflicts.

Much has been written since the war of the desira-
bility of codifying the law of war and neutrality. However desirable codification may ultimately be, the time
for it has hardly arrived. Any codification made in the
shadow of the World War would be a grave error, since
the great powers would attempt to write into the proposed code a justification of their own recent belligerent
conduct. Not until the late war has sufficiently receded
into the background will the interests of neutrals receive
any considerate attention at an international conference,
since at the close of the war there remained not a single
first rate power to espouse the cause of neutrals.

The uncertainty of the future development of neutrality is another reason for delaying codification of this
field of international law. Recent developments in Europe, such as the Locarno Pact, must necessarily modify
the old conception of neutrality, or they can never be
made successful, for the whole arrangement may be
vitiated if the "aggressor" state can, as heretofore, draw

---

[4] "Non-participation, on the other hand, which contemplates the
actual withholding of the resources of neutral territory from every
belligerent without discrimination possesses a power in that regard
which has never been exerted, and yet which may enable essentially
neutral states to maintain international peace". Hyde, II, 795.

munitions and supplies from non-member neutrals. The League of Nations and the other procedural experiments being made under it, ought to be given time to develop before codification is resorted to. The post-war development of the procedural side of international law is one of the most hopeful signs of the times.

DECLARATION OF NEUTRALITY OF THE NETHER-LANDS IN THE EUROPEAN WAR.   AUGUST 5, 1914.[1]

The ministers of foreign affairs, justice, marine, war, and the colonies, authorized to that effect by Her Majesty the Queen, make known to all whom it may concern that the Netherlands Government will observe strict neutrality in the war which has broken out between Great Britain and Germany and Belgium and Germany, powers friendly to the Netherlands, and that, with a view to the observance of this neutrality, the following dispositions have been taken:

Art. 1.   Within the limits of the territory of the State, including the territory of the Kingdom in Europe and the colonies and possessions in other parts of the world, no hostilities of any kind are permitted, neither may this territory serve as a base for hostile operations.

Art. 2.   Neither the occupation of any part of the State by a belligerent nor the passage across this territory by land is permitted to the troops or convoys of munitions belonging to the belligerents, nor is the passage across the territory situated within the territorial waters of the Netherlands by the warships or ships assimilated thereto of the belligerents permitted.

Art. 3.   Troops or soldiers belonging to the belligerents or destined for them arriving in the territory of the State by land will be immediately disarmed and interned until the termination of the war.

Warships or ships assimilated thereto belonging to a belligerent who contravenes the provisions of Articles 2, 4, or 7 will not be permitted to leave the said territory until the end of the war.

Art. 4.   No warships or ships assimilated thereto belonging to any of the belligerents shall have access to the said territory.

Art. 5.   The provisions of Article 4 do not apply to:

(1) Warships or ships assimilated thereto which are forced to enter the ports or roadsteads of the State on account of damages or the state of the sea.   Such ships may leave the said ports or roadsteads as soon as the circumstances which have driven them to take shelter there shall have ceased to exist.

---

[1] Naval War College, *International Law Topics*, 1916, pp. 61–64.

(2) Warships or ships assimilated thereto belonging to a belligerent which anchor in a port or roadstead in the colonies or overseas possessions exclusively with the object of completing their provision of foodstuffs or fuel. These ships must leave as soon as the circumstances which have forced them to anchor shall have ceased to exist, subject to the condition that their stay in the roadstead or port shall not exceed 24 hours.

(3) Warships or ships assimilated thereto belonging to a belligerent employed exclusively on a religious, scientific, or humanitarian mission.

Art. 6. Warships or ships assimilated thereto belonging to a belligerent may only execute such repairs in the ports and roadsteads of the State as are indispensable to their seaworthiness, and they may in no way increase their fighting capacities.

Art. 7. Warships or ships assimilated thereto belonging to a belligerent who may at the commencement of the war be within the territory of the State must leave within 24 hours from the moment of this declaration.

Art. 8. If warships or ships assimilated thereto belonging to different belligerents finding themselves at the same time, in the conditions set forth in Article 5, in the same part of the world and within the territory of the State, a delay of at least 24 hours must elapse between the departure of each respective belligerent ship. Except in special circumstances, the order of departure shall be determined by the order of arrival. A warship or ship assimilated thereto belonging to a belligerent may only leave the territory of the State 24 hours after the departure of a merchant ship which flies the flag of another belligerent.

Art. 9. Warships or ships assimilated thereto belonging to a belligerent to which Articles 5 and 7 are applicable may only be provisioned with foodstuffs in the ports and roadsteads of the country to the extent necessary to bring their provisions up to the normal limit in time of peace.

Similarly they can only be supplied with fuel to the extent necessary to enable them, with the stock they already have on board, to reach the nearest port of their own country.

The same vessel can not again be provided with fuel until a period of at least three months shall have elapsed since it was last provisioned in the territory of the State.

319

Art. 10.   A prize may only be brought into Dutch territory if such prize is unnavigable, or unseaworthy, or short of fuel or food-stuffs.

Such prize must leave as soon as the reasons which caused her to enter Dutch territory cease to exist.

Should such prize fail to do so, immediate orders shall be given her to leave.   In the event of a refusal, all possible means shall be employed to liberate the prize, with her officers and crew, and to intern the crew placed on board by the belligerent who has taken it as prize.

Art. 11.   It is forbidden, in State territory, to form a corps of combatants or to open recruiting offices on behalf of the belligerents.

Art. 12.   It is forbidden, in State territory, to take service on board warships or ships assimilated thereto.

Art. 13.   It is forbidden, in State territory, to equip, arm, or man vessels intended for military purposes on behalf of a belligerent, or to furnish or deliver such vessels to a belligerent.

Art. 14.   It is forbidden, in State territory, to supply arms or ammunition to warships or ships assimilated thereto belonging to a belligerent, or to come to their assistance in any manner whatsoever with a view to augment their crew or their equipment.

Art. 15.   It is forbidden in State territory failing previous authorization by the competent local authorities, to repair warships or ships assimilated thereto belonging to a belligerent, or to supply them with victuals or fuel.

Art. 16.   It is forbidden in State territory to take part in the dismantling or repairing of prizes, except in so far as is necessary to make them seaworthy; also to purchase prizes or confiscated goods, and to receive them in exchange, in gift, or on deposit.

Art. 17.   The State territory comprises the coastal waters to a distance of 3 nautical miles, reckoning 60 to the degree of latitude, from low-water mark.

As regards inlets, this distance of 3 nautical miles is measured from a straight line drawn across the inlet at the point nearest the entrance where the mouth of the inlet is not wider than 10 nautical miles, reckoning 60 to the degree of latitude.

Art. 18.   Further, attention is called to Articles 100, section 1, and 205 of the Penal Code; *Indisch Staatsblad*, 1905, No. 62; Article 7, section 4, of the law respecting the status of Netherlands national-

320

Appendix

ity (*Nederlandsch Staatsblad*, 1910, No. 55; *Indisch Staatsblad*, 1910, No. 296; Articles 54 and 55 of the Penal Code of Surinam; Articles 54 and 55 of the Penal Code of Curacao).

Similarly, the attention of commanding officers, owners, and charterers of ships is called to the dangers and inconveniences to which they would expose themselves by disregarding the effective blockade of belligerents, by carrying contraband of war, or military despatches (except in the course of the regular postal service), or by rendering them other transport services.

Any person guilty of the acts aforesaid would expose himself to all the consequences of those acts and would not be able, as regards them, to obtain any protection or intervention on the part of the Netherlands Government.

WAR BUOYING ON THE SCHELDT

Note addressed to the Belgian Government to announce that the Netherlands may be obliged to institute war buoying on the Scheldt. August 3, 1914.[1]

The Netherlands Government may be compelled, in order to maintain the neutrality of Dutch territory, to institute war buoying upon the Scheldt, that is to say, to move or modify a portion of the actual arrangement of buoys and lights.

At the same time this special arrangement of buoys has been so drawn up that when it is brought into force it will still be possible to sail up the Scheldt as far as Antwerp by day, but only with Dutch pilots who have been furnished with the necessary nautical instructions. In thus acting the Netherlands Government is convinced that it will be able to serve equally both the Dutch interests in the defense of Netherlands territory and Belgian interests in the navigation to Antwerp.

After the establishment of war buoying on the Scheldt, there would be no further reason to enter the tidal waters of Flushing at night, and as the presence of the lightships "Wielingen" and "Wandelaar" is not indispensable to navigation by day the Netherlands Government would be much obliged if the Belgian Government would be good enough, in the event of the establishment of war buoying, to wit, withdraw these boats in order to facilitate the maintenance of the neutrality of Dutch territory.

Telegram from the King's Minister at The Hague addressed to M. Davignon, Minister of Foreign Affairs, August 5, 1914.[2]

"War buoying will be instituted.
                    (Signed) BARON FALLON."

Telegram of M. Davignon, Minister of Foreign Affairs, addressed to Baron Fallon, the King's Minister at The Hague. August 6, 1914.[3]

"Please inform the Dutch Government as follows:
"The Belgian Government has taken notice of the institution of war buoying as on the Scheldt and of the measures which the Netherlands Government has taken to insure unobstructed navigation.

---

[1] *Belgian Gray Book*, Annex to No. 29.
[2] *Ibid.*, No. 50.
[3] *Ibid.*, No. 54.

Appendix

"It would be well if navigation could take place from 30 minutes before sunrise until 30 minutes after sunset, and that the exchange of pilots would take place at Bath.

"However much the Belgian Government may wish to meet the desires of the Netherlands Government, it is of the opinion, with a view to the coast harbors, the lightships *Wielingen* and *Wandelaar* must be retained, as well as the buoys in the Wielingen Channel.

(Signed) DAVIGNON."

ADMISSION OF FOREIGN WARSHIPS

Decree of July 30, 1914, for the temporary suspension of the Royal decree of October 30, 1909, (*Staatsblad*, No. 351), establishing new regulations with respect to the admission of foreign warships to the Netherlands territorial waters and the enclosed Netherlands water area.[1]

"We, Wilhelmina, by the grace of God, Queen of the Netherlands, Princess of Orange-Nassau, etc., etc.

"Upon joint recommendation of our Ministers of Marine, of War, of Foreign Affairs, and of Justice, on July 30, 1914;

"In view of the Royal decree of the 30th of October, 1909, (*Staatsblad*, No. 351) establishing new regulations with respect to the admission of foreign warships to the Netherlands territorial waters and the enclosed Netherlands water area,

"Considering, that in view of the general political situation in Europe it is desirable to make use of the provision referred to in the second paragraph of Article 14 of Our decree, aforementioned;

"Having approved and agreed to order:

"Article 1. The Royal decree of October 30, 1909, (*Staatsblad*, No. 351) is suspended until further announcement.

"Art. 2. During the period in which Article 1 of the aforementioned decree shall be suspended, foreign warships and ships assimilated thereto are prohibited from entering the Netherlands territorial waters and the enclosed Netherlands water area, from the sea, or from anchoring therein.

"Art. 3. The provision of Article 2 is not applicable:

"*a*) to cruisers engaged in police patrol of the North Sea fisheries for the powers authorized by the treaty of May 6, 1882, (*Staatsblad*, 1884, No. 40).

"*b*) to foreign warships exclusively employed on a religious, scientific, or humanitarian mission.

"*c*) to foreign warships in case of want, stress of weather, or unseaworthiness. As soon as these reasons cease to exist, in the judgment of Our Minister of Marine, the provisions of Article 2 again become operative.

"The exceptions to the noted prohibitions stated in points *a* and *b* are applicable only with respect to those powers which reciprocally extend the same treatment with respect to Netherlands warships.

"Art. 4. Foreign warships or ships assimilated thereto found in Netherlands territorial waters and the enclosed Netherlands water area in violation or anchoring therein, and not departing after the

---

[1] *Staatscourant*, No. 332.

first warning, expose themselves to such regulations of compulsion as the Netherlands Government shall find it necessary to use.

"Our Ministers of Marine, of Foreign Affairs, and of Justice are charged with the execution of this decree, which shall be published in the *Staatsblad.*

"The Hague, the 30th of July, 1914.
WILHELMINA.

The Minister of Marine,
J. J. RAMBONNETT.

The Minister of War,
BOSBOOM.

The Minister of Foreign Affairs,
J. LOUDON.

The Minister of Justice,
B. ORT.

Proclaimed the 30th of July, 1914.
The Minister of Justice,
B. ORT.

INSPECTION SERVICE.[1]

The Minister of War calls the attention of those concerned to the contents of *B. A. Z.*, No. 53, 1912, which are as follows:

During manoeuvres and practice, and also for other reasons, it may be necessary to forbid the entrance to Netherlands harbors and estuaries, or to permit entrance provisionally only.

When near the coast and in some conspicuous place near a channel, leading to a harbor or estuary, it is required to display three red balls during the day and three red lanterns at night, or light bundles, or to display signals, the meaning of which is not to be ascertained from the sailing instructions or light lists, to approach the harbor or estuary with especial care, or better, to anchor and wait for the morning, since obstructions may be found in the mouth of the port or harbor. It is thus forbidden to enter or depart without pilots and each ship may be subjected to inspection.

In so far as possible, information concerning the establishment of this inspection service will be given by vessels stationed at sea and displaying the said balls as well as the sign T. J. Y. during the day and the said lights at night; it is advisable to follow all the directions of these vessels and not to pass by those vessels without first having asked for directions.

When a ship is hailed by one of these vessels, or if a signal shot is given, then all within sight of these vessels must stop.

The establishment of this service for any particular harbor or estuary is never announced in advance.

The above inspection service is put into operation today.

---

[1] *Nieuwe Rotterdamsche Courant* of August 1, 1914.

Appendix

APPENDIX V

COAST LIGHT REGULATIONS

ANNOUNCEMENT[1]

The Dutch Government announces that, with a view to the international situation, the light ships "Terschellingerbank" and "Haaks" will be withdrawn, and that the shore lights, with the exception of those of IJmuiden, Scheveningen, Hoek van Holland, and Westhoofd, will be extinguished.

The navigation of merchantmen towards IJmuiden, on the Nieuwe Waterweg and by daylight towards Dordrecht, on the Scheldt and by way of the channel form Texel towards Harlingen remains provided with the necessary safety measures and open in accordance with pilotage directions.

---

[1] *Staatscourant*, 1914, No. 182.

AERIAL REGULATIONS

Decrees of the 3rd of August, 1914, concerning the prohibition of crossing the land frontiers by airships not belonging to the Netherlands land or sea forces.[1]

"We, Wilhelmina, by the grace of God, Queen of the Netherlands, Princess of Orange–Nassau, etc.

"Considering that it is necessary to prevent foreign armies from obtaining information concerning our preparations for war,

"Upon the recommendation of Our Minister of War of August 3, 1914, Kabinett, Litt. E 75;

"Having approved and undertaken to order that the crossing of the land frontiers by airships, not belonging to the Netherlands land or sea forces is prohibited for so long as the conditions named under paragraph 1 of Article 1 of the law of May 23, 1899 (*Staatsblad*, No. 128) exist.

"Our Minister of War is charged with the execution of this decree, which shall be published in the *Staatsblad* and of which a copy will be sent to the Council of State.

"The Hague, the 3rd of August, 1914.

WILHELMINA.

The Minister of War,
BOSBOOM.

"Proclaimed the 3rd of August, 1914.
The Minister of Justice,
B. ORT."

---

[1] *Staatsblad*, No. 354.

Appendix

APPENDIX VII

WIRELESS REGULATIONS

Prohibition of the Installation of Wireless Telegraphy

The Ministry of War—Announcement[1]

Since such will further the interest of the country's protection, the use within the Kingdom of installations for wireless telegraphy on land as well as on particular ships, is prohibited beginning today until further notice.

Established receiving stations must be so equipped that violation of this prohibition is not possible.

Supervision over the execution of the above shall be carried out by the military authorities, as well as the technical service of the Royal Telegraph.

> The Hague, August 5, 1914.
> The Minister of War,
> Bosboom.

The Minister of War supplements the announcement, appearing in the *Staatscourant*, No. 181, of August 5, with this notice that by the prohibition of the use within the Kingdom of installation of wireless telegraphy "Kingdom" is meant to include the territorial waters.[2]

> The Hague, August 8, 1914.
> For the Minister,
> The Secretary-General,
> A. J. Doorman.

---

[1] *Staatscourant*, No. 181.
[2] *Ibid.*, No. 185.

Neutrality of the Netherlands During World War

APPENDIX VIII

INTERNMENT REGULATIONS

A PROCLAMATION[1]

The Minister of War,

Has concluded under authority granted to him by Her Majesty the Queen, to institute the following:

Regulations concerning the internment of combatants and wounded subject to medical care.

Since war has broken out between Powers friendly to the Netherlands, the following rules, with an eye to the maintenance of a strict neutrality are established:

1. Transit across Netherlands territory may under no conditions be granted to sections of troops and military transports of war materials of belligerents.

In case such sections come upon Netherlands territory they must at once be disarmed and be conducted under guard to the internment depot at Alkmaar.

Only in case the local commander meets sections of the belligerents in the immediate neighborhood of the frontier and it clearly appears that the crossing of the frontier was the result of error, may such sections be permitted to leave Netherlands territory, and only if they depart immediately when ordered.

2. Unorganized soldiers belonging to belligerent armies, crossing the frontier, must be informed that they are upon Netherlands territory, and they must be ordered to leave. In case this order is not immediately obeyed steps must be taken to intern them as is provided under Article 1 for belligerent sections.

3. Every intentional violation of Netherlands neutrality must be resisted by force.

4. In case escaped prisoners of war come upon Netherlands territory they must be permitted to leave, if possible in the direction they themselves may choose.

In case they do not wish to leave Dutch territory steps must be taken to intern them as is provided under Article 1.

5. Whenever transit is requested by any of the belligerent parties for wounded or sick belonging to belligerent forces, such

---

[1] *Staatscourant*, No. 185.

transit must be provisionally detained and the approval of the superior officer, who must be informed of the strength and composition of the transport, must be sought at once.

6. The Geneva Convention is applicable to sick and wounded of belligerent forces brought into Netherlands territory for hospitalization.

As soon as they are no longer in need of medical attention, they must be sent to the internment depot, for internment.

7. The heads of military hospitals, where belligerent wounded and sick are cared for, as also the head of the internment depot, shall immediately upon the arrival of such sick and wounded and thereafter twice a month, send statements to the Red Cross Information Bureau giving all the details which may serve for the identification of such persons, as also details which may serve for the information and for the reassurance of their relatives at home.

8. The commander of the internment depot is responsible for his services to the Minister of War and will bring to this authority, among other proposals, proposals with respect to the granting of leaves of absence to interned officers on word of honor.

9. Directions will be given concerning the payment of salary or stipend to the wounded and sick under medical care, belonging to belligerent forces, and to the interned.

The Hague, August 8, 1914,
For the Minister,
The Secretary-General,
A. J. Doorman.

APPENDIX IX

REGULATIONS FOR THE VOLUNTARY AID TO BELLIGERENT SICK, WOUNDED, AND INTERNED PERSONS

Decree of the 27th of November, 1914, supplementing the Royal decree of the 19th of March, 1913 (*Staatsblad*, No. 113), containing regulations for the voluntary aid to sick and wounded persons, belonging to the land or naval forces of belligerent powers, with provisions, among others, for the supplying of aid and information service with respect to prisoners of war and interned persons.[1]

"We, Wilhelmina, by the grace of God, Queen of the Netherlands, Princess of Orange-Nassau, etc.

"Upon the recommendation of our Ministers of War and of Marine of October 6, 1914, First Part, No. 343, and of October 12, 1914, Bureau S. No. 77.

"Considering that the requirements serving the Netherlands Red Cross Information Bureau for sick and wounded also be extended to the supplying of aid and information service with respect to prisoners of war and interned persons:

"That to that end, as well as for several other reasons, Our decree of March 19, 1913, (*Staatsblad*, No. 113) requires supplementing;

"Having heard the Council of State (advice of October 27, 1914, No. 21);

"Having approved and decided to order;

"Article 1.   Article 3*b* is made to read as follows:

"*b*. to provide the necessary preparations, to make available in time of war trusted and skilled personnel, hospitals, and appropriate transport and medical supplies, and to establish an Information Bureau for the sick and wounded, which shall then operate as the Bureau of Information for prisoners of war and interned persons, and shall be charged with the supplying of such aid to these as shall be in conformity with Articles 14 and 15 of the Convention with respect to the laws and customs of war on land, established by the Hague Convention of October 18, 1907, made known by the Royal decree of February 22, 1910 (*Staatsblad*, No. 73).

"Article 2.   Article 3, 2*b* is made to read as follows:

"*b*. to establish and to maintain an Information Bureau for sick and wounded, like the Bureau of Information for prisoners of war and interned persons, and charged with the supplying of aid to these, one and another in conformity with Articles

---

[1] *Staatsblad*, No. 546.

Appendix

14 and 15 of the Convention with respect to the laws and customs of war on land, established by the Hague Convention of October 18, 1907, made known by Royal decree of February 22, 1910 (*Staatsblad*, No. 73).

"Article 3. To Article 6 is added a third line, as follows: "The Honorary Members of the Society shall be named upon recommendation of the Executive Committee.

"Article 4. After Article 17 of the Royal decree of March, 1913 (*Staatsblad*, No. 113), is added:

"The Executive Committee of the Netherlands Red Cross is given authority by us to bestow the decoration, "Service Cross," or to grant a "Service Medal" for valuable services in or for the Society.

"Our Ministers of War and Marine will be charged with the execution of this decree, of which a copy shall be sent to Our Ministers of Foreign Affairs, of the Interior, of Justice, of Colonies, and of Agriculture, Industry and Trade, to the Council of State, and to the General Executive Office, and that it shall be published in the *Staatsblad* and in the *Staatscourant*.

The Hague, November 27, 1914.
WILHELMINA.
The Minister of War,
BOSBOOM.
The Minister of Marine,
J. J. RAMBONNETT.

Proclaimed the 9th of December, 1914.
The Minister of Justice,
B. ORT."

APPENDIX X

PENAL AND DISCIPLINARY REGULATIONS WITH RESPECT TO THE INTERNED

Law of December 31, 1914, containing penal and disciplinary provisions with respect to military persons of a foreign power interned here on land.[1]

"We, Wilhelmina, by the grace of God, Queen of the Netherlands, Princess of Orange-Nassau, etc.

"To all, who may see or read this, greetings! Be it known:

"Whereas We having taken into consideration that penal and disciplinary provisions are desirable with respect to military persons of a foreign power interned here on land;

"Thus, We, having heard the Council of State, and in consultation with States-General, having approved and concluded, as also We approve and conclude by this:

"Article 1. Military persons of a foreign power interned here on land, with respect to the military laws and the recognition of their invested rank, will be placed on the same footing as Netherlands military persons:

"*a.* with respect to acts committed by them in violation of the general law;

"*b.* with respect to acts committed by them in violation of the provisions of Articles 84-86, 88-92, and 97-101 of the Fifth Title of the Criminal Code for war personnel at sea, or Articles 80-82, 85-89, and 99-103 of the Fifth Title of the Criminal Code for war personnel on land;

"*c.* with respect to acts committed by them in violation of the provisions of the Regulations for War-discipline, with the understanding that for military persons below the rank of officer the punishment of quarter-arrest, states-arrest, or ships-arrest may be replaced by the penalty of total or partial withdrawal of salary or stipend during a maximum period of two months and that the last named penalty may be imposed in addition to others;

"*d.* with respect to acts in violation of Article 3.

"In accordance with the military forces to which or under whose supervision they may find themselves, they will be considered as belonging to the land or sea forces.

"The subordinate relationship of Netherlands and foreign military ranks will be regulated by Us or by Our authority by Our Ministers of Marine and of War; the military authorities may, however, in certain cases, independent of this relationship, invest with a higher rank.

"Artcle 2. The commander of the internment depots, or the officers designated by them, as the commanding officers of a corps or of a warship are designated to apply this law.

---

[1] *Staatsblad*, No. 666.

Appendix

"The commander of an internment depot of the land forces determines which officers shall be designated for the application of the Regulation of War-discipline for combatants on land as the commanding officer of a company, and which officers will be designated as the higher officers of a corps.

"Article 3. Military persons of a foreign power interned here on land, who in violation of promises intentionally leave, or who absent themselves temporarily or permanently in violation of a promise given by them or in violation of the conditions under which leave of absence is granted, or who conspire to that end, shall be punished by military imprisonment of a maximum of six years.

"The misdemeanors described in this article are punishable even when committed outside of the Kingdom in Europe.

"Article 80 of the Penal Code is applicable in these cases.

"Article 4. In the application of this law such persons as have been freed upon word of honor or upon condition, are included under the term "persons of a foreign power interned here on land."

"Article 5. This law goes into effect on the day of its proclamation.

"Charged and ordered, that this shall be published in the *Staatsblad* and that all the Ministerial Departments, Authorities, Colleagues, and officials, whom it concerns, shall carefully execute it.

The Hague, December 31, 1914.

WILHELMINA.

The Minister of Justice,
B. ORT.

The Minister of Marine,
J. J. RAMBONNETT.

The Minister of War,
BOSBOOM.

The Minister of Foreign Affairs,
J. LOUDON.

Proclaimed the 3rd of January, 1915.
The Minister of Justice,
B. ORT.

335

THE RHINE CONVENTIONS

The articles of the different Rhine conventions which were the subject of dispute are as follows:

Vienna Congress Treaty, March, 1815, Annex XVI, Article VII, "Future Regulation of the Navigation of the Scheldt."

Everything relating to the Navigation of the Scheldt, which may need ulterior arrangement, besides the freedom of navigation on this river, specified in Article I, shall be definitely regulated in a manner the most favorable to commerce and navigation, and the most analagous to the regulations established on the Rhine.

Convention between the Riverian States of the Rhine, and Regulations for the Navigation of that River. Signed at Meyence, March 31, 1831. Preamble.

The completion of the definitive regulation for the navigation of the Rhine, in accordance with the stipulations of the Act of the Congress of Vienna, having experienced difficulties arising out of the manner in which the riverian Governments interpreted the general principles of that Act to the vessels coming from Germany and crossing the Netherlands in a direct line to the open sea and vice versa; considering that His Majesty the King of the Netherlands has maintained that his rights of sovereignty extended without any restriction whatever over the sea bathing his States, even where it mixes with the waters of the Rhine, and that, in accordance with the conferences previous to the Act of the Congress of Vienna, the Leck only was to be considered as the continuation of that river in the Netherlands; whilst His Majesty the King of Prussia, His Majesty the King of Bavaria, and His Royal Highness the Grand Duke of Hesse have maintained that the Act of the Congress of Vienna had placed certain restrictions on the exercise of those rights in so far as they might apply to vessels passing from the Rhine into the sea, and vice versa; and that under the denomination of the Rhine the said Act included the whole courses, also the branches, and all the mouths of that river in the Netherlands, without any distinction—views in which His Majesty the King of the French and His Royal Highness the Grand Duke of Baden now equally concur; the riverian States have thought proper to leave intact all questions mooted on the general principles of the Act of the Congress of Vienna bearing upon the navigation of the Rhine, as well as the inferences which might be drawn therefrom, and to concert all measures and regulations which the navigation of the Rhine can no longer dispense witɦ, on the basis of joint proposals reciprocally made and accepted, under the express reservation, nevertheless, that such understanding shall in no wise be prejudicial to the rights and principles maintained on either side.

Act of Accession on the Part of the Germanic Confederation to the territorial Arrangements Concerning the Grand Duchy of Luxembourg. Laid down in the Treaty of April 19, 1839, London.

Article IV, 1. The provisions of Articles CVIII to CXII, inclusive of the General Act of the Congress of Vienna, relative to the free navigation of navigable rivers, shall be applied to those navigable rivers which separate the Belgian and the Dutch territories, or which traverse them both.

2. It is also agreed that the navigation of the intermediate channels between the Scheldt and the Rhine, in order to proceed from Antwerp to the Rhine and vice versa, shall continue reciprocally free, and that it shall be subject only to moderate tolls, which shall be the same for the commerce of the two countries.

Convention between France, Grand Duchy of Baden, Bavaria, Grand Duchy of Hesse, Netherlands, and Prussia, relative to the Navigation of the Rhine. Signed at Mannheim, October 17, 1868.

Preamble. The Convention relative to the navigation of the Rhine concluded on the 31st of March, 1831, between the riverian Governments, having since then undergone numerous modifications, and a part of the stipulations contained therein being no longer in harmony with the actual conditions of the navigation, His Majesty the Emperor of the French, His Royal Highness the Grand Duke of Hesse, His Majesty the King of the Netherlands, and His Majesty the King of Prussia have resolved by common consent, to revise that Convention, maintaining nevertheless, the principle of the free navigation of the Rhine in matters of Commerce, and have to that effect, appointed Commissioners Plenipotentiary, namely: . . .

Article II. Vessels affected to the navigation of the Rhine, and rafts or floats of timber coming from the Rhine shall have the right to choose whichever route they wish in traversing the Netherlands on their way from the Rhine to the open sea or to Belgium, and vice versa. If one of the navigable channels connecting the open sea and the Rhine via Dordrecht, Rotterdam, Helvoetsluis, and Brielle becomes impracticable for navigation from natural causes or by reason of mechanical works, the navigable channel which is appointed for the use of Netherlands vessels in place of the obstructed channel shall be equally open for navigation by the other riverian States. Any vessel having the right to carry the flag of one of the riverian States and able to prove that right by a document issued by the competent authority shall be considered as affected to the navigation of the Rhine.

BIBLIOGRAPHY

I. PRIMARY SOURCES.

Brazilian Greenbook.

British Parliamentary Papers:

Miscellaneous No. 2 (1916) cd. 8145.
Miscellaneous No. 12 (1914) cd. 7627.
Miscellaneous No. 12 (1917) cd. 8594.
Miscellaneous No. 14 (1917) cd. 8690.
Miscellaneous No. 17 (1917) cd. 8693.
Miscellaneous No. 1 (1918) cd. 8909.
Miscellaneous No. 2 (1918) cd. 8915.
Miscellaneous No. 4 (1918) cd. 8985.
Miscellaneous No. 5 (1918) cd. 8986.
Miscellaneous No. 8 (1918) cd. 8989.
Miscellaneous No. 9 (1918) cd. 9023.
Miscellaneous No. 11 (1918) cd. 9025.
Miscellaneous No. 12 (1918) cd. 9026.
Miscellaneous No. 13 (1918) cd. 9028.

Carnegie Endowment for International Peace, Division of International Law, *Proceedings of the Hague Peace Conferences,* Vols. I, II, III. New York, 1920–1921.

Carnegie Endowment for International Peace, Division of International Law, *Resolutions of the Institute of International Law,* translated under supervision of, and edited by Scott, J. B. Washington, 1916.

Carnegie Endowment for International Peace, Division of International Law, *Report of the Commission of Responsibilities.* Washington, 1919.

Dutch Orange Books:

"Overzicht der Voornaamste van Juli tot October, 1915, door het Ministerie van Buitenlandsche Zaken Behandelde en voor Openbaarmaking Geschikte Aangelegenheden." Referred to as *Dutch Orange Book,* I, *or D. O. B.,* I.

"Overzicht van Eenige in het Tijdvak October, 1915, tot Juli, 1916, door het Ministerie van Buitenlandsche Zaken Behandelde Aangelegenheden". Referred to as *Dutch Orange Book,* II, *or D. O. B.,* II.

"Mededeelingen van den Minister van Buitenlandsche Zaken aan de Staten-Generaal Juli–December, 1916". Referred to as *Dutch Orange Book,* III *or D. O. B.,* III.

"Mededeelingen van den Minister van Buitenlandsche Zaken aan de Staten-Generaal December, 1916–April, 1918." Referred to as *Dutch Orange Book,* IV *or D. O. B.,* IV.

Neutrality of the Netherlands During World War

"Mededeelingen van den Minister van Buitenlandsche Zaken aan de Staten-Generaal April, 1918–Juni, 1919". Referred to as *Dutch Orange Book*, V or *D. O. B.*, V.

"Mededeelingen van den Minister van Buitenlandsche Zaken aan de Staten-Generaal Juni, 1919–April, 1920". Referred to as *Dutch Orange Book*, 1919–1920 or *D. O. B.*, 1919–1920.

"Mededeelingen van den Minister van Buitenlandsche Zaken aan de Staten-Generaal Mei, 1920–Mei, 1921". Referred to as *Dutch Orange Book*, 1920–1921 or *D. O. B.*, 1920–1921.

"Mededeelingen van den Minister van Buitenlandsche Zaken aan de Staten-Generaal Mei, 1921–October, 1922". Referred to as *Dutch Orange Book*, 1921–1922, or *D. O. B.*, 1921–1922.

"Recueil de diverses communications du Ministerie des Affaires Etrangers aux Etats-Generaux par rapport a la neutralite des Pays-Bas et au respect du droit des Gens". The Hague, September, 1916. Referred to as *Recueil*.

Dutch White Books:

"Diplomatieke Bescheiden Betreffende de Vaart in de Noordzee en het Kanaal in Verband met den Oorlogstoestand". The Hague, 1915.

"Diplomatieke Bescheiden Betreffende de Inbeslagneming door Britsche Autorieteiten van over Zee Vervoerde Brievenpost". The Hague, 1916.

"Diplomatieke Bescheiden Betreffende den Verscherpten Duikbootoorlog". The Hague, 1917.

"Diplomatieke Bescheiden Betreffende de Toelating van Bewapende Handelsvaartuigen der Oorlogvoerenden en Onzijdigen Binnen het Nederlandsche Rechtsgebied". The Hague, 1917.

"Opbrenging van de Nederlandsche Schepen *Elve* en *Bernisse*". The Hague, 1918.

"Doorvoer door Nederland uit Duitschland naar België en in Omgekeerde Richting". Tweede Vervolg. The Hague, 1918.

"Brief van den Minister van Buitenlandsche Zaken, No. 15. Zitting 1917–1918, 2. Staatsbegrooting voor het dienstjaar 1918, IIIde Hoofdstuk. The Hague, 1918.

"Brief van den Minister van Buitenlandsche Zaken, No. 16. Zitting 1917–1918, 2. Staatsbegrooting voor het dienstjaar 1918, IIIde Hoofdstuk. The Hague, 1918.

"Brief van den Minister van Buitenlandsche Zaken, No. 16. Zitting 1914–1915, 2. Staatsbegrooting voor het dienstjaar 1915, IIIde Hoofdstuk". The Hague, 1918.

"Brief van den Minister van Buitenlandsche Zaken, No. 22. Zitting 1917–1918, 2. Staatsbegrooting voor het dienstjaar 1918, IIIde Hoofdstuk. The Hague, 1918.

"Diplomatieke Bescheiden Betreffende de Uitzending van een Convooi naar Nederlandsch-Indië". The Hague, 1918.

Bibliography

United States Department of State, *Diplomatic Correspondence with Belligerent Governments Concerning Neutral Rights and Duties*, European War. Published as Special Supplements to the *American Journal of International Law*, IX, X, XI. Washington, 1915, 1916, 1917.

United States Department of Commerce. Bulletin, *Commerce and Industry of the Netherlands*, 1912–1918. Washington, 1920.

United States Naval War College. *International Law Situations, Topics, and Discussions*. Washington, 1901–.

United States Supreme Court Reports of Decisions. Referred to as *Dallas, Cranch, Wallace*, etc.

Hurst and Bray. *Russian and Japanese Prize Cases*. London, 1912.

Lloyd. *Reports of English Prize Cases*, I–X. London, 1924.

Roscoe. *English Prize Cases*. London, 1905.

Scott, J. B. *Cases on International Law*. St. Paul, 1922.

World Peace Foundation. *International Conciliation Pamphlets*, No. 172. Boston, 1909–.

II. SECONDARY SOURCES.

Albrecht. *Requisitionem von neutralen Privateigentum*. Berlin, 1913.

American Bar Association. *Reports*, Vol. 44.

Barclay, Sir Thomas. *Problems of International Practice and Diplomacy*. London, 1907.

Barnouw, A. J. *Holland Under Queen Wilhelmina*. New York, 1923.

Baty, T. *Britain and Sea Law*. London, 1911.

Beer Portugael, J. C. C. den. *Het Internationaal Maritieme Recht*. Breda, 1888.

Beer, Portugael, J. C. C. den. *La Neutralité sur L'Escaut*. The Hague, 1913.

Bernard, Montague. *A Historical Account of the Neutrality of Great Britain during the American Civil War*. London, 1870.

Blok, M. *Geschiedenis van het Nederlandsche Volk*, VIII. The Hague, 1913.

Bluntschli. *La Droit International Codifié*. Edited by Lardy. Paris, 1886.

Boeck, Ch. de. *De La Propièté Privee Ennemie sous Pavilon Ennemie*. Paris, 1882.

Bonfils, H. *Manuel de Droit International Public*, 7th Edition. Paris, 1914.

Bowles, T. Gibson. *Sea Law and Sea Power*. London, 1910.

Bowman, Isaiah. *The New World*. Yonkers-on-Hudson, 1921.

Briggs, H. W. *The Doctrine of Continuous Voyage*. Baltimore, 1926.

British Yearbook of International Law. London, 1920–.

Bynkershoek, C. van. *Dissertatio de Domino Maria.* The Hague, 1703.

Calvo, Ch. *La Droit International Theorique et Pratique.* Paris–Berlin, 1887.

Captain "Candid" of the Netherlands Army. *The Limburg Manoeuvre.* Utrecht, 1919.

Carsten, I. *Maatregelen ter Handhaving Onzer Onzijdigheid in den Huidigen Oorlog.* The Hague, 1916.

Chamberlain, J. P. *The International Rivers, the Rhine and the Danube.* Columbia University Studies, CV. New York, 1922.

Churchill, Winston. *The World Crisis.* New York, 1923.

De Visscher, Ch. *Belgium's Case—A Judicial Inquiry.* New York, 1916.

De Visscher, Ch. *The Stabilization of Europe.* Chicago, 1924.

Dupuis, Ch. *La Droit de la Guerre Maritime d'apres les Doctrines Anglaises Contemporaines.* Paris, 1899.

Einiche, P. *Rechte und Pflichten der neutralen Machte in See-Krieg.* Tübingen, 1912.

Fenwick, Charles G. *International Law.* New York, 1924.

Ferguson, J. H. *Manual of International Law.* The Hague, 1884.

Fiore, Pasquale. *Noveau Droit International Public.* Traduit de l'talien par P. Fradier Fodere. Paris, 1868.

Fisk and Pearce. *International Commercial Policies.* New York, 1923.

Francois, J. P. A. *Duikboot en Volkenrecht.* The Hague, 1919.

Garner, J. W. *International Law and the World War.* New York, 1920.

Garner, J. W. *Recent Development in International Law.* Calcutta, 1923.

Geffcken, L. H. *Das Seekriegsrecht und Die Neutralität* in Holtzendorff's *Handbuch des Volkerrechts,* IV. Hamburg, 1889.

Gessner, L. *Les Droits des neutres sur Mer,* 2nd Edition. Berlin, 1876.

Grotius, Hugo. *De Jure Bellis ac Pacis.* 1625.

Grotius Society. *Problems of the War, Transactions.* London, 1916–.

Grotius Annuaire International. The Hague, 1913–.

Hall, W. E. *A Treatise on International Law,* 8th Edition. Oxford, 1909.

Halleck. *International Law.* Revised by Sir Sherston Baker. London, 1878.

Hauteville, L. B. *Des Droits et des Devoirs des Nations Neutre en Temps de Guerre Maritime.* Paris, 1868.

Hendricks, Burton J. *Life and Letters of Walter Hines Page.* Garden City, 1922.

Hershey, A. S. *Essentials of International Public Law.* New York, 1914.

Bibliography

Hershey, A. S. *The International Law and Diplomacy of the Russo–Japanese War.* New York, 1906.

Hyde, C. C. *International Law, Chiefly as Interpreted and Applied by the United States,* I–II. Boston, 1922.

International Law Association. *Proceedings, 28th Conference.* Madrid, 1913.

Japikse, N. *Die Stellung Hollands im Weltkrieg.* Translated from the manuscript by N. Schwedemann. Gotha, 1921.

Keller, G. *Netherlands Oversea Trust.* The Hague, 1915.

Kent's *Commentary on International Law.* Edited by J. F. Abdy, 2nd Edition. Cambridge, 1876.

Kleen, R. *Lois et Usages de la Neutralité...* Paris, 1898.

La Question du Limburg. Published by Comité de Politique National Belge. Brussels, 1919.

Lawrence, T. J. *Principles of International Law,* 5th Edition. Boston, 1912.

Lawrence, T. J. *War and Neutrality in the Far East,* 2nd Edition. London, 1904.

Lisyt, F. Von. *Das Volkerrecht.* Berlin, 1918.

Louter, J. de. *Le Droit International Public Positif* (1910). Translated from the Dutch by the author and edited for the Division of International Law of the Carnegie Endowment for Peace, Washington, 1920.

Malloy, W. *Treaties, Conventions, International Acts, Proposals, and Agreements Between the United States and Other Powers, 1776–1909.* Washington, 1910.

Martens, F. de. *Traite de Droit International.* Paris, 1887.

Moore, J. B. *Digest of Internatial Law* (7 vols.). Washington, 1906.

Moore, J. B. *International Law and Some Current Illusions.* New York, 1924.

Nippold. *Development of International Law After the World War.* Carnegie Endowment for International Peace. New York, 1923.

Nys, E. *La Droit International.* Paris, 1912.

Nys, E. *L'Escaut en Temps de Guerre.* Paris, 1911.

Oppenheim, L. *International Law,* 2nd Edition. London, 1912.

Ortolan, T. *Regles Internationales et Diplomatic de la Mer.*

Parmalee, M. *Blockade and Sea Power.* New York, 1924.

Perels, F. *Das Internationale Offentliche Seerecht der Gegenwart,* 2te Auflage. Berlin, 1903.

Phillimore, Sir Robert. *Commentaries Upon International Law,* 3rd Edition. London, 1885.

Phillipson, Coleman. *International Law and the Great War.* London, 1915.

Pitt Cobbett. *Leading Cases on International Law,* 3rd Edition. London, 1913.

Quigley, H. S. *The Immunity of Private Property from Capture at Sea.* Madison, 1916.

Rivier, A. *Principes du Droit des Gens.* 1896.

Rolin. *La Droit de la Guerre.* Brussels, 1921.

Roxburgh. *International Conventions and Third States.* New York, 1917.

Salter, J. *Allied Shipping Control.* London, 1921.

Schucking, W. *Das Kustenmeer im Internationalem Recht.*

Scott, J. B. *Armed Neutralities of 1780 and 1800.* New York, 1922.

Scott, J. B. "The Trial of the Kaiser" in House and Seymour, *What Really Happened at Paris.* New York, 1921.

Snow, Freeman. *International Law.* Washington, 1888.

Struycken, A. A. H. *Holland, Belgium, and the Powers.* The Hague, 1919.

Temperley, A. *History of the Peace Conference at Paris.* Oxford, 1920–1924.

Tonnies, Ed. *Die Nederlandsche Uebersee Trust Gesellschaft.* Jena, 1916.

Senate Documents. No. 126, 67th Congress, 2nd Session.

Senate Documents. No. 3322, 64th Congress, 1st Session.

Ullmann, E. von. *Volkerrecht.* Tübingen, 1908.

Van Hamel. *Holland Tusschen de Mogendheden.* Amsterdam, 1918.

Verzijl, J. H. W. *Het Prijsrecht Tegenover Neutralen in den Wereld Oorlog van 1914 en Volgende Jaren.* The Hague, 1917.

Vier Brieven Over de N. O. T. Amsterdam, 1916.

Visser, L. E. *De Territoriale Zee.* Utrecht, 1894.

Voorst tot Voorst, Baron J. J. G. *Over Roermond.* The Hague, 1923.

Wehberg, H. *Das Seekriegsrecht.* Berlin, 1913.

Westlake, J. *International Law.* Cambridge, 1913.

Wilson and Tucker. *International Law,* 6th Edition. New York, 1913.

Woolsey, T. D. *Introduction to the Study of International Law.* London, 1875.

Wright, G., *Enforcement of International Law Through Municipal Law in the United States.* Urbana, 1916.

PERIODICALS

American Journal of International Law, published by the American Society of International Law. Washington, 1907–.

American Political Science Review, published by the American Political Science Association. Baltimore, 1907–.

Annuaire de L'Institut de Droit International, edited by E. Rolin–Jacquemin. Paris, 1877–.

Bibliography

Current History Magazine. New York, 1914–.

Fortnightly Review. London, 1865–.

International Law Notes. London, 1917–.

Journal de Droit International, formerly *Journal du Droit International Privé,* edited by E. Clunet. Paris, 1874.

Journal of Comparative Legislation and International Law, formerly *Journal of the Society of Comparative Legislation.* London, 1916–.

The Michigan Law Review. Ann Arbor.

The Minnesota Law Review. Minneapolis.

The New Europe. London, 1916–1920.

The New York Times. New York, 1851–.

The Pennsylvania Law Review. Philadelphia.

Revue de Droit International et de Legislation Comparee, edited by A. Rolin and E. de Visscher. Brussels, 1869–.

Revue Generale du Droit International Publique, edited by P. Fauchille and A. de Lapradelle. Paris, 1st series, 1894–1918; 2nd series, 1919–.

The South Atlantic Quarterly. Durham, 1902–.

The Yale Law Review. New Haven.

Zeitschrift fur Volkerrecht und Bundesstaatsrecht, edited by J. Köhler and others. Breslau, 1906–.

INDEX

Aircraft, above neutral territory by *force majeure*, 80; above neutral territory by mistake, 78 ff.; belligerent aircraft brought down by Dutch forces, 78–79; bombing of Dutch towns by belligerent aircraft, 8; prohibition of passage over Dutch territory, 77 ff.; violations of Dutch prohibitions, 80 ff.

Air regulations, convention for regulation of aircraft and radio, 84 ff.; 172, 182 *n.*; history of, 82–83.

Angary, Allied requisitioning of Dutch vessels, 296–303; history of the law of, 303–306; requisitioning of Dutch vessels chiefly British owned, 294–295.

Armed merchantmen, effectiveness of against submarines, 129; history of arming merchantmen, 124 ff.; Lansing's proposal with respect to armed merchantmen and submarines, 134–135; prohibition of entrance to Dutch territorial waters, 113 ff.; prohibition of entrance of neutral armed merchantmen to Dutch territorial waters, 123–124; right of belligerent to arm merchantmen, 113–114; right of neutral to exclude from territorial waters, 131 ff.

Armistice, juridical character of, 69 ff.; terms of, 49–51, 65, 67–68, 71, 75.

Asylum, of the Kaiser, 183 ff.

Base of operations, 176 ff.

Blockade, British blockade order, 196 ff.; continuous voyage in case of, 214 ff.; declaration of blockade zones by Germany and Austria-Hungary, 200 ff.; economic blockade of Holland, 205 ff.; extension of British blockade order, 202; German submarine blockade, 223 ff.; history of, 213 ff.; the future of, 225–226.

Cement, export of from Great Britain to Holland, 25–26.

Codification of international law, 316–317.

Commission of Inquiry, 91 ff.; 201, 204.

Commission of responsibilities, 186 ff.

Continuous voyages, 214 ff.; history of, 243–245.

Contraband, British Order in Council, Aug. 20, 1914, 228 ff.; British Order in Council, Oct. 29, 1914, 230–232; British Order in Council, Mar. 30, 1916, 232; French Decree, Aug. 25, 1914, 228 ff.; French Decree, Nov. 6, 1914, 230–232; French Decree, April 12, 1916, 232; French Decree, July 7, 1916, 233–236; German regulations of, 236–237; history of law of, 239–245; Maritime Rights Order in Council, July 7, 1916, 233–236.

INDEX

INDEX